LEV AND SONYA

LEV
AND
SONYA

The Story of the Tolstoy Marriage

by

Louise Smoluchowski

G. P. PUTNAM'S SONS / NEW YORK

G. P. Putnam's Sons
Publishers Since 1838
200 Madison Avenue
New York, NY 10016

The author gratefully acknowledges permission from the following sources
to reprint material in their control: Albin Michel for material from *Avec
Léon Tolstoi* by Tatiana Tolstoi, © 1975 by Albin Michel, English translation
by Michael Joseph Limited; Chatto & Windus: The Hogarth Press for material from *Tolstoy and the Novel* by John Bayley, © 1966 by John Bayley;
V.A.A.P., Central Soviet Copyright Agency, for material from *The Diaries of
S. A. Tolstoya*, © 1978 by Belles Lettres.

Library of Congress Cataloging-in-Publication Data

Smoluchowski, Louise.
Lev and Sonya.

Diaries translated from the Russian.
Bibliography: p.
1. Tolstoy, Leo, graf, 1828–1910—Biography—
Marriage. 2. Tolstoy, Leo, graf, 1828–1910—
Relations with women—Sof'ia Tolstaia.
3. Tolstaia, S. A. (Sof'ia Andreevna), 1844–1919.
4. Novelists, Russian—19th century—Biography.
I. Tolstoy, Leo, graf, 1828–1910.
II. Tolstaia, S. A. (Sof'ia Andreevna), 1844–1919.
III. Title.
PG3388.S6 1987   891.73'3 [B]   86–25475

ISBN 0–399–13236–8
Printed in the United States of America
1 2 3 4 5 6 7 8 9 10

For Nancy, who inspired my
interest in the Tolstoys, and
for those who made my book possible:
Alan, Bob, and especially Roman.

CONTENTS

NOTE ON TRANSLITERATION

To provide a certain atmosphere I have transliterated first names to resemble the Russian—Lev rather than Leo, and Aleksandr, Nikolai, Andrei and so on. Otherwise, I have tried to keep the transliteration natural for the English reader; where names are historically famous I use the familiar form (Peter the Great, Nicholas I) and I do not use the feminine ending for last names.

AUTHOR'S NOTE

Probably no marriage of a great literary figure has attracted more interest than that of Tolstoy. This is partly because he and his wife were extraordinary people and partly because we know so much about them. Lev and Sonya recorded a remarkable portion of their married life in their diaries and notebooks.

Like the Old Testament, the Tolstoys' accounts contain enough varied material to support almost any interpretation for which a reader seeks confirmation. A portrait of their marriage has to include this diversity; Lev and Sonya lived upon the larger scale. Although both Tolstoys were more inclined to write about their relationship when they were resentful, their diaries show that for a large part of their lives they lived together happily. When they were happy they were happy indeed, and the same was true of their resentments. When they were angry with one another they minced no words—but then, what marriage, however much based on love, is not sometimes rocked by emotional extremes? In this respect the Tolstoys' marriage followed psychological patterns common to all marriages. A major difference is that Lev and Sonya wrote nearly everything down and this narrative is based almost entirely on their own words.

The story falls into three parts. The first twenty years tell of love and an unusual partnership. Sonya provided the domestic and emotional surroundings in which Lev's genius flourished. During the middle years of their life together Lev's diary entries suggest that he suffered a severe depression in the medical sense which may have resulted from, or may have brought on, a crisis of confidence. In either case, he was unable to continue his literary work and he focused on his philosophical and religious convictions, convictions which had been growing since his youth but which assumed exaggerated importance when his artistic creativity was blocked. Sonya did not have the same sympathy for Lev the writer of moral essays that she had had for Lev the novelist and what appeared to be a philosophical gulf developed between the Tolstoys. The gulf had psychological roots as well; stress was inevitable during Lev's depression and the death of a favorite child brought Sonya close to breakdown. *Master and Man* (1895) marked Lev's return to writing great fiction and in the decade that began with his seventieth birthday the Tolstoys mellowed and once again their marriage was close and loving. This rapport might have continued until Lev's death but for the interference of their daughter Aleksandra and of Lev's disciple, Vladimir Chertkov.

As the Tolstoys' story unfolds in their diaries, the events they record appear in the context of their life at the time. Many periods of their marriage become more understandable: The discrepancy between Lev's religious convictions and his attitude toward Sonya at the time is less strange seen in relation to his depression; Sonya's hysteria in 1909 and 1910 becomes a desperate weapon rather than an illness; and even Lev's final, tragic flight from home no longer casts a disturbing shadow on his marriage but instead on those who manipulated him during the last year of his life.

In addition to the Tolstoys' diaries, notebooks and letters, I have used family material from books by four of their children—Aleksandra, Ilya, Sergei and Tatyana—and from *My Life at Home and at Yasnaya Polyana* by Sonya's sister, Tatyana Kuzminsky. My only other important source is the diary kept by Lev's secretary, Valentin Bulgakov, during 1910, the last year of Tolstoy's life. Although Tolstoy took his own experiences and transformed them in his novels, I have never used his fiction as source material for his life. Where Russian sources are listed in the bibliography I have used them and not English or French translations. Sergei Tolstoy edited his mother's diaries where the material was intimate and the Soviet 1978 edition generally respects Sergei's deletions. In some instances the Soviet edition omitted additional sentences; occasionally I found the deletions in Alexander Werth's translations of Sonya's diaries. The few times where I quote Werth are documented by referral to the notes. Otherwise, the translations are mine and I am responsible for any errors.

In order to avoid a cumbersome number of numerical references, citations of source material are selective. All quotations from Lev's diaries, notebooks and letters are from the Complete Works, those from Sonya's diaries and notes (with the exception noted above) are from the 1978 edition of her diaries and Sonya's letters to Lev are from her *Letters to L. N. Tolstoy*. Other correspondence is either from the Notes to Sonya's diaries or books by the Tolstoy children or Sonya's sister Tatyana.

Lev and Sonya is not a biography of Tolstoy, nor of his wife, nor is it a book about Tolstoy the novelist or philosophical thinker. It is about that part of his and Sonya's lives that touched on their marriage. By basing this story almost entirely on their own words, I have tried to give a picture of their marriage as they saw it themselves.

Chapter One

IN SEARCH OF LOVE,
1828–1862

1.

On 23 September 1862, in the Church of the Virgin Birth which stood inside the Kremlin, the fortified heart of Moscow that enclosed the Imperial Palace, state buildings and the houses of the aristocracy, a glittering and solemn candlelit ceremony united in wedlock Lev Nikolaevich Tolstoy and Sofya Andreevna Bers. So began one of the most famous of all marriages and a relationship that would know more love and happiness, pain and resentment, dramatic transformations and unexpected developments than it would seem possible to contain in the forty-eight years of the Tolstoys' life together.

To the family and friends who witnessed the ceremony and to those onlookers who wandered into the church from the palace grounds and parks the bridal couple may not have appeared to be the perfect match. The groom was thirty-four years old, a count descended from an old Russian family, widely traveled and experienced and already famous for his literary work. The bride was barely eighteen and her slim, girlish figure made her seem even younger. She was a doctor's daughter, reared within the Kremlin because of her father's position of physician to the court. Her knowledge of the world outside Moscow extended no further than Pokrovskoe, a small town eight miles from the city where the Bers family had a summer house.

In spite of the bride and groom's disparity in age and experience, they had enjoyed a long-standing familiarity with one another. All Lev's adult life, except during his military service and trips abroad, he had been in and out of the Bers household, both in Moscow and in the country. In fact, for many years he had been happily in love with the entire family—Dr. Bers, his wife Lyubov and their eight children. The Berses' appealing domestic life, its warm, bustling, teasing and loving atmosphere, had strengthened his desire for family happiness of his own. When Sonya was still a child, Lev began his search for the ideal woman with whom such happiness would be possible.

Lev's ideal of womanhood was rooted in his conception of his mother, Maria Tolstoy, who had died when he was only two, leaving no real memories but an image created from family tradition. Maria's qualities, however, had not been mere legends. She had been intelligent with high moral and intellectual standards and an unselfish devotion to her family. Not pretty except for her large, soulful eyes, she was five years older than Nikolai Tolstoy, the handsome army officer she married. The marriage was one of *convenance*, as Nikolai was greatly in need of his wife's money and she, at thirty-two, had no other prospects. There had been a flirtation between Nikolai and the penniless Tatyana Yergolsky, a ward of the Tolstoy family, but, like Sonya in *War and Peace*, Tatyana accepted the fact that her lover must marry for money. When Nikolai and his bride moved into Yasnaya Polyana, the estate some 130 miles south of Moscow that Maria inherited from her father Prince Volkonsky, they were accompanied by Tatyana Yergolsky, who made her home at Yasnaya for nearly all her life.

Four boys were born to Maria and Nikolai during the first seven years of their marriage—Nikolai, Sergei, Dmitry and Lev—and the boys were followed by a daughter, Maria, born just five months before her mother died. Although the marriage had been without romantic love, a deep affection developed between Nikolai and his wife and her death was as great a loss to him as to their children. Six years later Nikolai asked Tatyana Yergolsky to marry him and be a mother to his children. "Auntie" Tatyana, secure and happy in her position in the household, did not want to marry but she gladly agreed to care for the children. Although neither of the principals ever mentioned this proposal, a note in Tatyana's handwriting was found after her death, tucked into her small, pearl-embroidered purse:

16 August 1836

Nikolai made me a strange offer today—to marry him, to take the place of a mother to his children and never more leave them. I refused the first offer and promised to carry out the second for as long as I live.

The little Lev admired his dashing father from a distance. His nursery world was made up of women: his nurse; his grandmother Pelageya Tolstoy; her elder daughter, Aunt Aleksandra (the younger daughter, Aunt Pelageya, lived in Kazan) and Lev's favorite and best-loved "Auntie" Tatyana. Tatyana was another ideal creature, less intelligent and less educated than Lev's mother, but equally selfless. When Lev was old enough to join the company of his brothers, Nikolai, the eldest, introduced his younger brothers to another kind of idealism—the desire for a perfect world without pain where all human beings loved one another. Nikolai said that the secret of attaining this world was written on a green stick buried in the Yasnaya Polyana woods. This happy fantasy remained important to Lev all his life. Sixty years later he recorded in his diary his wish to be buried near the place where the green stick was supposed to be hidden.

In 1837, when Lev was nine, his father died. For a while Aunt Aleksandra was the children's guardian; at her death four years later Aunt Pelageya took her place. Aunt Pelageya moved the children to her home in Kazan, a busy port city on the River Volga about 450 miles directly east of Moscow. In Kazan the older boys attended the university and Lev, when he reached fourteen, was introduced to the delights of society—gambling, drinking, gypsy women and prostitutes—delights of which he partook with gusto and which he, before he reached nineteen, had learned to condemn with equal passion. By then a battle was engaged between his idealistic principles and his very normal human nature. This conflict set him apart from most aristocratic young men of nineteenth-century Russia. Turgenev, for example, seduced peasant women on his estates, fathered at least one illegitimate child and had a long affair with a married woman, all without besmirching his reputation. Such aristocratic detachment was not possible for Lev. The sexual indulgences that his class found normal and he set out to enjoy soon became sinful in his eyes. After his brothers took him to a brothel for the first time, Lev stood by the prostitute's bed and wept with pity for her.[1]

The diary he began during his third year at the University of Kazan was filled with resolves to live according to his ideals but, alas, as he noted, "It is easier to write ten volumes of philosophy than to put a single precept into practice." He wrote the first lines of his diary from a hospital bed:

17 March 1847. Kazan. Here it is six days since I entered the clinic and it is for six days that I have been nearly satisfied with myself. *Les petites causes produisent de grands effets.*

The small cause was gonorrhea. "I have gonorrhea for the reason, well understood, that one ordinarily has gonorrhea," and the great result was to be his reformation. At eighteen he began a lifelong occupation of recording his failings and setting anew his idealistic goals.

Lev's idealism did not extend to his university studies and his record was not brilliant. On this score he had little compunction, as he looked down upon most of the faculty and their teaching methods and he lacked the initiative to work for a diploma that for him would have no meaning. Today Lev's poor academic performance might be attributed to his failure to settle on a career or a goal in life. Without any deep religious attachment, bereft of father and mother, he struggled alone to establish a set of goals and moral values. "I have come to see clearly," he wrote in his diary, "that the irregular life which the majority of fashionable people take to be the result of being young is, really, the result of early corruption." [2] Lev blamed his corruption on the company he kept but admitted that character could not be changed simply by changing external influences. He kept asking himself, "What is the purpose of man's life?" The eighteen-year-old Lev decided that he could better discover the purpose of life away from the university. After three years of study he petitioned to leave, giving reasons of illness and "family considerations." The petition was granted in the spring of 1847 and Lev returned home to assume the responsibility of managing Yasnaya Polyana. According to a custom often followed in Russia, Lev, as the youngest son, had inherited the family home. [3] His first decisions were to improve the peasants' condition, increase the land's productivity and educate himself. He resolved to "fulfill everything which you have set for yourself," but confessed that his mental and physical will power might not be sufficient for his resolve. [4] His first daily schedule was ambitious but followed by a notation that nothing had been accomplished.

During the fifteen years between Kazan and Lev's marriage, his direction vacillated. He became interested in the education of children, developed an original method of teaching and tested it successfully in a school he founded for the peasant children at Yasnaya. While serving in the army in the Caucasus he wrote and published his first novel, *Childhood*, and overnight acquired a literary reputation. *Contemporary*, the literary magazine founded by Pushkin, published his stories from the siege of Sevastopol. Intellectual circles in St. Petersburg recognized Tolstoy as a stimulating and original thinker. He was also recognized in St. Petersburg and in Moscow as a hard drinker, a gambler, a devotee of gypsies and a profligate man-about-town. He recorded with self-disgust his indolence, indulgences and lack of moral restraint.

All this time Lev was acutely aware that he would be incomplete until he found that person who would be "the other" in his life. When he was twenty-eight he tried to talk himself into falling in love with Valeria Vladimirovna Arsenev, a pretty young woman who lived with her aunt and sisters not far from Yasnaya, but his diary and even his letters to Valeria betray the romance as too calculated.

Four years after this flirtation Lev felt the strongest physical attraction he had known. Aksinya Bazykin was a peasant woman living on the estate (her husband was serving in the army). Lev described their affair as similar to a married relationship, Aksinya bore him a son, but at the same time he called himself a "beast" and was ashamed to have taken advantage of a young woman. He never forgot or forgave himself for his involvement with Aksinya.[5] This affair when he was thirty intensified his longing for a relationship that would be without exploitation. Meanwhile he continued to dream of a wife with physical beauty, idealism and perhaps intelligence, too. Lev was devoted to a cousin eleven years his senior, Aleksandra Tolstoy, whom he jokingly referred to as "Granny" because he said that she was not old enough to require the respectful title of "Aunt." Granny was intelligent, perceptive, sophisticated, a maid of honor at court and at ease in fashionable and intellectual circles. She appreciated her young cousin and he, in turn, was always glad for her stimulating company. After visits to Granny he would become more aware of the loneliness of his single life, although merely imagining the ideal woman of his dreams could give him great joy. These exquisite dreams eventually mingled with the more realistic picture of domestic happiness reflected in the Berses' family life.

Lev's fondness for the Berses began in childhood when he played with Lyubov Islenev and her brother Konstantin. Lyubov was a few years older than Lev, who had a brief crush on her and once in a fit of jealousy shoved her down a flight of steps for not paying sufficient attention to him. Lyubov survived her punishment and when she was fifteen moved with her family to spend a winter in Tula, the provincial capital. Tula was only a few miles from Yasnaya, but there were no more childhood romps with the young Tolstoys. Lyubov's first winter in town she fell ill with a dangerous fever that none of the local doctors was able to cure. In desperation her father sent a message to Andrei Yevstafevich Bers, a Moscow doctor who was visiting the nearby Turgenev estate. Dr. Bers was a handsome man of thirty-five, tall and imposing with charm and poise. He had been, and perhaps still was, a lover of Ivan Turgenev's mother. It is hard to imagine what attraction Varvara Petrovna Turgenev held for Dr. Bers. She was a plain, willful woman who treated her thousands of serfs with grisly cruelty, had them flogged for invented offenses and once, in a rage, was reported to have tried to tear the mouth from the face of a peasant woman. The gentle Lyubov, who lay near death when the doctor first saw her, presented a dramatic contrast to Varvara. Moved by the young girl's predicament, Dr. Bers stayed in Tula caring for his patient until she was well. During this time he fell in love with her; when Lyubov confessed to returning her doctor's love, her mother and father were appalled. The Islenevs were large landowners, related to the aristocratic Sheremetevs, and they objected to Dr. Bers on grounds of class—he was a professional man without wealth or connections.[6] They also abhorred his German ancestry and disapproved of the fact that he was twenty years older than the young girl he wished to marry. But love won out and the wedding took place in August 1842. Lyubov settled down in Dr. Bers's Moscow apartment, which, because of his position as court physician, adjoined the palace. It was far from elegant, however, and seemed a cage to Lyubov, who was accustomed to spacious rooms and to a country estate with avenues lined with lime trees. At her husband's suggestion, she continued her studies until the babies started coming, thirteen in all, eight of whom lived. Of the first four, one was a boy, Aleksandr (Sasha), and three were girls—

Elizabeta, Sofya and Tatyana, more familiarly called Liza, Sonya and Tanya respectively. The last four children were all boys.

In *War and Peace* Lev modeled the Rostov family in part on the Berses—the hospitable household, the many children, relatives and family retainers, the constant guests who came with families and servants and stayed for months—but there were also dissimilarities. Count and Countess Rostov were typical landed gentry and more like Lev's paternal grandparents. Dr. Bers did not belong to this class nor was he ambitious to acquire a place in it through his marriage. He was interested in all sorts of people. Sonya's sister Tanya wrote her memoirs when she was in her seventies and she vividly recalled a gathering in her father's study that had included a peasant, a prince (Golitsyn), a violinist, a dean of Moscow University and an actor, all of whom were Dr. Bers's friends. Thus the Bers children grew up in an independent atmosphere where ideas and talents were more respected than social position and where education was considered important even for daughters. Both Liza and Sonya graduated with diplomas in childhood education. Liza was the most bookish but it was Sonya who, at age ten, read every word of *Childhood* and its sequel, *Boyhood.* Both of these books were especially exciting to the Berses because the author had modeled characters on the Islenev family. Lev once remarked to Lyubov that she must have recognized a lot that was near and dear to her.[7] When Lev paid a call on Dr. Bers soon after the publication of *Boyhood* Sonya tied ribbons onto the chair where he had sat. Lev made no mention in his diary of his call but noted instead:

> *18 February 1854. . . .* I remember nothing except that I am in Moscow. A disorderly existence both physically and mentally and I have spent too much money.

Two years later he found a visit to the Berses worth a comment:

> Went to Pokrovskoe . . . and had dinner at Lyubov Bers'. The children waited on us, such darling, gay little girls, and then we went for a walk and played leapfrog.

The darling, gay little girls were six years older in 1862. Liza and Sonya put up their hair and wore long dresses. Only Tanya clung fiercely to the prerogatives of childhood, clowned and teased, expressed her affections and whims freely and repressed none of her general exuberance. All three sisters were sensitive, intelligent and had a physical vitality and mental liveliness that made them attractive. One of Lev's closest friends, the Russian lyric poet Afanasy Fet, met the Bers daughters in 1862 and described their charm as *"quelque chose du chien,"* a slightly risqué phrase for sex appeal.[8]

The three girls, however, had grown into three quite different young women. Liza was coolheaded and sensible and at an early age had preferred to lie on the sofa reading while Sasha played with the younger sisters. Sometimes Liza reproved them for lack of manners and they in turn teased her and accused her of being haughty. A photograph reveals a trace of anxiety around her eyes and mouth; perhaps Liza had the insecurity for which haughtiness is the mask. Sonya was less beautiful but pretty with all the charms of vibrant health—rosy cheeks, luxurious dark hair and large, black eyes. Sonya was acknowledged to be the most sentimental daughter and her mood swings could be rapid. Dr. Bers once said that he thought his middle daughter might never be completely happy. Everyone's favorite was Tanya, the adorable imp, the vivacious young girl, the talented and irrepressible charmer who became a model for entrancing Natasha Rostov in *War and Peace*. Let Lev himself describe Tanya (Natasha):

> A plain but lively, black-eyed little girl with a wide mouth, childish, bare shoulders heaving out of her bodice from her fast run, with dark curls tossed back, thin, bare arms and little legs in lace pantaloons and open shoes, was at that pretty age when a little girl is already not a child but the child is not yet a young woman.[9]

Each daughter received individual attention from Lev. He discussed literature and serious subjects with Liza, talked about teaching children with Sonya or played piano duets with her, but he treated Tanya as if she were much younger than her fifteen years, carrying her piggyback and conniving with her to play tricks on the others. Sometimes he accompanied her when she sang and he nicknamed her "Madame Viardot" after Turgenev's mistress, a famous opera singer. He was as at home and happy in the household as if he had been a favorite uncle or cousin. Then, in the summer of 1862 during those most romantic Russian months when the lilacs have bloomed and the twilights grow long, the Bers family noticed a change in Lev. His visits were more frequent and his attentions more assiduous; in brief, he suddenly behaved like a man who had come courting. The family believed that he was courting Liza, the eldest daughter. Dr. Bers naturally assumed that no younger daughter would receive serious attention until the eldest was married; besides, to outward appearances Liza was the most suitable of the sisters to become Countess Tolstoy. She was beautiful, had a dignified bearing and was the most intellectual daughter. To confirm in everyone's mind that it *was* Liza, there was the gossip repeated by the two German governesses, one in the Bers household and one in the household of Lev's sister, Maria Nikolaevna. The governesses reported overhearing the count confide to his sister that he was so fond of the Bers family that if he married it would be to one of their daughters. To this remark Maria Nikolaevna had responded that Liza would make an excellent wife, she was so serious and sensible.

Serious and sensible was not enough for Lev, who had given only a passing thought to Liza before fixing his heart on Sonya. The Berses' servants, however, began to flatter Liza about Count Tolstoy's presumed interest in her. The austere older daughter softened noticeably; she took more care of her dress, arranged her hair in new ways and spent long periods in front of the looking glass. Her sisters teased her about Lev Nikolaevich whom they now referred to as *"le Comte."* Sonya, too, had a beau, a handsome young cadet, Mitrofan Andreevich Polivanov, and it was assumed that when Liza married *le Comte* Polivanov would seriously court Sonya. In the meantime Sonya and Mitrofan had an understanding that they were in love and Mitrofan unselfishly assured Sonya that he would not bind her if she should change her mind. So the summer of 1862 was full of romantic excitement for the Bers family. At Pokrovskoe there were guests for dinner and tea every day, Sasha (himself a cadet) brought other cadets for visits and Dr. Bers observed with approval the man he believed to be Liza's suitor. Mother Bers was less pleased, but acquiescent. The young people, and now Lev included himself among them, took long walks on moonlit nights or sat on the veranda talking until after midnight. At bedtime there were confidences in the room where the sisters slept. It was the sharp-eyed, intuitive Tanya who was the first to realize that all was not quite as it seemed on the surface. After Liza had fallen asleep Tanya whispered to Sonya, "Sonya, *tu aimes le Comte?"* and Sonya, without appearing surprised or shocked, whispered back, *"Je ne sais pas."* That night Sonya wept a little into her pillow before falling asleep and Tanya lay awake pondering the vagaries of love.[10]

Did Sonya's sensitive antennae pick up Lev's attraction to her even before he was aware of it himself? There is not a word in

Lev's diary to indicate when he first thought of Sonya as a wife. His diary for 1862 is almost empty until late August and by then Lev was in a torment of love. For Sonya the thought that she might become Countess Tolstoy was flattering and exciting and it was hardly surprising that her romance with Polivanov paled. On one score alone the young cadet had the advantage—he was handsome. Lev, apart from his piercing blue-gray eyes, was ill-favored. He had already lost many of his teeth, his beard was shaggy and he had the large, red hands of a peasant. As a young man Lev regretted not having the handsome appearance associated with heroism and distinction, but by 1862 he seldom referred to his looks. Besides, it was not appearance but personality that made him interesting to the Berses and they were particularly proud of his novels and his achievements in education. Liza and Sonya were regular readers of the education journal that Lev published at Yasnaya. All his accomplishments might have been reason enough to excite the Bers daughters but it was something more that set Lev apart from others. His extreme sensitivity to people and a certain inner fire, perhaps lit by the conflicts that divided him, made his presence electric and charming. Much later Tanya Bers wrote of him that, "Wherever he was, it was more lively and interesting." The Bers daughters were well attuned to respond to this interest and vitality, particularly the sentimental and reflective middle daughter.

2.

In early August something happened that speeded up the course of the romance. Lyubov Bers took her three daughters and two of their younger brothers to visit Grandfather Islenev and his second wife at Ivitsy.[11] What could be more natural than to visit Yasnaya Polyana, which was only a few hours ride from the Islenev estate? Lev's sister, Maria Nikolaevna, was staying with her brother; Lyubov was eager to see her childhood friend and she may not have been averse to promoting Lev's presumed courtship of Liza. Less pleased with the idea than her husband was, she still must have found it difficult to object for long to a prospective son-in-law who was a count, a member of one of Russia's oldest families and a famous author.

The Berses broke their journey with a stop at an inn in Serpukhov, a town halfway between Moscow and Tula. The children found staying at an inn, the smell of stables and hay and the early morning departure with cocks crowing and a mist hanging over the meadows, exciting. After a visit to Lyubov's family in Tula, it was only a short ride to the Tolstoy estate. The house stood in a sunny meadow surrounded by woods, a rambling white building overlooking a pond. Yasnaya Polyana means "bright glade"—the name described the location. Mother Bers found it quite familiar and nostalgic, although not entirely as it had been when she had played there with the Tolstoy children. Lev had since sold a part of the house to pay his gambling debts. This section had been completely removed and in its place Lev had planted trees and lilac bushes.

The Berses' visit was a surprise, received joyfully. Years later when Sonya wrote the story of her courtship and wedding she began with this August visit to Yasnaya Polyana:

> Maria Nikolaevna and Lev Nikolaevich welcomed us enthusiastically. Aunt Tatyana Aleksandrovna Yergolsky greeted us cordially but with more reserve and in a very proper French. Her companion, Natalya Petrovna, pressed me to her shoulder without saying a word. . . . They led us down to a big, vaulted room which was furnished not just simply but poorly. There were sofas painted white standing against the walls with, instead of backs, very hard cushions covered with blue and white striped ticking. A chaise longue was painted the same white. . . . It was the beginning of August and already the days were shorter. When we had had barely time to run around the garden, Natalia Petrovna took us to the raspberries. For the first time in our lives we ate raspberries from the bush. . . . When it began to get dark Mother sent me downstairs to arrange our things and to prepare the beds. Dunyasha (Auntie's maid) and I were busy getting ready for the night when suddenly Lev Nikolaevich came in and Dunyasha told him that there were three beds on the sofas but no place for a fourth.
>
> "But the chaise longue will do," said Lev Nikolaevich and he pulled it out at full length.
>
> "I shall sleep on the chaise longue," I said.
>
> "And I shall make up your bed," said Lev Nikolaevich and with clumsy, awkward motions he began to prepare the bed. The intimate way in which we made up the bed together made me shy but somehow pleasantly so. When

everything was ready we went upstairs. . . . The squint-
eyed little serving man, Aleksy Stefanovich, was putting
out the supper. . . . I took a chair and went out alone
onto the balcony to admire the view. . . . In my mood
there was something new, very significant, serious, happy
and infinite. Everyone went to supper. . . . Lev Nikolaevich called me to come to supper.

"No, thank you," I said, "I don't want to eat. It is so
lovely here." Lev Nikolaevich returned to the dining room
but he did not finish his supper. He came again to me
on the balcony. Of what we spoke, I do not remember in
detail. I only remember that he said, "How clear and simple you are." And this was very pleasant to me. How well
I slept on the chaise longue which Lev Nikolaevich had
prepared for me.

The next morning the weather was fine and Sonya woke in a
happy mood. Plans were made for an afternoon picnic, the carriage
was harnessed and Lev, who was to ride beside the carriage, suggested that Sonya ride with him on his horse Belogubka. She was
eager to comply but demurred because she did not have a riding
habit. She was wearing, she later recalled, a becoming yellow
dress with dark velvet buttons and a matching belt.

"It doesn't matter," Lev told her, "here in the woods there are
no dachas and no one will see you." He helped Sonya onto Belogubka. She felt incredibly happy galloping through the woods with
Lev Nikolaevich.

The others packed into the carriage and they drove until they
came to the chosen spot for the picnic, a rolling meadow with
old oak trees. Other guests arrived, the samovar was set up and
the supper put out. Everyone was in a gay mood and Lev persuaded
all of them to climb a large haystack and roll down, even his
sister and Mother Bers, but before they left the haystack they
crouched on the top, singing songs and watching the sun set.

Several days later the Berses went on to Ivitsy where Grandfather
Islenev and his second wife kept a more fashionable establishment
than that at Yasnaya. The day after their arrival, Lev unexpectedly
appeared astride his white horse. He was in good spirits, happy
and excited. As usual at Ivitsy there were many other guests and
at night there was dancing. For music those who could play took
turns at the piano. Sonya wore a white and mauve dress with
lilac bows on the shoulders from which hung ribbons, a style that
was called *suivez-moi*.

"How smartly all of you are dressed," Lev said, and he told Sonya with a smile that he wished Auntie Tatyana could be there to see and admire her. But he did not join in the dancing.

"Aren't you dancing?" Sonya asked.

"No, I'm much too old."

Tanya heard this and declared, "You don't look like an old man to me," but after staring at him quite hard she added, "but you don't look like a young man either." They laughed and Lev agreed to one turn of a waltz with Tanya, but then returned to his chair. Card tables were set up for those who were not dancing. The players kept score on the green baize covers using chalk that could be rubbed off. When it grew late, Mother Bers suggested that her daughters go to bed, but as Sonya was leaving Lev called her into the empty room where the card tables had stood. Unknown to them, Tanya followed and crawled under the piano to listen to their conversation.

"Sofya Andreevna," Lev said. "Wait here a little."

"What is it?"

"Read here what I am writing to you."

"All right."

"But I shall write only the first letters and you must guess what the words are."

"How is that? That's impossible. Well, all right."

Lev brushed the scores from the card table, took the chalk and began writing. They were both very serious and full of emotion. Sonya watched his large, red hand. Lev wrote: "Y.y.a.n.f.h.t.v.r.m.o.m.a.a.t.i.o.m.h." Sonya read aloud: "Your youth and need for happiness too vividly remind me of my age and the impossibility of my happiness." Her heart began to beat violently, the blood hammered in her temples and her face was burning. Later she recalled that she felt, "Outside of time, beyond awareness of the world; it seemed to me that in that moment I was able to do anything, understand everything, to embrace immensity."

"Now, once more," Lev said and he wrote, "T.e.i.y.f.a.f.o.a.-m.a.y.s.L. Y.a.y.s.T.m.d.m." Sonya easily read every letter: "There exists in your family a false opinion about me and your sister Liza. You and your sister Tanya must defend me." Lev listened to her without showing surprise. It was as though it were perfectly natural for Sonya to read his thoughts. The next morning he departed but not until he extracted from the Berses a promise to stop at Yasnaya on their return journey.

Lev's visit had not been long but he left the Bers daughters in a turmoil. Liza was frantic, convinced that Lev Nikolaevich was her lover but that Sonya was using unfair tactics to steal him from her. She wondered if she should fight for him aggressively as she felt that Sonya was doing. In desperation she turned weeping to Tanya. Had not Tanya observed that Sonya was taking *le Comte* from her? Had not she seen Sonya's flirtatious glances, her extra attention to her appearance? Tanya tried to reassure Liza that her "hurt would become less" but she had not the courage to tell her sister that Lev Nikolaevich had all but declared himself to Sonya. Instead she sought her mother when Lyubov was in bed and tried to tell her that the family was mistaken in thinking that it was Liza who was courted. Lyubov was not pleased and said that Tanya talked nonsense but, after remaining silent for a while, she asked, "Has Sonya told you anything of this?" Tanya admitted she had, but in secret. Tanya guessed that her mother's concern was for Dr. Bers, who adored his first daughter. He saw her ardent desire to be Countess Tolstoy and he firmly believed in the convention of the eldest daughter being courted first. He would not easily see Liza hurt and this worried his wife.

The Berses' second visit to Yasnaya was less rapturous. The adults were tired and the children anxious to be back in Pokrovskoe. As they piled into the coach Lev suddenly announced, "I am going with you. Really, how could I stay at Yasnaya now? It will be so empty and boring." Everyone but Auntie Tatyana and her companion departed, as Lev's sister also went along to prolong her visit with Lyubov. It was decided that Lev should sit on the outside seat, sharing it first with Liza and then with Sonya. When the cold evening came, Sonya was outside wrapped up cozily beside Lev, who told her long tales about his days in the Caucasus, about the beauty of the mountains and the primitive, wild nature there, and about his own exploits. Sonya recalled:

> I was so happy listening to his calm and husky voice, tender and moving and as if it came from somewhere far away. And then I would fall asleep for a few minutes and then wake up and once more his voice would be telling me beautiful and poetic tales of himself in the Caucasus. I was ashamed of being sleepy but I was still so young and, although I was sorry not to hear all that Lev Nikolaevich said, there were moments when I wasn't able to overcome sleep.

They drove all night. Near Moscow there was a final coach stop and all got out of the carriage to go into the station while the horses were changed. Liza had been riding outside and it was Sonya's turn, but Liza begged to continue outside, claiming that the coach was much too stuffy for her. Sonya did not find the heart to say no to her sister and got inside when they returned to the coach.

"Sofya Andreevna," Lev cried, "you know that it is your turn to ride outside."

"I know, but I'm cold," Sonya answered and the door of the carriage shut. From inside she could see that Lev stood for a few minutes in deep thought before he took his place beside Liza.

In Moscow Lev rented a room from a German shoemaker so he could be near the Berses at Pokrovskoe. On 23 August he picked up his neglected diary and made his first reference to Sonya, but did not use her name:

> *23 August.* . . . Spent the night at the Berses. A child! Just like a child! But a big mess! Ah, if only I could look at myself clearly and honestly. . . . I am afraid of myself. And what if it is this, the desire for love and not love? I try to see only her weak sides but even so, it is. A child! Just like a child!

Two days later he walked to the Berses' and Sonya gave him a story she had written. The heroine was Elena, who had beautiful black eyes. Her older sister, Zinaida, was cold and proud and the younger one, Natasha, was impish and spoiled by everyone. Elena was courted by an older man, Dublitsky, who was outwardly unattractive, rather vacillating in his opinions, but full of energy and intelligence. Also interested in Elena was a handsome youth, Smirnov, who proposed to her but whom she did not accept because of her attraction to Dublitsky. Zinaida thought Dublitsky was in love with her. Elena was torn by indecision—she admired Dublitsky but was uncomfortable before his sharp intelligence. She solved her problem by entering a convent. Dublitsky married Zinaida and eventually Elena left the convent and married Smirnov. The story could have been a thinly disguised warning to Lev to declare himself or Sonya would turn to Mitrofan Polivanov. Lev was disturbed:

> She gave me her story to read. What forceful truths and simplicity. She is tortured by uncertainty. I read every-

thing without getting upset, without a sign of jealousy or envy but "an extraordinarily unattractive appearance" and "vacillating opinions" hurt me famously. I calmed myself.

Perhaps because of Sonya's story Lev began berating himself for courting a young girl when he should be living an austere life devoted to work. But he had to admit that he was enthralled by Sonya:

27 August. Her shyness is not a good sign but she is firmly present everywhere.

At first he wrote "firmly present in my head" but he crossed out "in my head" and substituted "everywhere."

On 28 August he was thirty-four. He woke in a sad mood and noted, "I wrote in vain by initials to Sonya." He did not realize that his message had been clear to both Sonya and Tanya. He closed this entry with a rebuke to himself:

Wicked, ugly face, do not think about marriage, your calling is otherwise and has been amply rewarding.

But he continued to haunt Pokrovskoe. Sonya recalled a playful incident:

I remember one time when we were all very merry and in a playful mood. I kept repeating the same nonsense continuously. "When I am queen, I shall do now this, now that." My father's cabriolet from which the horse had just been unharnessed stood on the veranda. I settled into the cabriolet and shouted, "When I am queen I shall go driving in such a cabriolet." Lev Nikolaevich grabbed the shafts and in place of the horse he pulled me at a trot saying, "Here, I shall drive the queen myself." This incident showed how he was strong and healthy. "You mustn't, you mustn't," I cried. "It's too heavy for you." But I was very pleased and happy that Lev Nikolaevich drove me and that he was so strong. How wonderful were the evenings and the moonlit nights. Right now I can see that glade, all bright in the moonlight, and the moon reflecting in the nearby pond. How fresh, shining and brisk those August nights were. "What a mad night," Lev Nikolaevich often said, sitting with us on the balcony or walking with us around the dacha.

Near the end of August the Berses move
apartment, although they continued to sper
try. Lev was a frequent visitor in both p
wrote in his diary:

> Went to the Bers and with them to
> mind, never mind, silence. [An allusion to Gogol's *The
> Diary of a Madman*.] Not love as before, not jealousy, not
> even regret but something similar and sweet—a little hope
> (which must not be). Swine. A little like regret and sadness.
> But a marvelous night and a good, sweet feeling. . . .
> There was a family scene at their house.

There was tension in the Bers family. Dr. Bers waited for Lev to
propose to Liza, Liza grew more desperate in her hopes and Sonya,
still so much a child, nevertheless played her cards carefully and
correctly. Polivanov arrived and was there when his rival called.
Lev noted:

> S. toward P. did not make me jealous. I cannot believe
> that it is not myself. . . . We went for a walk, the summer
> house, and home for supper—her eyes, but night!

Like many a lover he began to fear that he had imagined Sonya's
interest in himself. They went for a walk and, finding the talk
trivial, Lev kept silent. Afterward he went riding and pondered
Sonya's attitude:

> I rode and thought: Either everything is accidental, or
> she feels emotions with an extraordinary subtlety, or it
> is the most trivial coquetry, one thing today and another
> thing tomorrow. In the main, where is she going, either
> by accident, or by coquetry, or with subtle intention?

Sonya's memoir does not describe what her feelings were like
during these days. She seemed to have been more confident of
the outcome and less tortured by doubts and introspection than
her lover. Dr. Bers and Liza and the servants had one idea about
Lev; Sonya, Sasha and Tanya had another. They were all waiting
for him to make a move. Meanwhile he temporized:

> Went for a walk: Either, either, either. And the day before
> happiness appeared so clearly that I did not sleep all night.
> In the evening we spoke of love. Still worse. . . . Today
> alone at home I somehow thought over my position in
> its proper breadth. I must wait.

He brooded on Sonya's story and the character of Dublitsky, so transparently himself:

> Dublitsky, don't intrude upon youth, poetry, love—these, old fellow, are for the cadets. . . . A monastery, work, here is your calling from which height you can calmly and joyfully watch the love and happiness of others—and I have been in that monastery and shall go back again. Yes.

This noble resolve did not fool him for long:

> Insincere diary. *Arrière-pensée*, that what I write will be hers, that she will be sitting by my side and reading this and—and that this is for her.

It irked Lev that Liza assumed a proprietary air with him as though he were already hers:

> My God! How she would be superbly unhappy if she were my wife. . . . Everything was seething inside me.

Every day his diary had references to Sonya:

> She blushes and is agitated. Oh, Dublitsky, do not dream. I am not able to leave Moscow. . . . Until three o'clock I did not sleep. Like a sixteen-year-old boy I dreamed and tormented myself. . . . Woke up at ten, tired from the agitations of the night. Worked lazily and, as a school boy waits for Sunday, I waited for the evening. . . . More in love than before. *Au fond*, hope remains. . . . I am in love as I did not believe it was possible to love. I am mad, I shall shoot myself if it continues like this. Was at their house this evening. She is delightful in every respect. But I am disgusting Dublitsky. I should have been careful before. At this point I cannot stop. Dublitsky, granted, but I am handsome through love.

He resolved to go to the Berses early in the morning and propose to Sonya at once but the next night he was forced to admit:

> *13 September.* Nothing happened. . . . Tomorrow I shall set off when I get up and say everything or shoot myself.

He had second thoughts about shooting himself and crossed out the last three words. He could not sleep that night. In the early hours of the morning he went to his diary:

Four o'clock in the morning. I have written her a lett(
Tomorrow I shall deliver it, i.e., today, the fourteent(
My God, how I dread to die. Happiness such as this seem(
to me impossible. My God, help me.

Sonya sensed her lover's dilemma and when he told her that he
must speak to her about something very important she guessed
what it was. She recalled:

He talked to me a long time that evening. I played the
piano in the drawing room while he stood, a figure leaning
on the stove all the time, and as soon as I stopped, he
repeated, "Play on, play on."

Sonya played, over and over again, the waltz song "Il Bacio,"
which she had learned by heart to accompany Tanya. Her hands
trembled with emotion and occasionally she stumbled. Lev left
the house without delivering his letter or speaking but he felt
more confident. The sixteenth was a Saturday. He spent the whole
day with the Berses, his letter in his pocket. At teatime Sonya
asked Tanya to sing "Il Bacio" and this obviously annoyed Lev.
He must have been sick of the tune if nothing else. Tanya was in
good voice and Lev soon lost his irritation and praised her. Years
later he told Tanya that he had vowed to himself, "If she takes
that final note well, then I shall deliver my letter today." Tanya's
final note was clear and beautiful. Lev waited for his chance to
catch Sonya alone. Sasha arrived with friends and the dining room
table was spread with a repast for the hungry cadets. Tanya began
serving tea and Lev called Sonya into her mother's empty room.
Sonya described his proposal in her memoir:

He began, "I have wanted to speak to you but I cannot.
Here is a letter which I have already had in my pocket
for several days. Read it. I shall wait here for your answer."
I grabbed the letter and swiftly dashed downstairs to the
room I shared with my sisters. Here is what the letter
said:

Sofya Andrevna,[12]
It has become unbearable for me. For three weeks every
day I say, today I shall tell her everything and I set off
with the same fright, ruefulness and happiness in my
heart. And each night, as now, I go through the past
day, I torture myself and I say, why didn't I speak and

how and what should I have said? I have brought this letter with me so that I can hand it to you if once more it is impossible for me or I lack the courage to tell you everything. *Your family's false opinion about me* consists, it seems to me, in this: that I am in love with your sister Liza. This is not fair. *Your story dwells in my head* because reading it I was convinced that I was Dublitsky, that I could not dream of happiness, that your *beautiful* and poetic need for love . . . [Here part of the letter is illegible.] . . . that I do not envy nor will I envy him with whom you are in love. It seemed to me that I would be able to rejoice for you, as for a child. At Ivitsky I wrote, "Your youth and need for happiness too vividly remind me of my age and the impossibility of my happiness." But both then and now I lied to myself. Even then I could have broken off everything and once again gone back to my cloister of solitary labors and my passion for work. Now I am unable to do anything and I feel that I have upset your family, that the simple attitude that I had for you as a friend and an honest person is lost. And I cannot leave and I cannot stay. You are an honest person, tell me, hand on heart—do not hurry, for God's sake, do not hurry—what should I do? This is not a laughing matter but serious. A month ago I should have died laughing if anyone had told me that it was possible to be tormented as I am tormented at this time, and happily tormented. Tell me, as an honest person, do you wish to be my wife? Only say yes if you do so fearlessly with all your soul; otherwise, if you have a shadow of a doubt, it will be better to say no. I expect it and will find the strength to bear it. And if I could never be loved as a husband as I love, that would be terrible.

I didn't read this letter thoroughly at once but ran my eyes over it to the words, "Do you wish to be my wife?" I wanted to return upstairs at once to Lev Nikolaevich with the answer yes when I met my sister Liza in the doorway. She asked me, "Well, what is it?" and I answered her quickly, *"Le Comte m'a fait la proposition."*

Tanya arrived in time to hear these words. She had seen Sonya dash from their mother's room with a letter, had seen Liza's pursuit and, guessing what had happened, she put down the tea tray and ran after her sisters. According to Tanya's account (Sonya generously omitted this part), Liza became hysterical and screamed, "Refuse him, refuse him instantly!" Sonya received a different message from her mother:

> My mother came in and at once knew what had happened. Taking me firmly by the shoulders she pushed me toward the door and said, "Be off and tell him your answer."

If Mother Bers feared that the procrastinating suitor might change his mind and flee the house, Sonya obeyed her as if the same thought had occurred to her:

> As though on wings, with a frightful speed, I came running up the stairs, flashed past the dining room, the living room and ran into my mother's room. Lev Nikolaevich stood waiting for me leaning on the wall in the corner of the room. I went to him and he took me by both hands. "Well, what?" he asked. I replied, "Of course, yes." After a few minutes everyone in the house knew what had happened and all began to congratulate us.

3.

Not everyone took part in the congratulations. Liza remained in her room and Dr. Bers claimed that he was not feeling well and shut himself in his study. That night Lev described his happiness in a minimum of words:

> *16 September.* Spoke. She—yes. She is like a wounded bird. Never mind writing. None of this can be described or forgot.

"Wounded bird" is an odd description for a young woman who must have had a sense of triumph, unless the second "she" referred to Liza or Lev was thinking of Sonya's youth and inexperience. The next day he came down to earth:

> *17 September.* Engaged, presents, champagne. Liza is pitiful and wretched, she should detest me. She kisses me.

This must have cost Liza an effort. All day she put up a good front. The seventeenth was Sonya's nameday as well as her moth-

er's and the family friends came with their congratulations. Liza
and Sonya were dressed alike as was their custom on festive occa-
sions; both wore mauve and white with bows on their shoulders.
Dr. Bers avoided the occasion but Liza stood bravely in line with
her mother and sister to greet the guests.

It was at this party that the Berses announced Sonya's engagement. Mother Bers did not always handle the situation tactfully;
she sometimes spoke of her daughter's engagement, forgetting to
mention which daughter. Both Liza and Sonya blushed at the
confusion of the guests who first turned to Liza with their good
wishes only to be directed to Sonya. The old university professor
who had taught French to all the daughters was distressed that
Count Tolstoy was marrying Sonya Bers. He remarked frankly,
"C'est dommage que cela ne fût Mlle. Lise. Elle a si bien étudié."

The wedding preparations began in haste, most of them boring
to Sonya. Her family took her to shops where she tried on dresses,
lingerie and bonnets with complete indifference. Lev, too, was
impatient with formalities and persuaded the Berses that the engagement need last for only one week. Both he and Sonya were
immersed in their love and their new relationship.

Lev's ideal of marital bliss included complete openness between
husband and wife, a sharing of their innermost thoughts by reading
one another's diaries, writing frankly and holding nothing back,
and he was anxious that they start this openness at once. He brought
his diaries to Sonya and asked her to read them. She recalled
later:

> Lev Nikolaevich came every day and once he brought me
> his diaries. I remember how reading these diaries, which
> he gave me to read before our wedding from an unneces-
> sary conscientiousness, shocked me terribly. And it was
> wrong of him, I cried a lot looking at his past.

Indeed, Lev erred naively and cruelly in thinking that he should
share his past life, a life he recalled with shame and disgust, with
his fiancée, a sheltered young woman who had just celebrated
her eighteenth birthday. It is a tribute to Sonya that she gave
their love and her hopes for their marriage priority over these
revelations.

Sonya was not the only one weeping. Her family and friends
shed tears as though she would be lost to them forever. When
Lev arrived and found Sonya comforting a hysterically sobbing
girlfriend, he said dryly, "It is as though you were burying her."

He was also puzzled by the need for a large trousseau. "Surely she has clothes," he told Mother Bers. "She has always been properly dressed." But in spite of his impatience with conventions, Lev did not neglect his own part, as Sonya remembered:

> Lev Nikolaevich was also going to a lot of trouble. He bought a handsome *dormeuse* [a sleeping coach] for the wedding trip, ordered a photograph of our family and gave me a brooch with diamonds. He took his own portrait which I asked him to set in the gold bracelet given to me by my father.

Sonya was absorbed in her love and, already, by a fear of losing her husband's love. After Lev's death she wrote:

> This fear stayed in my heart all of my life although, thank God, in the forty-eight years of our married life we kept our love for one another. When we talked about our future, Lev Nikolaevich offered me a choice of where I wanted to be after the wedding: to stay living in Moscow at first with my relations or to go abroad or to go straight to Yasnaya Polyana.

Sonya chose to go straight to Yasnaya Polyana and this pleased Lev profoundly.

The day of the wedding arrived, the twenty-third of September, and Lev was beset by qualms. He went at once to Sonya and found her in the room where the luggage stood ready for the coach. Together they sat on the trunks and he tormented her with doubts about her love for him. Sonya recalled:

> It even seemed that he wanted to escape, that he was afraid of marriage. I began to cry. Mother came in and rebuked Lev Nikolaevich. "You have found a fine time to upset her!" she said. "Today is the wedding, so exhausting for her, and a long journey still to go and she is all in tears." Lev Nikolaevich appeared to be ashamed. He went away quickly.

The only blood relation that Lev would have at the wedding was his Aunt Pelageya from Kazan, who drove with Sonya to the church. His brother Sergei had gone to Yasnaya to prepare to receive the married couple. The other Tolstoy brothers had died, Dmitry in 1856 and Nikolai in 1860. Lev chose a friend, Timiryazev, to be best man. The customs of the day were adhered to except that

Sonya insisted on doing her hair herself. After six o'clock her sisters and girlfriends began to dress her, pinning on her flowers and the long tulle veil. The wedding dress was also tulle with open neck and sleeves. Sonya observed that her girlish shoulders and arms had a pitiful, bony appearance. At last all was ready and the bridal party waited for the best man's announcement that the bridegroom was at the church. Sonya recalled:

> An hour and more passed, and no one. The thought flashed through my mind that he had escaped—he had been so queer in the morning. But in place of the best man . . . [Lev Nikolaevich's] valet appeared . . . in a state of excitement and asked us to quickly open a suitcase and give him a clean shirt. In all the preparations for the wedding and the departure they had forgotten to leave out a clean shirt.

Another wait and the best man came to announce that the groom was waiting at the church. Sonya went to say good-bye to her father, who claimed illness as an excuse not to attend the wedding:

> I went to him in his study to say good-bye and he seemed mollified and touched. They prepared the bread and salt, Mother took the icon of the martyred Sofya. Standing by my Uncle Mikhail Aleksandrovich Mother held the icon and they blessed me. Solemnly and without a word we drove to the church which was within two steps of home. I cried all the way.

It was expected then that a bride should cry on leaving her family and Sonya had more reason than most. The Berses were particularly close and affectionate and Sonya was a little frightened of her fiancé, who was not only sixteen years older than she but a famous person. There were also his diary confessions of his dissolute past and, besides, with her entire engagement squeezed into one week, she wept from excitement and exhaustion. Added to all this emotional tension was the fact that Sonya was about to be the central figure in a fashionable ritual that would be attended by many people whom she barely knew, members of the palace staff, and strangers who had wandered into the church. Sonya described the ceremony and her feelings:

> The winter garden and the courtyard of the Church of the Virgin Birth were splendidly illuminated. Lev Nikolae-

vich met me in the courtyard of the winter garden, took my hand and led me to the church's door where the priest met us. He took both our hands and led us to the lectern. [In the Russian Church the altar is in the sanctuary behind a screen.] The court choir was singing, two priests assisted and everything was elegant, elegant and solemn. . . . Lev Nikolaevich described our marriage ceremony perfectly in his novel *Anna Karenina* where he described the wedding of Levin and Kitty.

During the ceremony Sonya felt numb:

It seemed to me that by this time, after all the days of agitations, I had experienced so much that, standing under the crown [the ritual crown used in the Orthodox ceremony] I experienced nothing and felt nothing. It seemed that something was happening that was beyond question, inevitable, like a spontaneous phenomenon.

Among the bride's attendants, according to Russian custom, were two men. One was her brother Sasha and the other his good friend and Sonya's rejected beau, Mitrofan Polivanov.

The ceremony over, the bride and groom were congratulated and Lev drove back to the Berses' in the carriage with Sonya. She recalled:

He was very sweet and seemed to be happy. At home in the Kremlin the preparations were all there that were usual at weddings: champagne, fruit, bonbons, and so forth. There were not many guests, only relations and the closest family friends. They changed me into my traveling dress. . . . Six post horses were brought by a postillion and harnessed to the new *dormeuse* just bought by Lev Nikolaevich, the shiny, black, newly acquired trunks were fastened to the top of the carriage and Lev Nikolaevich began to hurry the departure. . . . I had purposely waited to the end to say good-bye to my mother. Just before I took my seat in the carriage, I threw myself around her neck. We both wept. . . . The autumn rain never ceased to pour, the dim street lights and carriage lights were reflected in the puddles. The horses made impatient noises with their hooves and those in front with the postillion pulled forward. Lev Nikolaevich slammed the doors of the carriage on us. . . . I hid myself in the corner and,

all spent from exhaustion and grief, I wept without stopping.

Lev did not understand Sonya's grief at leaving her family. He
declared that apparently she did not love him very much if it
was so terrible for her to leave home. Sonya thought that he could
not understand her crying because he had lost his father and mother
when so young. She dried her tears and marveled at the darkness
of the road as they left Moscow. It was the first time she had
traveled at night in autumn or winter. Until their stop at Birulevo
they barely conversed. Sonya remembered that "Lev Nikolaevich
was particularly solicitous and tender with me." If Lev had bought
the sleeping coach in order to make love to his bride at once, the
circumstances were not favorable. His last-minute fears of marriage, Sonya's desperate grief at parting from her family, her obvious fright and exhaustion produced a strained atmosphere. Lev
found the intensity of Sonya's grief abnormal and he may have
suspected that reading his diaries had destroyed some if not all
of her love for him. He could have been referring to her knowledge
of his diaries when he wrote in his diary two days later that "she
knows everything; it is simple." He was wrong if he believed that
it would be simple for Sonya to forgive and forget his diary revelations. That she knew "everything" could have referred not only
to the diaries but to marital relations. Sonya was a doctor's daughter, she had a sensible mother and she would have been instructed
as to the facts of married life even though her mother was a nineteenth-century woman and would have encouraged her to be afraid.
Sonya later recalled her fear but she also recalled that her husband
had been "particularly solicitous and tender" with her. Although
she wrote this many years later, there is no reason to believe it
was not true. Her first draft of her courtship story was written
in Lev's lifetime and read to him for his approval. Sonya was
never loath to discuss her resentments with Lev nor was she prudish
about discussing physical relations, as her diaries show. When
Lev and Sonya had been married for twenty-seven years and *The
Kreutzer Sonata*, with its unflattering portrait of a wife, was published, Sonya feared that she would be identified with the wife
in the novel. In retaliation she wrote a story (which she decided
not to try to publish) about a physically repulsive, lecherous man
who married a pure young woman and raped her in their wedding
coach. Sonya intended this as a false picture of her husband and
she wrote it to sting him to the realization of how painful it was

to be unfairly described. If Lev had actually behaved in such a manner, Sonya's purpose would not have been achieved. She wanted him to feel the pain of *un*true accusations.[13]

When they stopped in Birulevo, the innkeeper was so impressed by a titled couple arriving in a carriage drawn by six horses that he gave them the royal suite. Sonya described it:

> . . . A big empty room with very uncomfortable, red plush furniture. They brought the samovar and prepared the tea. I hid in the corner of the sofa and sat silently like one condemned. "Come along," Lev Nikolaevich said, "play the mistress, serve the tea." I obeyed and we began to drink tea but I was shy and afraid.

The next day they arrived at Yasnaya Polyana in the evening. Auntie Tatyana was at the door to meet them, holding the icon of the Mother of God, and beside her stood Lev's brother Sergei with the bread and salt. Sonya curtsied to them, crossed herself and kissed the icon and Auntie Tatyana. Lev did the same and then they went together to Auntie's room. The next morning Lev summarized his engagement week:

> *24 September 1862.* Incomprehensible how the week has gone. I remember nothing, only the kiss by the piano and the appearance of Satan [Lev referred to the physical desire aroused by the kiss], then jealousy of the past, the doubt of her love and the thought that she deceives herself. . . . On the day of the wedding, fear, distrust and the desire to escape. Festive rites. She tear-stained. In the coach. She knows everything; it is simple. In Birulevo. Her fear. Something unhealthy about it. Yasnaya Polyana. Seryozha [Sergei] tender, Tatyana already speaks of sufferings. Night, a distressing dream. Not her.

By "sufferings" was Auntie Tatyana referring to Sonya's difficult new role as mistress of a household, or to her own position now that Lev was married? And of whom did Lev dream? What is telling about the entry is what it confirms about Lev; his desire to be pure and loyal to Sonya even in his dreams and, failing this, his need to share with her what he felt was a sin, albeit a subconscious one. Because he and Sonya had agreed to read each other's diaries regularly, to hide nothing from each other, he knew that she would see what he had written. At the end of their first day at home he went back to his diary:

Morning coffee—awkward. . . . Walked with her and Seryozha. Dinner. She grew much less shy. After dinner, I
slept, she wrote. Unbelievable happiness. And again she
writes beside me. It cannot be that all of this will end
only with life itself.

And five days later:

30 September. At Yasnaya. I do not recognize myself. All
my mistakes are clear to me. I love her as much as ever
if not more. Work I cannot. Today there was a scene. I
felt sad that everything in our house was like other people's. I told her she offended my feelings for her, I wept.
She is charming. I love her even more. But could it be
not real?

Chapter Two

LOW TIDES AND HIGH TIDES,
1862–1863

1.

On Sonya's first morning in Yasnaya Polyana she found herself the uncomfortable recipient of a cock and hen decked out in colored ribbons, a gift from the peasant women of the village. The women, similarly adorned with ribbons and following an old custom, had come up the tree-lined avenue singing their welcome to the new countess. Sonya was forced to stand holding the flapping, frightened birds while the women clapped and danced. "Here's a count for you," they cried, "picking up such a beauty for himself in Moscow." Sonya blushed and did not know what to say. Peasant customs and manners were strange to her. Inside the Kremlin the servants had clean fingernails and were less forward than the people who belonged to the land.

Peasant life was not the only aspect of the country that was strange to Sonya. The stillness at night amazed her and there were no street lights to relieve the darkness. Even the Berses' house at Pokrovskoe was within the reaches of city life and Sonya was used to constant visitors and company her own age. This may have been her hardest adjustment, having to live with only her husband and Auntie Tatyana and Auntie's companion, Natalya Petrovna. Auntie Tatyana was a tiny figure, old-fashioned and romantic. She always wore a shawl and bonnet and, although she spoke impeccable French, her conversation was trivial. Natalya Petrovna was also tiny. She came from a minor gentry family, took snuff and liked a glass of vodka before dinner. At the table she bored the company jabbering about people she had known. Occasionally she chewed tobacco. The two old ladies were not stimulating company.

Lev, at home in the place he loved above all others, had few adjustments to make. He preferred country life to Moscow or St. Petersburg and the simple atmosphere of Yasnaya suited him perfectly. Everything was fondly familiar, the old furniture from his childhood, and even the leather couch on which he had been born. The actual room of his birth had been in the part of the house he sold, but he often pointed to the trees and bushes covering the spot where the room had been and said, "Do you see that larch tree? Well, up there about where that branch is was the room in which I was born." The portraits that gazed from the walls had been there for as long as Lev could remember—his grandparents, Count and Countess Ilya Tolstoy, and his maternal grandfather, handsome, austere Prince Volkonsky. In Lev's study there was a picture of his dashing father and a silhouette of his mother as a child, today the only existing picture of Maria Tolstoy.

Lev's familiar world extended outside the house to the Yasnaya Polyana school which he had founded, the teachers and pupils, the pilgrims, holy beggars who roamed throughout Russia and for whom there was always a welcome at Yasnaya, and the peasants, many of whom had known Lev Nikolaevich since his birth. The only novelty for Lev was his wife and he was passionately in love with her.

More than physical attraction, however, had propelled him to her and her to him. Lev had long before resolved to marry a very young woman whom he could fashion to his own liking and, as a matter of principle, to marry outside of his class.[1] The Berses mingled with Kremlin society because of Dr. Bers's position as physician to the court but they were not of the aristocracy. On Sonya's side she had always wanted a husband whom she could hero-worship. Lev's fame, his age and his literary accomplishments all suited her. And, in spite of their differences, the Tolstoys shared many traits. Both were idealistic, sensitive, volatile, easily jealous and prone to self-analysis. Granny, Lev's cousin Aleksandra Tolstoy, once told him that his constant self-analyzing would turn his heart into a dry sponge. Now he had a wife with the same habit of dissecting and examining her thoughts and emotions.

From the beginning Sonya tried to find her place in her husband's world. Besides writing (Lev had turned again to *The Cossacks*, started years before in the Caucasus) he was actively managing his estate and Sonya became his assistant. She handed out the supplies from the storeroom and for a while she checked the milking of the cows. Inside the house she rearranged the furniture to make the rooms cozier. She had been married only two days when she wrote to Tanya and described her happiness as a wife:

> How are you, sweet Tatyanka? Sometimes I am very sad that you are not here. In spite of the fact that my life is wonderful above all, it would be even more so if I could hear your nightingale voice and sit chatting with you as it used to be. . . . Today we have already made tea upstairs around the samovar, as it should be in a happy family. Auntie is so contented, Seryozha so nice, but about Levochka I do not want to speak, it is frightening and confounding that he loves me so much. Tatyana, do you see why? What do you think? Is it possible that he could stop loving me? . . . For the first time I sign myself importantly,
> Your Sister,
> Countess Sonya Tolstoy

Lev added a postscript to the letter:

> If you should ever lose this letter, our charming Tanychka, then I shall not forgive you for a century. But do me a favor, read the letter and send it back to me. . . . Today she has a cap with crimson trimming—not bad. And this morning, how she played the grownup, perfectly and just like the mistress of the house.

To his cousin Granny Lev wrote:

> I lived for thirty-four years and did not know that one could love so much and be so happy.

There was love and happiness but there were also misunderstandings. These were inevitable between two such sensitive persons. It was a misunderstanding followed by a "scene" that swept Sonya into a blue mood. She turned to her diary and began the journal of her married life. This was the beginning of a remarkable dialogue between the Tolstoys that was at the center of their marriage and yet something apart for both of them. Because of their vow to read one another's diaries and to write honestly, their entries were often cruelly frank. To an extent this proved to be positive, particularly during the first year of marriage when it was easier to describe some feelings by pen than face to face. Certainly they learned much about one another through these private confessions. The confessions were also dangerous and at times misleading. The truth at noon one day is not always the truth at breakfast several days later and yet sometimes many days elapsed between the writing and the reading of an entry. This would put Lev and Sonya out of step with one another or have one reacting to something the other had already forgotten. Both poured out every bad mood and every criticism of the other and all this seemed more serious and permanent in writing, so the diaries did not always contribute to domestic harmony.

Sonya began writing in her journal on 8 October 1862:

> Again a diary and I find it tiresome to return to a former habit which I have given up entirely since I married. I used to write in my diary when I was unhappy and now, most likely, it is for the same reason. . . . For a long time I dreamt of a man whom I could love as a perfect whole, a fresh, pure man. . . . Now that I am married I should admit that all my former dreams were foolish and renounce them but I cannot. All of his, my husband's, past is so terrible for me that it seems I can never be reconciled to it.

Sonya's complaints about Lev's past led him to doubting her love, which in turn brought tears from Sonya. She even accused him of deliberately tormenting her, but accusations and *contretemps* ended in blissful reconciliations. Sometimes Sonya's love overwhelmed her:

> Yesterday with Grandpa [Grandfather Islenev visited Yasnaya] I came from upstairs purposely to see him [Lev] and when I looked at him I was seized by such a special feeling of strength and love. I loved him so much that I wanted to draw near to him but it seemed that if I touched him I would not then be so happy.

Her overwhelming love made her vulnerable to jealousy. She wished that she had been Lev's first and last love as he was her first and last. She wrote:

> He kisses me and I say to myself that I am not the first one to captivate him.

Sonya's jealousy was not unreasonable. If she had not read about her husband's past, she would probably have accepted the fact that there must have been women before her. It was reading Lev's diaries that gave her too vivid a sense of his earlier affairs, particularly his relationship with the peasant woman Aksinya who was still living on the estate with the child Lev had fathered. When Sonya's thoughts turned to Aksinya, Lev's diaries were there at hand with passages such as the following to tempt her morbid curiosity:

> Caught a glimpse of Aksinya. Very beautiful. All these days I have waited in vain. Today in the old forest of tall trees—I am a fool. A beast. The rosy sunburn of her neck—I am in love as never before in my life. . . . Decided I must make love and work, that is all. Already, how many times! . . . Had a dream—the strawberries—the road, she.[2]

Perhaps Sonya taunted Lev with some of these passages and there was a scene with tears and explanations because the day after writing about her jealousy she felt better. Another problem for her was Lev's physical reserve:

> I am listening to him sleeping. It's frightening to be alone. He does not allow me to approach him and this is hard for me. All physical demonstrations are so offensive.[3]

Sonya, eighteen, newly awakened to love and coming from an affectionate family, seems to have been more demonstrative than her husband. Physical demonstrations did not always offend Lev, however. The Tolstoy children remembered their father being demonstrative with their mother and sometimes kissing her hand tenderly. During the first months of marriage Sonya needed the reassurance of constant signs of her husband's love for her. The slightest imagined coolness frightened her:

> He does not love me. I expected this but did not think it would be so terrible. Why do people believe in my enormous happiness?

But people did believe in her happiness; to visitors like Fet she seemed to be a radiant wife. Her own strengths, particularly her good brain and her youthful energy, asserted themselves. Much as she dramatized her fears and doubts she did not nurse them and soon would be happy again throwing herself into the role of mistress of the household. Organization came naturally to her and, inside the house and in the garden, Sonya delighted in adding her own touches to the simple, almost crude, style of life that had existed at Yasnaya Polyana. Two months earlier she had run about the garden with her sisters and younger brothers and she was still the same exuberant, healthy young person. Now, with keys tied to her belt like a chatelaine, she ran across the meadow to join her husband leaping the hedges as easily as if she had worn trousers.[4]

In mid-October Lev wrote in his diary:

> There have been two clashes at home 1. because I was rude and 2. because of her *n*. [Probably *n* is for *naïveté*.] Still, I love her more and more although it is a different kind of love. . . . Such happiness takes my breath away.

It was a breathtaking happiness for both of them. Lev's love for Sonya spilled over to include her family. A few weeks after his marriage he wrote to Liza Bers begging her not to abandon her habit of writing to him and suggesting that they use the familiar "thou." He signed his letter, "Your brother, L. Tolstoy." A letter to Tanya written the same day with Sonya looking over his shoulder was in quite a different mood:

> Tatyana, darling friend!
> Pity me, I have a stupid wife. (*Stu*—I am pronouncing it thus [emphasis on first syllable] as you pronounce it.)

Here Sonya took the pen from his hand and wrote:

> He is stupid himself, Tanya.

Lev continued:

> This news, that we are both stupid, must grieve you very much, but after sorrow comes consolation and we are both quite satisfied that we are stupid and do not want it otherwise.

Sonya took the pen away again to write, "But I want him to be intelligent."

> Here then is a problem. Do you sense how we are rocking with laughter at this. I am sorry that they have cut out your lump. [Tanya had just had a tonsillectomy.] Send me a piece. . . . Sonya says that it is insulting to write to you in this tone.

To make up for the "tone," Lev ended his letter by saying, "It's true, one could not quickly find another Tanya so satisfying or such a connoisseur as L. Tolstoy." This affectionate raillery was tolerable to Sonya because it was addressed to Tanya, who was still almost a child and was her favorite sister.

A disparity between Lev and Sonya that was difficult to change was Sonya's entire absorption in her marriage while Lev balanced his married happiness with his literary career and his duties as manager of the estate. The Tolstoys' first daughter, Tatyana, wrote about her mother:

> In those days the goal of every young girl was marriage. And my mother was also drawn to that ideal by instinct. To her marriage was a sacrament. Her entire education had been a preparation for life as a wife and mother and she brought to that family life all the treasures of her virgin body and soul.[5]

Sonya recognized the problem of her dependence on her husband:

> The truth is, I am not able to find something to do. He is happy because he is clever and talented. But I—neither the one nor the other. One cannot spend life on love alone but I am so limited that for the time being I think only of him.

When Lev complained of not feeling well, Sonya at once feared that he would become ill and die. When he was happy, she worried that his mood would change. Now pregnant, she blamed her fears on her condition but also on her idleness:

> It isn't hard to find something to do, lots to do, but one must first be enthusiastic about trifling things—raising chickens, strumming on the piano, reading . . . pickling cucumbers. All of this will work out, I know, when I forget the idle life of my girlhood and become accustomed to the country. . . . My husband loves me too much to be able to give me direction right away and, oh, but it is hard to work things out oneself.

But Sonya did try to work things out. She counted on their coming visit to her family in Moscow at Christmas and felt that there she would find a better perspective on her situation. In the meantime she found a new cause for jealousy—Lev's devotion to the pilgrims who stopped at Yasnaya and whom Sonya referred to as "the people." Why should Lev have such warm love for these strangers? All his love belonged to her:

I live for him, I live by him and I want him to be the same way.

Sometimes she felt oppressed by the house with the two old ladies inside and the students and pilgrims outside. She wrote in her diary that in such a mood she ran from the house:

> I ran away because everything and everyone began to be odious to me. . . . When I quietly ran alone from the house I all but laughed for joy. L. isn't odious to me but I suddenly felt that he and I are on different sides, i.e., that his people could not be everything to me. It's very simple, if I am not everything to him, if I am a doll, if I am only a wife and not a person, then I am living as I am not able to live and as I don't want to live.

She resolved that whenever she felt the house was oppressive or that her husband was preoccupied with his thoughts and ignoring her, she would go riding or for a walk. The first time she did this she began at once to worry that perhaps Lev missed her. Was he concerned for her, did he wonder where she was? She ran home to find him wistful but he made no comment on her absence.

Sonya could have found ample to do in being Countess Tolstoy, organizing the house and preparing for the baby. But she never wanted simply to play house. Even when she had many children and gave time and energy to their needs she still found reserves for what was then her most satisfying role—that of being her husband's helpmate, the one who shared his life and at times his thoughts. During the first months of marriage Sonya had not found that role and Lev saw that she was restless with time on her hands. He tried to find for her what diversions he could. When the winter snows came, on moonlit nights he bundled his wife in furs and they took the troika sleigh racing across the frozen fields. Sonya's breath would come fast with excitement and her cheeks were scarlet from the wind.

In December an unfortunate incident occurred. The village women came, as was their custom, to wash the floors and Aksinya was among them with a small boy. Lev had given orders that Aksinya was not to be brought to the house, but either the orders were forgotten or Aksinya deliberately sneaked in. She must have had some curiosity about the new mistress. Sonya recognized her because of her child's resemblance to Lev and she rushed to her diary:

I think that someday I shall kill myself from jealousy. "I am in love as never before in my life." And simply a broad, pale peasant woman—it is horrible. I looked with such pleasure at his daggers and guns. One thrust—it would be easy. While there is no child. And she is here, a few yards away. I am simply insane. . . . I wish I could burn his journals and all of his past.

Sonya was not the only one complaining:

I am all the time discontented with my life and even with her. I must work—.

But their happiness was more resilient than Sonya's jealous tirade or Lev's fussing would suggest. It was a month before Sonya felt the need to open her diary and in the middle of December, just three months after their engagement, Lev noted:

Another month of happiness.

2.

On 23 December the Tolstoys arrived in Moscow for their Christmas visit. Sonya's elation began when they drove between the cannon that stood on either side of the Kremlin gate. Lev, laughing, told the Berses, "When Sonya saw her familiar cannon, near which she was born, she almost died of excitement." The Berses' apartment was full so the Tolstoys took rooms in a nearby inn but had their meals with the family. Sonya was the center of attention, home for the first time since her marriage. Reunited with her family, and especially with her beloved Tanya, she asked for nothing more. Lev, however, had many calls to make on his Moscow friends and he wanted Sonya with him. The calls, particularly those on Lev's intellectual friends, were a strain for Sonya and she bolstered her confidence with a new bonnet.

"What?" Lev cried when he saw Sonya admiring herself in a looking glass. "Is Sonya going to make her calls in that tower of Babel?" Mother Bers assured him that the tower of Babel was the latest fashion but this did not pacify Lev, who continued, "Why, really, it's a monstrosity. Why can't she go in her fur cap?" Both Sonya's mother and Tanya laughed at the idea of making calls in Moscow in a fur cap so Lev relented.[6] He was less easily pacified when Sonya allowed her old beau Polivanov to flirt with her mildly. Lev fumed in his diary:

> *27 December.* . . . I was very dissatisfied with her. I compared her with others, I almost repented of it [his marriage] but I knew this was temporary and I waited and it passed. . . . Tanya I watch very intently.

Three days later he mentioned Tanya again:

> A stupid evening at the Berses. Fear of Tanya—sensuality. Sonya's fear touching. Only the difference hurts me. I shall always love her.

Lev watched Tanya "very intently" and he was afraid of her. In her youthful good spirits Tanya was flirting with the world at large and with her brother-in-law in particular, and Sonya saw this and was upset. The difference that hurt Lev he did not explain. Perhaps it was a sensual response to Tanya that the sixteen-year-old imp unconsciously aroused and Lev, characteristically, noted his response. He was not insensitive to Sonya's feelings and on 3 January he began his diary for the new year with comments that showed his understanding of what was happening:

> At present everything is good but all of a sudden there will be grief or worse. She kissed me while I was writing. I sensed that it was not for fun. I glanced back, she was crying. Tat [Tanya] pesters me.

Sonya wept from jealousy of her younger sister's attentions to Lev and he reacted with annoyance toward Tanya. But Tanya was gradually becoming more than a sister-in-law to Lev and in a way that need not have given Sonya concern. Tanya was insinuating herself into Lev's creative imagination. The same day he noted in another entry:

> The epic genre is becoming the only natural one for me.

Lev was digesting ideas for a new novel. *Childhood, Boyhood* and the last of the trilogy, *Youth,* had won him fame and charmed readers with their simple and haunting evocation of childhood and adolescence but they were not major works. For six years Lev had been trying to finish *The Cossacks.* Now something about his married happiness, his sense of completeness on having found his "other," stimulated his creativity. He was able to finish *The*

Cossacks in a few months and turn his thoughts to a longer work; in particular, to a novel about the Decembrists, a group of Army officers, all aristocrats with liberal leanings, who, hoping for a constitutional monarchy, tried to prevent the accession of Nicholas I. On 14 December 1825 they assembled in St. Petersburg's Senate Square joined by about seven hundred soldiers. They were too late as that morning both church and state had sworn allegiance to Nicholas and the new czar himself led his troops to put down the rebellion. Five leaders were executed and others banished to Siberia. Lev had always been fascinated by the Decembrists; now he spent long daytime hours in libraries reading about the period and in the evenings he sought out acquaintances who could supply him with information on the rebellion. His researches, however, did not dominate his thoughts. On 5 January he wrote a poetic tribute to Sonya:

> Family happiness absorbs me entirely and it is not possible to work. . . . I love her at night or in the morning when I get up and see her—she looks at me and she loves me. And no one, above all not I, as she knows, stops her from loving me in her own fashion. . . . I love her when she sits near me and says, "Levochka," and she hesitates— "why aren't chimney pipes built straight?" or "Why do horses have to have such a long, hard life?" and so on. I love her when we are alone and I say, "What are we to do, Sonya, what are we to do?" She is laughing. I love her when she becomes angry at me and, suddenly, in the twinkling of an eye, she has both a harsh thought and a harsh word for me. "Stop it, it's boring" and after a minute she is already smiling shyly at me. I love her when she does not see me or know it and I love her in my fashion. I love her when she is a little girl in a yellow dress and thrusts out her lower jaw and tongue, I love her when I see her head tossed backwards and her face is serious, startled, childlike and passionate. I love her when—

He broke off here. Perhaps Sonya was once more reading over her husband's shoulder and interrupted him.

The blissful happiness and the doubts and jealousy common to the first year of most marriages were experienced by both Tolstoys. Lev, like Sonya, had overblown reactions. After a spat over a dress he refused to compliment, he decided:

> *She no longer loves me.* [Lev's underlining.]

Sonya read this and was full of remorse:

> Yesterday I misbehaved terribly, never before to such an
> extent. Is it possible that I have such a detestable disposi-
> tion or is it ordinary nerves because I am pregnant?

Whatever the reason, she was nervous and quick to jump to conclu-
sions. Lev went calling alone one evening and Sonya waited for
him at her family's apartment. For a while she chatted happily
with Tanya. "But you know, Tanya," she confessed, "sometimes
it bores me to be grown up, the silence at home [Yasnaya] annoys
me, I'm filled with an irrepressible need for gaiety and movement,
I run and jump, remembering you and how you and I used to go
crazy together and you called it being carried away. But Auntie
Tatyana looks at me, laughs good-naturedly and says, 'More carefully, quieter, *ma chère* Sophie. Think of your child.'"

As the evening wore on and Lev did not return as soon as he
had promised, Sonya became alarmed and told her mother and
sister that another woman was detaining him. Mother Bers replied
at once, "Enough of that, Sonechka, you are just inventing nonsense." When Lev finally strode into the apartment at one in the
morning Sonya began to sob. Lev kissed her hand and soothed
her. "Sweetheart, darling, calm yourself." He explained that he
had met Zavalishin, one of the actual Decembrists, and had quite
forgotten the time.[7] Sonya was calmed and later confessed to her
diary that she was "afraid of horrors because I am pregnant."
Her greatest horror was still the thought of Aksinya and she described a nightmare that revealed how much she was haunted
by her husband's former passion:

> *14 January.* . . . Today I had such a nightmare. The peasant
> women and girls from our village [Yasnaya] came to us
> in an enormous garden and they were all dressed like
> grand ladies. They went somewhere, one after another,
> and the last to leave was A. [Aksinya] in a black silk dress.
> I talked with her and such a malice took hold of me that
> I took her child from her and began to tear it to pieces.
> Everything came off, the feet and the head, as I was in
> such a fury. Levochka came in and I told him that I would
> be banished to Siberia but he collected the feet, arms,
> all the pieces and said, "It doesn't matter, it's a doll." I
> looked and, indeed, instead of a body everything was cot-
> ton and kidskin.

Sonya admitted that she was indulging in self-torture when she thought of Aksinya and in the same diary entry she marveled at her married happiness:

> I am always thinking that it is accidental, passing or else too wonderful. It is terribly strange that one person, for no reason except his personality and his face, is able to suddenly take me in hand and fill me to the brim with happiness.

At the same time Lev wrote in his diary that he had the "best" relations with his wife and that the "low tides and high tides do not astonish me." Sometimes he felt guilty about his happiness, afraid that it distracted him from his work, from his ideal, which was to

> Do everything that *I must* for others in order to fully enjoy what I am given and to return to others, to *everyone*, by means of my work that which they have given to me.

About his marriage he wrote that each little quarrel left a cut in their love:

> The least little cut always remains in love, love that is the best thing that exists in the world. I know this and shall cherish our happiness and you know this.

After writing this, Lev went with Sonya for dinner at the Berses and felt no cuts in his happiness. He proudly watched Sonya describe their life at Yasnaya Polyana. That evening he noted about Tanya:

> Tanya—the charm of her *naïveté*, egoism and flair. How she takes the tea from L. A. [Mother Bers] or spills it. I love and am not afraid.

Lev could love his sister-in-law without being afraid. His troubling, involuntary response to her childish flirting was sublimated and almost ready to emerge in the creation of the heroine of an epic work. Meanwhile Sonya noted that her only problem was that Lev loved everyone and everything and she wanted him to think and live and love only for her. At rock bottom Sonya was too sensible to demand this and she added that she could not expect Lev to

> . . . follow the course of our relationship in its subtlest details as I do, thanks to having nothing more to occupy me.

Lev came to the same conclusion about the dangers of idleness:

> I used to think, and now that I am married I am even
> more convinced, that in life and in all man's relationships
> the foundation of all is work.

Sonya read this and resolved that she would no longer live an
idle, frivolous life as she had as a girl because:

> Levochka has given me to feel that one cannot be satisfied
> by a life only with family and husband or wife but that
> it is necessary to have something else.

Here Lev inserted in Sonya's diary:

> Nothing is necessary besides you. Levochka talks a lot of
> nonsense.

A few days later the Bers family crowded onto their apartment
porch to watch the Tolstoys' departure for home. As the sleigh
and hired post horses moved away, Tanya burst into tears and
called to them, "Now I shall not see you until spring." Lev shouted
back, "You will come flying to us with the swallows."

3.

Both Tolstoys were glad to be home. Lev marveled that he was
no longer interested in the Yasnaya Polyana school and he dismissed it as a passion of his younger, unmarried years. He wrote
in his diary:

> *8 February.* . . . She is everything. She doesn't know and
> doesn't grasp that she transforms me, incomparably more
> than I her. Only it is not consciously. Consciously we are
> both powerless.

Sonya, too, was rapturous:

> Life is so easy for me, it is so good to live on earth. I
> was reading his diary and began to feel happy. I and his
> work, he is occupied with nothing more. . . . I am glad
> that he is writing.

In March Lev wrote a strange and fanciful letter to Tanya to
which he never received a reply. In *My Life at Home and at Yasnaya*

Polyana Tanya placed the letter a year later and quoted an abridged version. In the main, it is an example of Tolstoy's rich, nonsensical imagination running away with itself. Parts are almost surrealistic:

> In the center of the earth one finds the alatyr stone and in the center of man one finds the navel. How impenetrable are the ways of Providence! Oh, young sister of the wife of her husband! In *his* center sometimes one finds objects as well. . . . I had a dream: There came in the mail coach two doves, one dove was singing, the other was dressed in a Polish costume, and a third, not so much a dove as an officer, smoked cigarettes. [The three doves were Tanya, her cousin Sasha Kuzminsky and her brother Sasha. The three had visited Yasnaya Polyana recently.] From the cigarettes came, not smoke, but oil and the oil was love. . . . Tanya, my dear young friend, you are young, beautiful, gifted and sweet. Keep safe yourself and your heart. Remember the words of Katerina Yegoroven: It is never necessary to add sour cream to a schmantkuchen. [A German cream cake.] . . . Pardon me, sweet Tanya, that I give you advice and try to develop your mind and your higher faculties. If I allow myself this, it is only because I love you.
>
> Your brother,
Lev

When no reply came to this letter, Sonya began one to Tanya:

> What is it, Tanya, are you depressed—you don't write to me at all, but I so love to receive your letters and Levochka hasn't had an answer to his wild epistle. I understood exactly nothing of it.

Sonya had not been amused by the nonsense. She did not continue the letter to Tanya, but Lev picked up the pen and wrote a story about Sonya in which she was sleeping beside him and turned into a china doll. This letter, beautifully written in the guise of a fairy tale, charmed not only Tanya but all the Bers family. Taken together the two letters suggest an explanation of why they were written. From early in her marriage, Sonya had enjoyed physical relations with her husband. Apart from her fear the very first day, there is nothing in her diary complaining of this side of married life and Lev's comment in his diary—"I love her when I see her head tossed backwards and her face is serious, startled, childlike and passionate"—does not imply that she was a cold lover. But now she was six months pregnant and her clumsy body concentrated on the coming event of giving birth. She, the more demonstrative and responsive of the pair, was less so but Lev seems to have understood why. Although there is an accident and the doll falls from a table and breaks her leg, Lev is reassured by a servant that with white of egg the leg can be repaired. The letter shows a tender, sympathetic attitude toward the doll (Sonya). The first letter to Tanya, on the other hand, suggests a subconscious fantasy of desire. In six months this fantasy would settle firmly on Natasha in *War and Peace*. Perhaps she and Pierre and Prince Andrei already occupied their creator's imagination. But Tanya/Natasha never threatened the constancy of Lev's love for Sonya. Soon after writing these two letters Lev wrote in his journal:

> *24 March.* I love her more and more. Today it is seven months and I feel once again what I have not felt for a long time, a sense of annihilation in front of her. She is so impossibly good and pure and whole beside me. In these moments I feel that I cannot possess her in spite of the fact that she has given all to me. I do not possess her because I dare not, I do not feel worthy of her.

Sonya copied these words from her husband's diary and carried them with her. In return she wrote:

> Levochka gives me too much happiness. I love his cheerfulness, his bad moods, his goodness, his kind face, his gentleness, his vexations, all of which he expresses so well that he *hardly* ever offends one's feelings.

They had been married for little more than half a year but their passionate infatuation was becoming love.

4.

Lev once compared his writing to childbirth; each period of creativity involved suffering similar to the pain of labor. During the spring and summer of 1863 he busied himself with his farming but the labor pains for *War and Peace* had begun. He was restless, preoccupied, depressed at times and in his periods of depression he fussed about his health. Sonya, with three months left before the baby was due, was also restless with waiting. Both Tolstoys made good resolutions. Lev listed in his diary the qualities that he should have:

1. Order 2. Industry 3. Resolution 4. Constancy 5. The desire to do good and to do good for others. I shall cultivate these attitudes in myself.

Sonya resolved that she would try to join her husband as much as possible in the farming. She feared that he was not well:

I am afraid to let him know how I feel, but his blood pressure frightens me very much.

Dr. Bers, now reconciled to Lev's choice of Sonya over Liza, paid an April visit to Yasnaya. While Lev went to Tula to meet his father-in-law, Sonya indulged in the dangerous pastime of reading the love letters he had written to Valeria Arsenev, the young woman Lev had halfheartedly courted when he was twenty-eight. Fortunately, the letters were not passionate; in fact, they were sometimes bossy, and Lev's diary entries about the affair did not disturb Sonya. She could read his summary of Valeria without anxiety:

The trouble is that she is like noodles, without bones and without fire.

Sonya commented in her journal that Lev's love for Valeria had been simply a love of family life and a desire to have a wife:

As though it were not in any way V. but the woman he had to love, myself rather than V.

Sonya did not mention whether or not her father reassured her about Lev's blood pressure. After Dr. Bers's visit Lev threw himself more strenuously into farming, but Sonya found that her big belly made her participation impractical most of the time. Brooding alone, she decided that Lev was hostile toward her pregnancy because it was so far advanced now that physical relations were forbidden by the doctor:

29 April. . . . For him the physical side of love plays a big part. It's too bad—for me none, the opposite. But morally he is sound—that's the principal thing.

Sonya was probably writing as she thought she *ought* to feel. It was hardly true that physical relations meant nothing to her. A month later she was confessing to her diary:

With the return of good weather and good health, there
will be the joy of putting the house in order, the baby
and the return of physical pleasures—that's disgusting.

Sonya scolded herself for the "disgusting" thought but she wrote
"physical pleasures," not physical relations. Without sexual relations, Sonya needed more demonstrations of affection and she was
hurt when her husband seemed to neglect her. She wrote dramatically, "It's a shame to drive away a dog when it fawns." Sonya
compared her lot to what her mother's had been and decided
that her own was probably easier, as Dr. Bers' practice had been
more demanding in taking him away from home than Lev's absences to manage the estate. More depressing than his absences
were Lev's sullen moods and he himself recognized that he was
poor company:

Either because of inertia or because of something in myself
morally awful and hopeless, all this time has been a depressing period for me. . . . It seems to me now that I
have wakened up. I love her and the future and myself
and my life.

One reason for Lev's improved mood was the arrival of Tanya,
Sasha and some of their friends for a summer visit. This company
diverted Lev but Sonya felt isolated from them and she had a
slight twinge of her jealousy of Tanya. Lev was hunting, riding
and walking with the young people and Sonya, sitting at home
waiting for her baby to arrive, felt relegated to a position of unim-
portance. But as the time of delivery approached, she felt a surge
of energy and excitement. Once more enjoying her normal vitality,
she spent an evening in animated conversation with A. S. Erlen-
wein, a young teacher at the Yasnaya Polyana school, and Lev
was jealous. He used his jealousy as an excuse to focus all his
frustrations on his marriage. He complained in his diary:

Where am I, the other self which I know and love, which
sometimes comes to life and frightens and gladdens me?
I am petty and nothing. And I have been this way since
I married the woman I love. . . . I have been ruining myself
in a bout of running the estate for nine irreparable months.

Lev did not choose to recall that even before marriage it had been
a struggle to live according to his ideals. His self-reproach, however,
was interrupted by domesticity. On 27 June Sonya felt her first

labor pains. Lev begged her, "Sweetheart, wait until midnight." He believed that twenty-eight was his lucky number; he had been born on 28 August 1828 and he wanted his first born to arrive on the twenty-eighth of the month.[8] Sonya obliged and it was two in the morning on 28 June when she gave birth to a boy, Sergei, on the very leather couch where her husband had been born. Tanya was awakened by the commotion and came from her room to be told by Auntie Tatyana, *"Le bon Dieu a donné un fils à Sophie et Léon."* Tanya dressed and went to the dining room where her mother was talking to the doctor. A distraught Lev, his eyes red from weeping, joined them. Champagne was served and then all filed into Sonya's room where the new mother lay, exhausted but happy.

Lev could not bring himself to write an account of the birth until a month later, but chronologically it belongs here:

> On the night of the 26th of June we felt particularly agitated. She had pains in her stomach, she was tossing about, we thought that this was just because of her having eaten berries. In the morning she got worse and at five o'clock we got up, already having decided to fetch the others. She was flushed, in her dressing gown and she uttered a scream and then it passed, she smiled and said, "It is nothing."

Lev called a servant to stay with Sonya and went to Tula to fetch the midwife and notify the doctor. He described himself as

> . . . occupied with petty things as one is before a battle or at the moment of approaching death. I was annoyed at myself that I felt so little.

He returned home and Auntie greeted him with the news that the labor had begun in earnest.

> My darling one, how she was seriously, honestly, touchingly and fiercely beautiful. She was in her dressing gown, unfastened, a little jacket with lace insets, her dark hair disarrayed, her face flushed with red patches, big burning eyes. She paced back and forth gazing at me.

Sonya admitted to Lev that the labor pains were very strong:

> She kissed me simply, calmly. While everyone swarmed about, it [the labor] started up again. She caught hold

of me. As in the morning I kissed her but she was not thinking about me and there was something severe and serious about her. Maria Ivanova [the midwife] took her to her bedroom. . . . "The birth has begun," she [Sonya] said softly and solemnly with concealed joy that she would be the star when the curtain rose. She attended to everything, bustled about the dressers, made her preparations, squatted and, always, her eyes shone solemnly and calmly. There were several labor pains and each time I held her and felt how her body trembled, expanded and contracted and the impression of her body on mine was entirely different from during the time both before and after marriage. In the intervals I ran about, fussed over setting up in her room the couch on which I was born but all the time I kept having a feeling of detachment, reproach toward her and irritation. I wanted everything to be considered and done a little quicker and a little more efficiently. They made her lie down, she herself had thought . . . (I am not finishing this and am not able to write any longer about that which was truly torture).

Lev's suffering for Sonya was so acute that he never continued this diary entry; a dozen years later, however, he recalled Sonya's experience when writing about the birth of Kitty's first child in *Anna Karenina*. In her autobiography, Sonya described her first labor:

The suffering continued all day, it was terrible. Levochka was with me all the time and I saw that he was very sorry for me. He was so tender, tears shone in his eyes and he wiped my forehead with a handkerchief damp with cologne. I suffered for hours and at 2 o'clock in the morning of the 28th of June I gave birth to our first child. Lev Nikolaevich sobbed loudly, embracing my head and kissing me.

The euphoria of being parents of a new baby soon gave way in the Tolstoy household to a normal sense of letdown. The unexpected demands of the newcomer, the implicit responsibilities to be faced and the disruption of their former routines all underscored the fact that life had changed. Sonya went from elation to depression. She was impatient to resume physical relations with her husband and ashamed of her eagerness:

14 July. It is all done, I have suffered, I have given birt
I am up and about and enter anew into life a little. . .
I don't feel natural because I am afraid of my vulgar lov
of mother for child and I fear that my love for my husban
is unnaturally strong.

To make matters worse, Sonya's physical recovery was slow and
she had trouble nursing the baby. Lev disapproved of mothers
who did not breast-feed their children and Sonya agreed with
him in theory. She struggled to her feet when still weak and did
her best to nurse. Mother Bers was furious. "Lyovochka always
has to be eccentric. He wants to make Sonya's life like that of
the peasant women but with us the mother's care for a child is
not the same as that of a peasant woman in the village; besides,
neither is our strength." [9] There was a gloomy air about the household. Mother Bers, Tanya and Auntie Tatyana all tried to persuade
the Tolstoys to engage a wet nurse but Lev refused to listen to
them and Sonya adopted a stance of tragic martyrdom. She agreed
that it was abnormal not to want to nurse one's baby; she certainly
wanted to feed her child herself, but she asked what she could
do against a physical liability. Her nipples were sore and infected,
nursing was torture and she resented Lev's lack of sympathy and
his disappointment. On 3 August she wrote in her journal:

It seems to me now that I don't even love him. One cannot
love a fly that is every minute biting.

But having given vent to her resentment, she added:

I wanted to write this because I was angry. It is raining.
I am afraid that he will catch cold. I am no longer hurt—
I love him. God bless him.

When Lev read this passage he wrote after it:

Sonya, forgive me. I only now know that I am guilty and
how guilty I am. There are times when one lives as though
with no free will but impelled by an irresistible outside
law. This was how I was in regard to you—and it was
really me! But I have always known that I have many
failings. Still, I thought I had a tenth of a part of sensitivity
and generosity. I was rude and cruel and to whom? To
the one person who gave me the most happiness in life
and who alone loves me. Sonya, I know that it cannot
be forgotton or forgiven but I know you better and I under-

stand my meanness, Sonya, little pigeon. I was guilty, I was wicked, only there is in me a different man who sometimes is asleep. Love him and don't reproach him, Sonya.

Alas, Sonya did not read this note in her diary in time to prevent her from letting another quarrel arise. In a childish pique, Lev crossed out all that he had written. Sonya wrote next to his comments:

Somehow he became angry and crossed out everything. This was when I had terrible mastitis, pain in my breasts and was not able to nurse Sergei and this made him angry. . . . I deserved those few lines of kind words and repentance on his part but in a fresh moment of anger against me he deprived me of them before I read them.

Dr. Bers was furious when he learned that Sonya was trying to nurse her baby in spite of mastitis and that his son-in-law was making a tragic drama out of her failure. He wrote and scolded them in words that would have brought back a sense of proportion to any but the most strained of sensibilities:

As to the question of whether or not to take a wet nurse, you are like Hamlet bellowing "to be or not to be" and you have been performing this tragedy for six entire weeks. . . . I see that you both have gone out of your minds and that I must come to see you in order to set you to rights.

At the end of his letter he had some words for Tanya:

Tanya, stay at the heels of your restless sister, scold her constantly for indulging her whims and angering God; but Levochka, simply hit him quickly with whatever is at hand that he may become wiser. He is a great master of language and writing but he turns out to be otherwise in deeds. Let him write a story in which a husband torments his sick wife and wants her to continue to nurse her child; all the womenfolk will cast stones at him.

This affectionate, teasing letter did not restore the Tolstoys' sense of humor. They were both irritable and plagued with failure, Lev's failure to start writing and Sonya's failure to feed her baby. Sonya began complaining about everyone—the servants, her maid Dushka (who did not comb her hair properly), Auntie Tatyana, Tanya and Lev. Her husband likened her "grumbling and chiming resentments" to those of his sister in a bad mood. In the middle of the night he went to his diary and wrote that he was afraid to enter Sonya's room:

> She is snoring peacefully but will begin to groan if she hears me.

Finally Mother Bers persuaded her son-in-law to send for a doctor who examined Sonya, pronounced that she had a severe mastitis and forbade her to continue breast-feeding. The wife of a driver on the estate was engaged as "milk mother" to Sergei, who later became close friends with her son Misha, his "milk brother."

Equilibrium returned to the household until a new problem arose. Russia, because of a rebellion in Poland, massed troops on the frontier. Lev, frustrated by his failure to get started on his novel, threatened to join the army if war was declared. Sonya, who suspected that she was already pregnant again, was horrified. She pictured herself a widow with one child and another on the way. (The pregnancy was a false alarm.) In her diary, she argued:

> What is behind this craziness? Is he unbalanced? . . . I don't believe in this love of country, this *enthousiasme* at age thirty-five. Are not one's children the same as one's native land? Are not they just as Russian?

Lev was not really serious about going to war and he dropped the notion as he had dropped his worries about Sonya's inability to nurse their baby. A major work was at last on the tip of his pen and he needed only the impetus to start writing. In October he reread the harsh words he had written about Sonya in August and was ashamed of them:

> All that is past and all false. I am happy with her but terribly dissatisfied with myself. . . . Vacillation, timidity, laziness, weakness. These are my enemies.

His enemies would not frustrate him much longer.

Chapter Three

AN IDEAL WIFE FOR A WRITER, 1863–1869

1.

The years 1864 through 1867 were a golden period in the Tolstoy marriage. A year of living together had accustomed Lev and Sonya to one another and their love was firmly established. There was a baby in the nursery, Sonya was at ease as mistress of the house and a constant flow of summer guests began the long tradition of Yasnaya Polyana hospitality. More important to the household's well-being than anything else, Lev was writing.

War and Peace took six years to complete. Lev's enemies, those personality traits that he blamed when unable to write, returned more than once. When his inspiration dried up and his writing stalled, Lev became despondent and filled his diaries with worries about his health. When the writing went apace, he forgot his dizzy spells and coated tongue and was the happiest of men. He told Sonya and her family that he was writing about the war of 1812. The subject pleased the Berses and Dr. Bers wrote to his son-in-law in September 1863:

> It so happened that my father used to tell us a lot about the year 1812; really, it was a remarkable and interesting epoch. You have chosen a lofty subject for your novel, God give you success.

Dr. Bers collected material for Lev's research and sent him books on the period and family letters from the years 1812–1814.

Meanwhile, some of the material for *War and Peace* was being lived and observed. During the autumn of 1863 the Tolstoys were invited to a ball in Tula at which the czarevich was to be present. Sonya shyly begged off, using her health as an excuse, and that would have been the end of the matter if Tanya, at the suggestion of the hostess, had not persuaded Lev to take her in Sonya's place. What excitement for the ebullient Tanya! She ran through the house shouting to everyone that Lev Nikolaevich was taking her to a ball. Soon Sonya was regretting that she would stay behind. Bravely she saw her husband and sister depart in their finery and then she collapsed in tears of self-pity. In her autobiography she recalled her disappointment:

> Altogether many close friends and relatives would be at this ball in Tula and when Lev Nikolaevich put on his dress coat and left for the ball with my sister Tanya I began to cry bitterly and I cried all evening.

Sonya was more philosophical the next day. Her health was really frail at the time and, besides, there was another reason she could not have gone. She confessed to her sister, "But you know, Tanya, I would not have been able to go even if I had been well. You know Levochka's opinions. Would I have been able to put on a ball gown with a bare neckline? This is really inconceivable. How many times he has censured married women who bare themselves, as he puts it." Sonya's missed opportunity, however, was the novelist's gain. Although Lev changed the circumstances and the people, Tanya's first ball was his inspiration for Natasha's first ball in *War and Peace*.

Lev was disappearing into his study every day and not discussing his work with anyone. Sonya knew that his spirits were good, that the writing had begun in earnest and that he was, in his own words, "restored to life." In October she wrote:

> He says, "I am restored to life." What for? . . . How is he restored to life? He says, "You will understand."

Sonya wanted to share his work at once and wondered if she had been as mature as Aleksandra Tolstoy (Granny) he might not have discussed his writing with her right away:

> I should like to embrace everything about him, understand him so that he can be with me as he is with Aleksandra but I know that this is impossible and I don't take offense.

Sonya referred to her husband's correspondence with Granny, which touched on many of Lev's ideas. Lev would never share his writing with Granny, however, to the extent that he shared *War and Peace* and *Anna Karenina* with Sonya. Not only did he eventually discuss the writing of these novels with her, but both masterpieces were enriched by the insights Lev had gained through his marriage to Sonya. In *Tolstoy and the Novel* John Bayley wrote:

> *War and Peace* is dominated by the female principle; it is a profoundly feminine view of life.

This feminine view is the view of Tolstoy, the genius, but there is no telling how much Lev was influenced by reading Sonya's journal and looking at the world not only through his own masculine eyes but through hers. In April 1863, when Lev's creative imagination was absorbed by his plans for a major novel, he made a note that he had read several of Sonya's diaries and added, "They are excellent." [1] These particular diaries described the low tides and high tides of Sonya's adjustment to marriage and, indeed, may have been excellent reading for a writer sensitive to feminine psychology.

But when Lev began writing the first pages of *War and Peace* he hesitated to show his work even to Sonya. When he disappeared behind his study door, she felt rejected and resentful. She described Lev as "cold, almost calm, heavily occupied" and herself as "depressed and angry." On 28 October she wrote in her diary:

> My mental weakness is awful, I am disgusted with myself. If I am disgusted it must be that my love grows weak. No, I love him very much. There can be no doubt of that. If only I could pull myself together once again. My husband is so dear, so terribly dear. Where is he at? A history of 1812? He used to tell me everything—now I am not worth it.

Lev actually had very little to show but some weeks later he delighted Sonya by handing her the first few pages of his novel and asking her to make him a fair copy. "The foundation of all is work," he wrote in his diary during the first months of marriage and now both he and Sonya would be at work to the same purpose. For twenty years, until her daughter Tatyana shared this chore with her, Sonya made the fair copies of her husband's work. Once she said that she had copied *War and Peace* seven times. This meant not only the material that went into the final version, but pages and pages of incidents and characters that lived for a while in their author's imagination, only to be rejected. Tatyana Tolstoy described her mother settling down to her evening task of copying:

> We had scarcely finished wishing her goodnight before that pretty head, its hair so black and smooth, was already bent over the table again, her shortsighted eyes peering to decipher my father's manuscript, those pages crammed with writing, scrawled with erasures, the lines of script sometimes crisscrossing in every direction. In the morning my father would find the sheets back on his desk, plus a neat and legible fair copy which he then proceeded to work over again, adding whole new pages black with his vast, illegible scrawl, sometimes deleting other pages completely with a single stroke of the pen.[2]

Making and remaking fair copies was not Sonya's only new chore. She took on more of the family responsibilities including all the management of the house, some of that of the estate and, eventually, the raising of the children.[3] More important, she protected her husband. When the writing mood was right for him, she allowed no one to enter his study. When his inspiration faltered, Lev was free to refresh himself as he chose; he could ride, hunt or go for walks and the household carried on without him. If he wanted Sonya's company, she dropped what she was doing and went to his study.

Perhaps Sonya's greatest contribution to Lev's masterpieces was the example of herself. Describing his creation of Natasha, Lev said, "I took Tanya, ground her up with Sonya and out came Natasha."[4] Natasha is superficially much more like Tanya than like Sonya (Kitty in *Anna Karenina* would be more like Sonya), but Sonya made her contribution to all of Lev's great women characters. Lev's knowledge of his wife's psychology, through his access to her diaries as well as because of his close relationship with her, enabled him to get inside the skin of his heroines. Through Tanya Lev observed Natasha and through Sonya he became Natasha.

While Lev was writing, Sonya was satisfied to put his needs before all else. *War and Peace* was barely half-finished when she began to suspect that it would be an extraordinary work and she looked upon her role as one of great importance. Because of her youthful energy—she was just nineteen in August of 1863—she could meet Lev's demands without neglecting her domestic duties.

Only her diary was neglected, a sure sign that she was happy, but it was there to turn to when her spirits dropped or she felt restless as she did shortly before Christmas 1863:

> I have lit two candles, have sat down at the table and I begin to feel lighthearted. . . . I want to flirt, even with Alyosha Gorsky [a half-witted peasant from the village] and I want to be cross even if just at a chair or anything at all. . . . When I think of Tanya, it makes me sick, something stings.

Tanya was a very real worry. She and Lev's brother Sergei had fallen in love during the summer. They were engaged to be married, but secretly as the Berses had persuaded them to wait at least a year before an announcement. Besides a great difference in their ages (Sergei was Lev's older brother and Tanya was Sonya's younger sister), there was a more serious obstacle. Sergei lived with a gypsy woman, Masha, who had borne him several children. The relationship was comfortable, perhaps even rewarding, and Sergei's conscience troubled him when he thought of abandoning the woman who had been his common-law wife for fifteen years. Although Tanya knew of Masha's existence, Sergei concealed from her the extent of the relationship. But Sonya's mood as she wrote in her diary that December evening was not one for facing up to Tanya's problems. The thought of her sister stung, but:

> I even put that aside, I am in such a silly mood. . . . I feel so young today that I need to do something crazy. Instead of going to bed I should like to turn somersaults. But with whom?

Tanya in turn had her worries about Sonya. She believed that her sister humbled herself too much before her husband and his demands, that Sonya should not always take Lev's wishes as law, that "You also have your own self, as he has his. Be your natural self, just as you are, and all will be well." Sonya believed that she had rewards dearer to her than the self-fulfillment that Tanya suggested. She smiled and showed her sister the lines from Lev's diary that she kept with her always, the lines in which he described her as impossibly good and pure.[5]

Sonya's frivolous and rebellious moods never lasted for long. All through the winter life at Yasnaya Polyana revolved around the novel. Lev was writing, Sonya was copying and recopying, and the old ladies hovered respectfully. It pleased Auntie Tatyana that Lev, when undecided about something in his work, came to her room and laid out a game of Patience. Then he would say, "If this Patience comes out, then I must change the beginning" or "If this Patience comes out, then I must give it a title." Playing Patience seemed to concentrate Lev's faculties and he would return to work with renewed energy. Another spur to inspiration arrived in the spring—Tanya came for her annual visit. "Tanya will be here with the swallows" was now a family saying, although Auntie sometimes said, "Our Tanya will be here with the grasshoppers." This time Tanya feared that she would be in the way (Sonya was expecting a second baby in October) and she wrote begging to be given a small, downstairs room. When Lev greeted her he said, "What nonsense you talk! You are never in anybody's way here. But then, do you think that you are living with us free of charge? I am writing down everything about you." [6] Two months after her wedding, Sonya had written to her sisters, "Girls, I am telling you secretly and I don't intend it to be repeated; Levochka may describe us all when he is fifty." [7] It seems that Lev had had some thoughts about putting his wife's family into a novel as early as 1862 and discussed them with Sonya. Now that he was writing *War and Peace* Sonya made no mention of the similarities of the characters in the novel to members of her family. She may have known intuitively that fiction does not copy life but transforms it.

Lev put aside his writing when the good weather came and Sonya was not concerned. She believed that creativity was restored by relaxation and summer interruptions to writing were not to be compared to those times when inspiration failed and depression took over. After the long and lonely winter, Yasnaya was astir with company and happy activity. Besides Tanya, there was Liza Bers, Lev's sister Maria Nikolaevna and her daughters, and the Diakov family. The Diakovs were aristocratic neighbors and good friends of the Tolstoys. In the daytime there was hunting, picnics, long walks and rides and in the evening charades, singing, music and animated conversation. Lev participated in everything and after one successful evening of charades he proposed that they should put on a play. Since there were no suitable plays in the Yasnaya library, Tanya suggested that Lev write one for them. Three days later Lev finished a comedy, *The Nihilists*. There was a shortage of men so both Liza and Sonya took men's parts. Like many shy people, Sonya felt at ease on the stage and according to her sisters was a talented actress. Maria Nikolaevna agreed to take a part if she could ad lib her role. "Do not write my part," she said, "I would never learn it. You select my appearances and I myself will think of what to say." The rehearsals were hilarious and none enjoyed them more than Lev. After the performance had been greeted with enthusiastic applause, the script was thrown away. Not even Sonya, who saved every page of *War and Peace* that Lev discarded, bothered to save Tolstoy's first play.[8]

Sonya took her second pregnancy with ease. She walked and played croquet and managed to run a household that often numbered twenty at dinner without complaining. Sometimes she even joined the hunting parties and amused everyone with her behavior. She had none of the others' eagerness to succeed—in fact, she was delighted when the prey escaped, but she enjoyed the beauty of the outdoors in summer and would fall into a dreamy state while the rabbit raced by and the others were shouting at her to release the dogs.

At the end of summer Lev opened his diary:

> *16 September 1864.* It will soon be a year that I have not written in this book. And a happy year. Relations with Sonya have become consolidated, stronger. We love one another, i.e., for one another we are the dearest people in the world and we see one another clearly. No mysteries and nothing for which to be ashamed. During this time I have begun a novel, I have ten printed pages [Lev meant what would amount to ten printer's galleys] but now for a while I am making corrections and revisions. This is agonizing.

The ten printer's sheets or galleys amounted to what was to be Book One of Lev's novel, about one hundred pages out of over thirteen hundred which comprised the completed work. During one of his breaks from his "agonizing" corrections, Lev was riding across the countryside when his horse stumbled and threw him. Half fainting from the pain of a broken shoulder, Lev lay helpless until a peasant found him and carried him to a hut. When Sonya arrived a woman bonesetter was massaging the dislocated joint. Sonya at once sent for a Tula doctor who made eight torturing attempts to set the shoulder before giving up. Although her baby was almost due to arrive, Sonya spent the night in the hut with

Lev. In the morning she sent for another doctor who was able to put the joint in place.

As soon as this crisis appeared to be over, the Tolstoys' second child arrived, on 4 October. The birth was much easier than before; Sonya had no depression afterward and she was able to nurse the baby. It was a girl named Tatyana, called Tanya, after Lev's beloved Auntie Tatyana and Sonya's favorite sister. Lev had some lingering pain in his shoulder but he was able to write and Yasnaya hummed with productive activity. The satisfaction that Sonya felt when her husband's writing went well permeated her whole life. Her vitality never flagged. Lev attributed this to her Islenev blood and once remarked, "My goodness, what a vital energy is this Islenev blood and it flows in all of you black Berses." [9] The black Berses were those with dark hair and eyes: Sonya, Tanya, their mother.

Lev's shoulder continued to hurt him and in November 1864 Sonya sent him to her family. Dr. Bers urged trying exercises before surgery but Lev was impatient to have the shoulder reset and done with. Dr. Bers sent for three surgeons who performed the operation in Mother Bers' room. Both she and Tanya remained in the room to watch all the procedures; Lev had instructed them that Sonya would want to know every little thing. The first problem was getting Lev to fall asleep under the chloroform. He suddenly jumped from the armchair where they had placed him and cried out in delirium, "My friends, to live like this is impossible. I think, I have decided—" He did not finish his sentence, and back in his chair he finally fell into a deep sleep. While Mother Bers calmly held the patient's head, two servants, instructed by the doctors, pulled on the arm until the joint came apart. Tanya was horrified, fearing that her brother-in-law might regain consciousness. The arm was successfully reset and Lev was soon well enough to give the Berses and their friends a first reading from his novel. Tanya described it in a letter to Polivanov:

> When everyone was seated Levochka began to read. He began somewhat feebly, as though embarrassed. I quailed. I thought, all is lost. And then it was as though he recovered himself and he read so firmly and with such absorption that I felt as if he had begun to carry everyone along with him. . . . Everyone said that the Rostov family are living people. And how close they are to me! Boris reminds

me of you in appearance and manner of behaving. Vera—
you know this is absolutely Liza, her sedateness and her
relations to us. . . . Pierre they liked least of all. But to
me he was the best of all, I love this type.

To Tanya Lev dictated his letters home and sometimes parts of
his novel. Years later Tanya recalled the sessions when he had
dictated *War and Peace:*

I can see him as though he were here now: With marked
concentration on his face, supporting with one hand his
injured arm, he walked back and forth in the room dictating to me. Not paying any attention to me whatever, he
spoke aloud: "No, commonplace, it won't do!" or he simply
said, "Strike out." His tone was imperious, his voice audibly impatient and often, dictating, he altered the same
thing three or four times.

To Sonya Lev wrote on 7 December:

My darling Sonya,
What a clever girl you are in everything about which you
want to think. That is why I say that you are indifferent
to intellectual interests but you are not only not narrow-
minded, you are intelligent, very intelligent. And it is the
same with all of you black Berses, to me especially sympathetic. The black Berses are L.A. [Mother Bers], you, Tanya.
. . . I remember how you said to me that everything military and historical [in his novel] about which I struggle
so will be poor and the rest will be excellent—the family
life, characters, psychology. That is so true, it could not
be more so. And I remember how you said that to me
and I remember everything about you that way. And, like
Tanya, I want to burst out crying, "Mama, I want to be
in Yasnaya, I want Sonya." I began writing to you in a
low mood but I am finishing an entirely different man.
My dear heart. Only love me as I love you and nothing
else matters and everything is wonderful. Good-bye, it is
time to go on with work.

Sonya missed Lev terribly during their three-week separation, and
she wrote to him frankly:

I write to you in the study, I write and weep. I weep
because of my happiness and because you are not here.

. . . Does your shoulder make you unhappy? I imagine that you are thinner.

She told him every detail of domestic life at home, what the babies did and what the nurse said. Finally she could write to him:

Darling friend, Levochka,
At last I am comforted and made happy by a letter that you are coming. How I have waited for this for so long and I have been afraid to send for you.

Lev was home before Christmas. In February 1865 the first part of Book One of *War and Peace* appeared in *The Russian Messenger* and immediately attracted widespread attention.[10]

Lev continued working steadily all through the winter; Sonya was busy copying and sometimes she gave her husband critical comments. She did not think Prince Andrei a sufficiently defined character but, on the other hand, she found Princess Maria perfectly realized.[11] Lev's old friend, the poet Fet, agreed with Sonya about Prince Andrei:

I do not think Prince Andrei was a pleasant person to live with, a conversationalist, etc., but least of all a hero able to constitute the thread by which to hold the reader's attention.

Lev replied:

I am glad for your opinion of one of my heroes, Prince Andrei, and I benefited from your criticism. He is monotonous, tedious, and only *un homme comme il faut* for all of the first part. This is true but he is not to blame for this, I am. Besides my plan for the characters and their actions, besides my plan for the clashes between characters, I have another historical plan which complicates my work extraordinarily and with which, it seems, I am not coping.[12]

Nevertheless, as the novel progressed, Lev became exhilarated and told Sonya that he felt young. She wrote in her journal in February 1865:

And he said that this feeling of youth signified, "I can do anything." And I want and can do anything. But . . . I see that I cannot nor do I want to do anything except nurse the family, eat, drink, sleep, love my husband and children.

Lev's exhilaration disappeared in the spring. He had lost his writing momentum. Sonya noticed his somber mood, his irritability, and she feared one of his depressions. When he spoke of possibly living in Moscow the following winter she admitted to her diary that she dreaded living in the city without a nice apartment, a carriage, good clothes and all the trappings she wanted with Moscow life. She confessed with rueful admiration that such things did not matter to Lev:

> Levochka is amazing. It's all the same to him; this is true wisdom, even virtue.

She marveled at her husband's character and compared herself to a weak worm beside him. Sonya had been ill when she wrote this and was staying at home while Lev took his evening walk. The house was quiet, the children asleep and she thought of herself as worthless and insignificant. Then Lev returned and she relaxed and was happy:

> Fresh air surrounded him and he himself made an impression on me of fresh air.

Lev was determined not to give up writing until the summer months. In March he noted in his diary:

> For three days I have stuck to it, not slacking but not stretching myself too much. I write, I redo. Everything is clear to me but the amount of work that I anticipate is terrifying.

He became so preoccupied with his work that Sonya complained in her diary:

> He's cool toward me and indifferent. I am afraid to say, *he doesn't love me.* This tortures me all the time and that is why I'm shy and indecisive in my relations with him.

Lev was aware of the coolness between them but wrote:

> I wait calmly for this to pass.

Sonya waited less calmly:

> Levochka quite destroys me with his complete indifference.

The following day the truth came out:

> Levochka has begun to be affectionate. He kissed me; this hasn't happened in a long time. But it is all poisoned by

the thought that he hasn't slept with me for such a long time.[13]

Perhaps Lev read this paragraph and repaired matters because the next day he noted:

Sonya and I are fine again.

He did not say the same of his novel. For a while he enjoyed the spring weather and let his mind wander to other subjects. He contemplated a history of Napoleon and Czar Alexander I and noted that he had great thoughts about this stirring theme. Some of the thoughts eventually found their place in *War and Peace*. While the creative urge was stalled Lev turned to his farming. Sonya noted in her diary in March 1865:

Levochka is very occupied with the cattleyard workers while his novel is being written without much enthusiasm. He has all the ideas but when will they be put down? Sometimes he discusses his ideas and his literary plans with me and I am always terribly pleased.

Discouraged comments appeared in Lev's diary:

Did not write. . . . Wrote a little. . . . Not in the mood but I must hang on. . . . Writing is going badly. I must get it out.

He began to record the worries about his health that went with moods of frustration. He had rushes of blood to his head, sounds in his ears and poor digestion. He was not irritable with Sonya, however. He wrote in his diary:

I love Sonya very much and we are *so* happy!

Tanya arrived in May for her summer visit and once more some raw material for Natasha's story took center stage. Her secret engagement with Sergei continued, but Sergei's relationship with Masha was not resolved, a fact that troubled both Tolstoys. Lev spent a lot of time with Tanya, riding and hunting and observing her carefully. Their constant pleasure in one another's company rankled Sonya:

I am angry with Tanya. She insinuates herself too much into Levochka's life. . . . They have gone to the woods alone. God knows what thoughts come to my head.

An event in June diverted Sonya from these thoughts. Tanya and Sergei finally announced their engagement and Sonya rejoiced in her sister's happiness. Alas, although Sergei had found the courage to become formally engaged to Tanya, he still lacked the courage (and perhaps he even lacked the desire) to break his long-standing relationship with Masha. When Tanya discovered this truth and realized that another woman and her children had a prior claim on Sergei, she was horrified and deeply hurt. She broke her engagement. Sonya shared Tanya's grief and raged in her diary against Sergei:

> He is detestable. "Wait a little, wait a little" he kept saying and only with the intention of leading Tanya by the nose to amuse himself at the expense of her feelings. [Sonya did not believe for long that Sergei had been this heartless.] . . . They had already been engaged twelve days. They had kissed one another, he had reassured her and said all the conventional things, he was making plans. An all-round scoundrel.

Sonya's sympathy for Tanya led her to marveling at her own happiness:

> For what am I given such happiness? . . . We have been so loving, the summer weather is warm and everyone and everything around is wonderful.

Summer ended, the guests departed and Lev returned to his novel but without satisfaction. He complained:

> *19 September.* . . . I don't know whether it's because I am sick that I can't think correctly and can't work or if I am so undisciplined that I can't work. If I could work as I should, how happy I would be!

Some days later he felt a little better. He read over what he had done so far and decided that it was "not bad."

> It need not be done over. I must add to Nikolai a love of life and the fear of death on the bridge. And to Andrei—recollections of the battle of Brünn.

With Sonya all was well:

> We two are so happy, such happiness is true for one out of a million. . . . Yesterday evening I wanted to write but only sketched an outline. Today I began but gave up.

The less he wrote, the more he fretted about his health. He had a stitch in his back, a coated tongue and indigestion. He worried that he could not urinate, that he had diarrhea or that he was constipated. In October he gave up writing entirely and read Trollope:

> I am reading *The Bertrams*. Glorious. . . . Trollope kills me with his mastery. I console myself that he has his way, I mine.

Lev decided that a program of strict hygiene might restore his health and with it his inspiration. Finally on 1 November he could note that he was writing with abandon. He was almost back in stride, although worried about his dry mouth. A few days later he reported that his tongue was looking better and that he had made an excellent *selle* [stool]. On 12 November 1865 he made his last diary entry for eight years:

> I am writing, my health is good and I don't fuss over myself. I finished the third part. Much is clearing up very well. Killed two hares in half an hour.

He stopped examining his tongue every morning, he became excited about his novel and Sonya was happy to have copying again. Both Lev and Sonya were still concerned about Tanya—her despair after her breakup with Sergei, her failing health and even an abortive suicide attempt. This concern did not interfere with Lev's burst of creativity. In fact, Tanya's bittersweet love affair was being put down in *War and Peace*.

2.

Sonya took a deep satisfaction in surrounding her husband with domestic comfort and happiness. Whether she herself was aware of it or not, she was reconciling his inner conflicts and freeing him to be creative. Lev's writing was going well throughout the winter of 1865 and Sonya was copying *War and Peace* with a growing appreciation. Sometimes Lev came to her fresh from finishing a chapter and radiant with satisfaction. This was the case when he finished the description of the Rostov hunt. When he read aloud to Sonya the pages describing Prince Andrei lying wounded on the battlefield, his voice became choked with tears. Buoyed with self-confidence, Lev wrote a joking letter to Fet on 23 January:

> I am very glad that you love my wife. Although I love
> her less than my novel, she is my wife all the same, you
> know. Someone is coming. Who is it? My wife.

Lev could write thus to Fet because he knew that his friend regarded
Sonya highly (Fet dedicated some of his poems to her) and he
knew that Fet understood the strength of Lev's love for his wife.
Indeed, to family and friends the Tolstoys' union seemed perfect.
Lev's sister Maria Nikolaevna admonished her daughters not to
be in a hurry to marry, that it took time to find such a marriage
as the Tolstoys' who made an ideal couple.[14] Sonya's brother,
Stefan Bers, wrote some years later when he was an adult:

> The mutual love and closeness of this couple have always
> served as my ideal and model of married happiness.

Christmas 1865 was spent in the Kremlin. The new railway that
was to connect Kursk to Moscow was finished as far as Serpukhov
and the Tolstoys went by sleigh to Tula to board the train for a
seventy-mile ride to Serpukhov. They completed their journey in
a horse-drawn coach, a most unpleasant experience. The horses
traveled at such a speed that all the family was thrown against
the walls of the coach and little Sergei was sick to his stomach.
This time they stayed in the Berses' apartment until February
and then moved into a rented flat. After the holiday festivities,
Lev spent his time collecting material for his novel, taking a class
in sculpture and giving readings of *War and Peace* for family and
friends. Everyone enjoyed the readings except Sonya, who by now
knew the work by heart and sometimes fell asleep. Sonya's old
beau Polivanov visited the Berses and she was unable to resist
some lighthearted flirting. Lev was jealous. Sonya admitted that
she seemed unable to behave herself in Polivanov's presence but
she declared that in her heart

> There's not a single blemish nor ever was there for a minute
> of my married life, and Lev judged me too severely and
> sharply.

This was a very minor tempest. Back in Yasnaya, Sonya summed
up the visit in her journal:

> *12 March.* . . . It was good in Moscow. I loved my family
> and they loved my children. . . . All of our life went well,
> I loved everything in Moscow, even our Dmitrovka Street
> apartment and our stuffy sitting-room–bedroom and the

study where Lev modeled . . . and where we sat talking together in the evenings.

In April she gloated:

> Everyone envies our happiness. All of this makes me wonder, why are we so happy and what does it actually mean?

After the birth of another son, Ilya, on 22 May 1866, Sonya felt well as she had after Tanya's birth. Indeed, as she wrote to her sister Tanya, she was too busy to be depressed; she had her weaning, nursing, washing, caring for the children, jam making, sweets making and copying for Lev. The copying stopped in the summer while Lev relaxed with their guests. A newly hired estate manager brought along with him someone who became a thorn in Sonya's side. She confided to her diary:

> We have a new estate manager with a wife. She is young, attractive. . . . She has long, inappropriately long, animated conversations with Levochka about literature, beliefs in general. The conversations are tormenting to me and flattering to her.

The Tolstoys were sleeping in separate bedrooms after Ilya's birth (the doctor had forbidden their physical relations for a period) and Sonya mused that in her husband's bed she would have confessed her resentment and jealousy and cleared the air. She didn't, however, and Lev, who could not have been reading her diary, innocently suggested inviting the new manager and his wife to dinner. Sonya growled in her diary:

> I wish her every kind of harm but when I am with her for some reason I am especially sweet.

A month later Sonya was laughing at what she called her almost groundless jealousy. In August she marveled again at her happiness:

> There are days when I am so happy and well that I want to do something so that everybody will be admiring and astonished.

The house was full of guests. Besides the Bers family there were the Princesses Gorchakov, whom Sonya had met in Moscow, Prince Lvov and V. A. Sollogub, a writer who came with his two adolescent sons. Sollogub told Sonya that she was the ideal wife for a writer, "a nursemaid of talent." [15] To Lev he exclaimed, "What a fortunate man you are! Life has brought you all you desire." To this Lev replied that it was not that he had all he desired but that "I desire all that I have."

On Sonya's nameday in September Lev surprised her with a party on the terrace which included music and dancing. After the summer guests had all left and Lev had returned to writing, Sonya found time to describe her fete in her journal.

> Music at dinner which so surprised and pleased me, Lev's sweet and loving expression, the evening on the terrace lit by lanterns and candles, the youthful figures of the vivacious young girls in demure white dresses. . . . Above all, the lively, beloved face of Levochka who all the time and everywhere was trying his utmost to make everyone happy. . . . It seems to me that it is impossible to live so close in spirit as I live with him. We are so awfully happy in every way. . . . These days I am spending a lot of time every day copying (without first reading) Lev's novel. This is a great delight for me. Mentally I live through the entire world of impressions and ideas while I copy. Nothing moves me so much as his thoughts, his talent. And this happened recently. Either I myself have changed or the novel really is so very good—that I do not know. I write very quickly and that is why I follow the novel sufficiently fast to pick up everything interesting and sufficiently slowly to think over, deeply feel and review all of his ideas. We often talk about the novel and he, for some reason which makes me proud, very much trusts and listens to my opinions.

In November the first of a series of English governesses joined the household. Hannah was the daughter of a gardener at Windsor Castle to whom Lev had offered the position of governess by mail. Lev was in Moscow when Hannah arrived and Sonya wrote to him:

> She is very young [actually about Sonya's age], rather sweet, a pleasant, even pretty face, but our mutual ignorance of languages is terrible.

Sonya kept a Russian-English dictionary at hand and soon was thinking of Hannah as almost another sister. When the long winter months came and Lev was in his study writing, Sonya was glad to have Hannah's company. But Sonya did not begrudge the time Lev spent on his novel; through her copying she was eagerly following the development of *War and Peace*. In mid-January 1867 she noted:

> Levochka has been writing all winter, with irritation, with tears and emotion. I think that his novel must be magnificent. Almost every part he reads to me moves me also to tears and, I do not know, is it because I am his wife that I can sympathize with it or is it because it really is excellent? I rather think the latter.

That winter Lev would have agreed with Sonya's opinion of his novel, but there may have been a tiny crack in his confidence. It was not anything that disturbed the progress of his work, nor anything that he discussed with Sonya, intelligent black Bers that she was, but in January he wrote to Y. F. Samarin a letter that he never sent but kept among his papers and which contained the following confession: [16]

> Up to this time, and I shall soon be forty, I have loved truth more than all else and I have not despaired of finding it and I seek it, I seek it. Sometimes, and never more than this present year, I succeed in raising a little the corner of the curtain and I peep there: But I am alone and it is painful and frightening and, it seems to me, that I am led astray.

He felt alone and it was frightening to be still searching for the truth and certainty that he had tried to discover in his youth. Since his marriage the certainty had seemed to be in love and in family happiness; but was love, family happiness and fame sufficient to justify a man's life? And if not, what was? This crack in Lev's confidence was tiny, however, and his good feeling about marriage and work remained.

During many games of Patience Lev would promise himself that if the game came out he would give his novel a title, but until March of 1867 the work was nameless. Then he chose the title *War and Peace*, probably influenced by a popular work by the French socialist, Pierre-Joseph Proudhon, which was called *La Guerre et la Paix*.[17] Now that the novel had a name it began to assume its final shape, although Lev continued to correct and revise his manuscript and would do so even after the entire novel was printed.

There was a wedding at Yasnaya in the summer of 1867. Tanya, her health and spirits restored after her ill-fated love affair with Lev's brother, married her childhood sweetheart, Aleksandr (Sasha) Kuzminsky. Neither the Bers nor the Tolstoys approved at first; both families had hoped for someone more distinguished, but the marriage was happy and Lev and Sonya had always been fond of Sasha. The Kuzminskys lived first in Tula where Sasha practiced law and later, when he became a judge, in Kiev and St. Petersburg. Except for a short time when Sasha took a position in the Caucasus, he and Tanya spent their summers at Yasnaya, their children growing up with the Tolstoy children. Before Tanya's wedding, a brief incident put a close to her romance with Sergei. When she and Sasha drove in a cabriolet to meet the priest who would perform their wedding ceremony, they passed Sergei coming from the opposite direction in an open carriage. All three bowed before speeding past. Sergei was returning from seeing the same priest and he, too, had made arrangements for a wedding, his own to his gypsy wife.

At the end of summer Lev left home to visit the battlefield of Borodino before writing his chapters on the battle. Sonya was pregnant again and her mood sank; she missed her sister, she missed the summer guests and excitements, and she missed her husband. She was hurt that he had left full of enthusiasm for his trip. She complained in her diary that her love did not mean enough to him:

> I am nothing but a miserable, crushed worm whom no one wants, whom no one loves, a useless creature with morning sickness, a big belly, two rotten teeth, a bad temper, a battered sense of dignity and a love which nobody wants and which nearly drives me insane.[18]

A letter from Lev dispelled her gloom:

> Moscow, 27 September 1867
> I have just come from Borodino. I am very satisfied, very, with my trip and in spite of the fact that I had to survive without sleep and decent meals. If only God gives me good health and tranquility, I shall write a battle of Borodino such has never been done before. Always boasting!

Lev returned and life at home was so productive and happy that Sonya ignored her journal. In the summer of 1868 she reread through parts of it:

It makes me laugh to read my journal, how contradictory it is, as though I were an unhappy woman. But is there a happier one than I? Could one find a marriage more agreeable and happy? Sometimes I stay alone in my room and I begin to laugh with joy and cross myself. May God give me this for a long, long time. . . . Soon we shall have been married six years. And I only love him more and more. He often says that this is surely not love but that we are so accustomed to one another that we couldn't exist without the other.

As *War and Peace* appeared in installments, readers were enthusiastic. There were also some negative comments, these mostly from people who were offended by the realism. Turgenev, not always one to praise Tolstoy, wrote to the literary critic P. V. Annenkov: [19]

I have just finished the fourth volume of *War and Peace*. There are insufferable things in it and there are marvelous things and these marvelous things which, in essence, predominate are so magnificently good that nothing better has ever been written in our country and it is doubtful that anything so good has ever been written.

One of the most enthusiastic readers of *War and Peace* did not live to see it finished. Dr. Bers died in 1868. The Tolstoys said good-bye to him in his study in the Kremlin where he lay paralyzed, an old man with a white beard and pale blue eyes. Sonya does not seem to have mourned her father greatly; another man dominated her life. In May 1869 she had a fourth child, Lev, and at the end of the year *War and Peace* appeared in its entirety. Except for those critical reviewers who found it too realistic, too conservative, too radical or too disrespectful of Russia's leaders, there was a national furor of acclaim. Most readers recognized the greatness of *War and Peace* at once even though, as Tolstoy admitted, it was not a novel in the conventional sense nor was it pure history. Lev had applied his genius to the task of showing how, at a crucial time in Russian history, events happened in spite of the human wills at work and not because of them. He did not overly concern himself with a central plot, climax or dénouement; these seem to occur as inevitably as in life. It is with the force of life that *War and Peace* rolls on until it comes to an end.

When the novel was finished but not yet published in one volume, Lev had an experience that showed that the tiny crack in his confidence was widening. This time his anxiety was more terrifying than what he had expressed in his letter to Samarin in 1867. Lev was traveling to the province of Penza to look at some property that was advertised for sale and he wrote to Sonya while on his journey:

4 September 1869

I write to you from Saransk, darling friend. . . . How are you and the children? What has been happening? For two days I have been tortured with anxiety. The day before yesterday I spent the night in Arsamas and something extraordinary happened to me. It was two o'clock in the morning, I was very tired, I wanted to sleep and nothing was hurting me. All at once there came over me such a terrible, melancholy terror as I have never experienced. I shall tell you the details of this feeling later on; but it was an agonizing sensation such as I have never felt before and, God grant, I'll never feel again. I jumped up, called for the carriage horses. While they were being harnessed I fell asleep, and woke up feeling sound. Yesterday this feeling returned to a lesser degree but I was prepared and did not give way to it, especially so because it was weaker. Today I feel well and happy, so far as I can apart from my family.

Lev always referred to this incident as the "Arsamas misery" and twelve years later he made it into an autobiographical short story, *The Memoirs of a Madman.* Lev reproduced his own feelings in a hero who is overcome by terror without understanding from what or whom he wants to flee. When he runs into the corridor asking himself what it is that he fears, the voice of Death replies, "Me. I am here." Such an episode as Lev had in Arsamas would not be unusual as a symptom of prolonged stress, an understandable stress after six years spent producing a work such as *War and Peace.* The terror that disappeared after a good night's sleep did not, however, go away forever. The Arsamas misery would return to torment Lev and remind him of the fears and anxieties with which he faced the puzzling question: What is the purpose of life?

Chapter Four

A COMPLICATED INNER LIFE,
1870–1878

1.

Sonya was proud to be her husband's "nursemaid of talent," as the writer Sollogub had called her. She knew that she had a kind of interior barometer that responded to the risings and fallings of Lev's needs. Now that *War and Peace* was finished she stood ready for the next great work, aware of the important role she played but also humble about it and happy with her designation of nursemaid.

Lev saw Sonya's part in his life and work in a deeper sense and recognized his emotional dependence on her. In 1870 he was not keeping his diary but he never gave up his notebooks, his grab-bags of estate information, ideas for writing and philosophical musings. In February he wrote in a notebook:

> *14 February.* The ties of husband and wife are not founded on a contract and not on carnal union. In carnal union there is something frightening and blasphemous. The blasphemy is missing only at the time when it produces fruit. But nevertheless it is terrifying, as terrifying as a corpse. It is a mystery. The tie of mother's breast and child is still obvious. When the child is hungry the mother has milk. The same tie exists between husband and wife. One never hears that father, mother, their beloved children, friends, brothers and sisters all die at once. But who has not heard of a thousand instances of the death of a husband

and wife (who have lived happily) almost at the same instant.

Lev wrote this at a time when he was discussing his ideas for a new work, and discussing them for the most part with Sonya. He seemed to be saying in a different way what he had said six years after his marriage—that they could not exist without one another. On the same day that Lev wrote his note about the ties of husband and wife, Sonya started a new project. In a notebook separate from her diary she began writing what eventually became her notes for a future biographer of her husband. She started with an explanation of her purpose:

> The other day I was reading a biography of Pushkin when it occurred to me that posterity will be interested in a biography of Levochka and it would be useful if I wrote down, not his everyday life, but his intellectual life so far as I am able to observe it.

This might seem a tall order but Sonya did not make the mistake of attempting something beyond her abilities. At twenty-five she still wrote a direct, simple, almost childlike prose and she did not embroider her information. Her notes show the many directions taken by Lev's restless imagination and the manner in which he approached his writing. They also show how much he discussed his work with Sonya. She felt that

> Now is a good time to begin. *War and Peace* is over and there is not yet any serious enterprise.

Lev might have said there was because, even before finishing *War and Peace*, he had begun planning a novel set in the time of Peter the Great. Sonya's insights told her that it was too soon to take these plans seriously. In fact, she did not mention the interest in Peter the Great at the beginning of her notes, but instead described Lev's reading in philosophy. She wrote that he delighted in Schopenhauer but that he referred to Hegel as "mere verbiage." She realized that it was a tremendous intellectual struggle for Lev to settle on his next work:

> He often says that his brain aches, that he feels a terrible burden; that it is all over for him and that it is time for him to die and be gone.

The terrible burden could have been the sense of obligation that went with Lev's genius. Even before he began *War and Peace*, he had written in his diary that he must "return to others, to *everyone,* by means of my work that which they have given to me." One masterpiece had not relieved him of his sense of obligation. Another problem plagued him: his rich imagination gave him an embarrassment of ideas. When he was reading Russian folk tales, a story led him to think of doing children's books on four levels, beginning with the ABC's. Another tale gave him an idea for a play and he began reading Molière, Shakespeare and Pushkin. He told Sonya about an idea for a comedy but she noted that the material was frivolous and she thought that he would not consider it for long. She was right. Lev told her, "No, having tried something of the epic sort it is hard to take up drama." Early in February 1870 Sonya made a note that Lev had called her into his study especially to talk about history and historical figures. She noticed that he was reading a history of Peter the Great by Ustrylov. If Sonya was anxious for him to choose his subject and get started, she kept this to herself. Often Lev exclaimed to her, "How much work there is ahead!" Suddenly Sonya felt hope:

> Yesterday evening he said that he had thought of the idea of a woman, married, upper class but lost to herself. He said that the problem for him would be to make this woman not guilty but merely pitiable. As soon as he had conceived this character, all the faces of the masculine characters that he had been imagining before, took their places grouped around this married woman. He said, "Now everything is clear to me."

Sonya drew a line across the page after this entry in her notes and added:

> He said, "They reproach me with fatalism; but perhaps no one is more of a believer than I am. Fatalism is an excuse to do evil, but I believe in God, in the words of the gospel that not a single hair falls but that it is God's will and that is why I say that everything is predestined."

Sometimes Sonya forgot that she intended to confine her notes to her husband's intellectual life:

> We have just been skating. He tries to do everything, on one foot, on two feet, backward, in circles and so forth.

Unwittingly she drew an analogy to Lev's wandering thoughts. All year his notebook reflected two searches—to find a theme for his new work and to make sense out of the problem of life. Was there a purpose to existence? He wrote in a notebook on 26 March:

> Everything that is rational is powerless. Everything that is senseless is creatively productive. . . . In other words, the main point of life is incomprehensible to reason, but nothing is comprehensible to reason but reason itself.

In November Lev returned to his Peter the Great material and wrote to Fet:

> 17 November 1870
> You cannot imagine how difficult it is for me, this preliminary work of deeply plowing the field which I am *compelled* to sow. It is terribly difficult to think about, and to rethink, everything that may happen to all the future people in a work in progress, and a very big work, and to think about millions of possible combinations from which to choose one millionth. And with this I am occupied.

Sonya was relieved to be able to write in December:

> Today it seems to me that for the first time he begins to write seriously. . . . All this time of inactivity, which I would call intellectual relaxation, has been very tormenting to him. He said that he was ashamed of his idleness and not only in front of me but in front of everyone. Sometimes it would seem to him that inspiration was returning and he would rejoice. Sometimes it would seem to him— and this always happened when he was away from home and family—that he was going mad and the fear of madness was so strong in him that afterward when he told me about it I was overcome with horror.

Sonya's horror was justified; Lev's anxieties were increasing, but apparently he only discussed them with Sonya. Externally life was much the same. Lev wrote to Fet that the weather was depressing but that everything at home was fine and all were well.

The serious writing that had encouraged Sonya in December turned out to be one of twenty-five versions of the start of a novel set in the time of Peter the Great. This version was soon tossed aside and Lev, on a sudden impulse, took up the study of Greek. Sonya was recovering from giving premature birth to a second daughter, Maria (Masha), in February 1871. The baby was sickly and Sonya dangerously ill with puerperal fever, though six weeks later she had regained her strength sufficiently to be pressed into service as Lev's tutor. She listened to and checked his oral translations of Greek. Sonya was impressed by the speed with which Lev mastered the language but she knew that

> He wants to be writing and often says so. He dreams chiefly of a work so clear and elegant that there would be nothing superfluous, a work like all the ancient Greek literature, like the Greek art.

This was in March 1871. A year later, in March 1872, Lev wrote an isolated sentence in his notebook: "Wild animals and birds are not frightened." Surely wild animals and birds experience fear but perhaps Lev was envying them their lack of *psychological* fears, the kind of fears that were besetting him. Sonya did not need to read his notebooks to know that her husband was not in good health, either mentally or physically. In the summer of 1871 she persuaded him, after much resistance on his part, to go to the Samaran steppe and take a cure that consisted of drinking fermented mare's milk, kumys.[1] Lev took with him his young brother-in-law, Stefan Bers. From the steppe he wrote to Sonya:

> We live in a tent. We drink kumys. . . . The inconveniences would horrify your Kremlin heart. There are no beds, no china, no white bread, no spoons. . . . Each day we dine on lamb which we eat with our fingers from a wooden bowl.

In his first letters Lev admitted that he was still depressed. Soon the vigorous and primitive outdoor life restored his physical health and, apart from missing his family, he seemed to relish the new experiences. One letter to Sonya described the native hospitality:

> When one arrives the host kills a plump, fat-tail sheep, sets out a huge tub of kumys, lays rugs and cushions on the ground, seats his guests on them and does not let them leave until they have eaten the sheep and drunk the kumys. He invites his guests to drink from his hands and with his fingers (without forks) he puts lamb and fat into their mouths, and one must not offend him.[2]

No doubt Sonya's Kremlin heart was horrified, but in spite of, or perhaps because of, this hospitality Lev became so fond of Samara that he purchased over seven thousand acres of land in the province. He remained there through July, drinking the kumys and studying Greek. Sonya urged him to relax and drop his studies. "Have you given up the hateful Greeks?" she asked and he wrote back that her letters missing him were more harmful than all the Greeks could be. At the end of his letter he said, "Suddenly, I want to weep, I love you so much."

When Lev returned to Yasnaya, Sonya did not believe that he was healed:

> *18 August.* . . . His disease remains. I cannot see it but I can sense his indifference to life which began last winter and his lack of interest in everything. Something has come between us like a shadow which divides us. . . . He says that it is old age. [Lev was forty-three.] I say that it is illness.

Aging, illness or depression, Lev was content neither with himself nor with his efforts to write fiction. In 1871 and 1872 he put aside his literary work and concentrated on his idea of composing primers for young children. These books grew out of Lev's educational theories, which were once again close to his heart. Some years later, in 1876, when *Anna Karenina* was nearly finished, he described his schoolbooks as the "only truly good and useful thing" that he had ever done.

Both Tolstoys were upset by the departure of the Kuzminsky family for the Caucasus. Sasha, now a public prosecutor, had been transferred to Kutaisi. There was no one, as Sonya often said, who could lift their spirits as Tanya could. Other visitors helped. Lev's sister came for Christmas, 1871 bringing her three children and the Diakovs were guests for the end-of-the-year festivities. Sonya organized the usual theatricals, concerts and fancy-dress parties but Lev seemed happier when the season was over and he reopened the Yasnaya Polyana school. This time he enlisted his family as teachers, including Sergei and Tanya, who were nine and seven respectively. Sonya wrote to her sister Tanya:

> Tanya and Seryozha teach fairly decently. In a week everyone knew the letters and syllables by ear. We teach them downstairs in the front hall which is huge, in the small dining room under the staircase, and in the new study. The main thing that spurs us to teach them reading and writing is that there is such a need and they all have a desire to learn and learn with such pleasure.

Thirty-five children came to the house every day. The peasant pupils brought presents for the Tolstoy children and played with them after class. Sonya found them rather "rowdy" but was impressed by how quickly they learned. She was also helping her husband with his primers and noted:

> We stayed up until four o'clock in the morning correcting the ABC books.

This was in April 1872, and Sonya, seven months pregnant, was losing some of her enthusiasm for the school. She wrote to her sister that it was difficult to have to supervise her own children's lessons every morning and have the school in the afternoon. But Sonya did not want to give up and was pleased that all the pupils could read and write. At the same time she noted in her diary:

> This winter has been a happy one; again we live harmoniously and Levochka's health has not been bad.

The school had given them a sense of accomplishment which was a distraction from the worrisome thought that Lev was not writing. Sonya's diary was full of simple family pleasures: gathering flowers with the children, going for moonlit walks with Lev, Lev bringing home flowering branches and Lev sitting up all one night to study the stars in preparation for writing a lesson. In June 1872 a sixth baby arrived, Pyotr (Petya), and that summer Lev hired a tutor for his older children. Until then the Tolstoys had educated their children themselves, most of the task falling on Sonya—although Lev gave an occasional lesson in mathematics or composition. The first tutor was followed by others, all of whom lived at Yasnaya and ate with the family. The favorite governess, Hannah, had been plagued with a cough which turned out to be a symptom of tuberculosis. Sadly Sonya sent her off to the Kuzminskys and the warmer climate of the Caucasus. There Hannah recovered and two years later she married a Georgian prince.

In the autumn and winter Lev took his place at his writing desk nearly every day but had little to show for his efforts. Sonya wrote in her notes:

> He has made about ten beginnings but is always dissatisfied. Yesterday he said, "The machine is ready, now to bring it to action."

Sonya yearned for Lev to be writing. When his life was productive artistically, hers was at its most satisfying. His long periods of inactivity left her without her sense of her highest purpose. She was twenty-nine and her glossy, black hair and perfect complexion made her look younger. Sometimes a tempting discontent came over her. She was aghast at her thoughts but recorded them in her diary:

13 February 1873. Levochka has gone to Moscow and without him I sit all day in melancholy with fixed eyes and with thoughts in my head which agitate and torment me and do not give me peace. And always in this mental state of anxiety I turn to my journal. Into it I pour out all my bad mood and I sober myself. And my mood is sinful, stupid, dishonest, terrible. Where would I be without his constant support, utmost love, without his wisest and clearest view of everything? And sometimes during a time of anxiety I suddenly peep into my heart and ask myself: what is it that I want? And I answer aghast—I want to be gay, I want frivolous chatter, I want clothes, I want to be attractive, I want people to say that I am beautiful and I want Levochka to see and hear all this. I also want him to sometimes leave his preoccupied life, which depresses him at times, and spend his life together with me, the way many people live all the time. And with a cry from my heart I renounce all this with which I, like Eve, am tempted by the devil. . . . And what could beauty bring that I need? My darling little Petya loves his old nurse as if she were beautiful. Levochka could get used to a wife with the ugliest face if she would be quiet, submissive to him and would live a life that he chose for her.

Sonya resolved that she would get rid of all her pettiness but she added:

Little ribbons delight me, I want a new leather belt and, now, after writing all of this I want to cry—. The children sit upstairs and wait for me to teach them music and I am writing all this nonsense in the study downstairs.

The cure for Sonya's discontent came within a month. In her notes for 19 March 1873 she wrote:

Yesterday evening L. suddenly said to me, "Oh, I have written one and a half sheets and it seems to be good." I thought that this was a new attempt to write about the time of Peter the Great and I did not pay much attention. But then I learned that he had begun an epic novel about contemporary private lives.

This was the beginning of *Anna Karenina*.

2.

Anna Karenina was a more conventional novel than *War and Peace*. Its two stories in counterpoint so easily and naturally blend together that neither that of Anna and Vronsky nor that of Kitty and Levin can be called the minor theme. A book set in Tolstoy's own time and concerning the private lives of fictional characters, *Anna Karenina* did not demand the research and study that was necessary for *War and Peace*. This second major novel posed another kind of challenge. All the questions about the purpose of life that were tormenting Lev he tried to answer through the development of his character Levin. In this respect *Anna Karenina* was a greater emotional challenge than anything Lev had done before. Sometimes during the writing he was as happy as he had ever been, but there were other times when he despaired of finding answers to those questions that disturbed Lev/Levin. At these times he fell into deep depression and Sonya had to fight not to lose hope herself.

The plot for *Anna Karenina* was worked out in the spring of 1873 at the beginning of the writing. In an undated paragraph among Sonya's notes, she described the event which suggested to Lev the name of his heroine and the circumstances of her suicide. A neighbor of the Tolstoys who was a widower had taken as his housekeeper a relative of his dead wife. Her name was Anna and she became her employer's mistress as well as housekeeper. When Anna discovered that her lover had fallen in love with and planned to marry a beautiful German, she went to the railway station and threw herself onto the tracks in front of an approaching freight train. Sonya wrote in her paragraph:

> They did an autopsy on her body and Lev Nikolaevich saw her lying in the Yasenki barracks, naked and with her skull crushed. It made a terrible and profound impres-

sion upon him. Anna Stepanovna was a tall, plump woman with Russian features and characteristics, a brunette with gray eyes, not beautiful although very attractive.

This experience diverted Lev from the novel set in the time of Peter the Great and he returned to his idea of a sinning but pitiable married woman, first considered three years before he began writing *Anna Karenina*.

The writing went smoothly all spring. In the summer of 1872 the Tolstoys decided that the entire family would accompany Lev on what was now an annual visit to Samara for the kumys cure. The trip would be by coach, train and boat. For the last lap, where there was no transportation, a huge *dormeuse* would be sent ahead to wait for them. Sorrowful news interrupted the preparations for this ambitious journey. Tanya wrote from the Caucasus that her six-year-old daughter Dasha had died. Lev tried to console his sister-in-law and wrote to her on 18 May 1873:

Beloved friend Tanya!
I am not able to write you the feelings which were produced in me by the news of the death of charming, my darling, my favorite (as I am now pleased to remember) Dasha! I would never have thought that this death could affect me so much. I feel how close you and your children are to me. Each day I can't think of you and her without tears. I have the feeling that, very likely, now tortures you; I forget and then remember and then ask myself with horror—is it possible that it is true?

Lev urged prayer, religious consolation:

For what does a child live and die? It is a frightening enigma. And for me there is only one explanation. It is better for her. However commonplace these words, they are always new and profound if one understands them. And it is better for us and we must become better after these sorrows.

Lev's letter to Tanya shows one direction his thoughts were taking before the enigma of death. Sonya's reaction was less resigned, but life with six active children did not permit the Tolstoys to indulge their sorrow. Lev had been to Moscow to shop for the trip; he had bought coats and hats, shoes, suitcases, trunks and picnic baskets. He wrote to Fet:

I was in Moscow, I made forty-three purchases for 450 r[ubles] and after this, it is really impossible not to go to Samara.

To amuse the children on the long journey Sonya painted a series of pictures in several notebooks. As long as she had young children or grandchildren Sonya made these picture books. She had no talent for drawing and her perspective and proportions were inaccurate, but the dramatic scenes of wolves carrying off children into a dark wood, of a fire with children manning the bucket brigade and of hares stealing vegetables from the garden were all a huge success with her young audience. Besides this and other entertainment for the children, the Tolstoys had with them everyone's personal belongings, their bed linen, dishes, cooking utensils—everything that was needed for three months of living except for the minimal furniture they would find in the house where they planned to stay.

The journey was a rigorous adventure. The children ranged in age from ten-year-old Sergei to the one-year-old baby, Petya, who was still nursing. From Tula they took the train to Nizhny Novgorod (now called Gorki), a journey of over 350 miles; from there they embarked on a steamer for an equally long trip down the Volga to the town of Samara. In Samara they spent the night in a hotel. The big *dormeuse* was waiting in the courtyard for the final stage of their trip, about eighty miles eastward across the Samaran steppe. Their destination was a plain wooden house, too small for the whole family, so Lev and Stefan Bers slept in a tent of the Bashkirs, a Mohammedan tribe living in Samara, and the three older boys lodged in an empty shed. The hot climate and change in food brought immediate digestive troubles but Sonya had remembered to bring her medical supplies. There would be no doctor within reach for the summer. Years later in his *Sketches of the Past* Sergei described the country:

The rich, deep black earth was covered with thick grasses, various herbs, feather grass, couch grass, wild oats and every possible kind of wormwood. Brown and white bustards, the size of turkeys, flew over the steppe and large, white-beaked golden eagles. Hawks soared everywhere and the air was filled with the noise of sparrow-hawks fluttering and the chatter of grasshoppers. In spite of the scorching heat breathing was easy on the steppe; the air was dry and even on the very hottest day a breeze was blowing.

Life wasn't easy but even the city-raised Sonya surmounted the primitive conditions, including the insects that pestered them while they ate or slept. When they returned to Yasnaya at the end of August, Lev wrote to Fet:

> In spite of . . . the drought, the discomforts, all of us, even my wife, were pleased with the trip and still more pleased to fall back into our old ways of life and work.

September was the month when Lev usually returned to writing but he found it difficult to settle down. He sat for his portrait by the painter Kramskoe, he served a term of jury duty, but both activities were excuses to delay writing.[3] Then, on 9 November 1873, the first death struck the family. Eighteen-month-old Petya, the baby whom Lev had described in a letter to Granny as a "colossus, a big, fat baby, adorable in his bonnet," died of the croup. The small corpse in a tiny coffin lined with silver cloth was placed on a table in the sunny living room where the children came to say good-bye to their baby brother. Little Tanya noticed that the tiny hands crossed on the baby's chest had black fingernails. Lev wrote to his sister-in-law Tanya:

> I had not expected that, besides the sadness of losing him, our noisy little Petya would leave such a void in the house for his father.

Sonya wrote in her diary:

> *11 November.* On the ninth of November at nine o'clock in the morning my little Petushka died of a throat illness. He was sick for only two days, he died quietly. . . . My darling, I loved him so much and now emptiness. Yesterday they buried him. But I am not able to connect the living him with the same him dead, both near and dear to me but how different was the living, bright, loving creature from the dead one, quiet, solemn and cold. He was very attached to me. Was he sorry that I remained behind and that he had to leave me?

Lev made no mention of the baby's death but after an entry on 17 November, he drew a line across the page and wrote a separate comment:

> After death perhaps there is a chemical life following the physical life on earth. The father has many mansions.

A month later he wrote in his diary:

> If a man thinks that his life is only a transient phenomenon—the sound of Plato's lyre, then it follows from this that the life of all men seems to him to be only the sound of a lyre; but if he loves or is loved the meaning of his life becomes for him profound.[4]

As Levin would in *Anna Karenina*, Levin's creator hoped to find the meaning of life in love.

Sonya openly grieved for Petya while Lev tried to console himself with philosophical submission, but the loss brought them closer and eventually Lev could write to Granny that Sonya, apart from the natural, physical pain she felt as a mother, shared his belief that they must submit to death and see it as significant and beautiful. The parents were able to forget their grieving in the spring when Lev got back some of his enthusiasm for *Anna Karenina*. In March 1874 he delivered the first part of the novel to the printer. Until the book was finished, however, Lev had a vacillating attitude toward the work. At times he seemed to feel that in charting Levin's growing understanding of life he was gaining understanding himself. At other times he lost all interest in the book (in a letter to writer and historian P. D. Golokhvastov he called it "offensive and nasty") and turned to education and the management of what had grown to be seventy schools in the Yasnaya area. The needs of children, he said, were more urgent than the lives of his imaginary characters.[5] Even Sonya never had the same admiration for *Anna Karenina* that she had for *War and Peace*. She recognized Levin as a self-portrait of the author, but she did not warm up to him as a character. "Levochka," she said teasingly, "you are Levin but plus talent. Levin is an unbearable person."

A new baby, Nikolai, arrived in May, but the next month the wings of death again brushed Yasnaya. The previous year Auntie Tatyana had suddenly begun to age and, aware that she would not live much longer, she moved her bedroom from a large, sunny room upstairs to a small one on the ground floor. She insisted on moving, explaining to Lev, "I want to move in order that my death won't spoil for you your beautiful, outside room." She died in June 1874—the loss of Lev's closest tie to childhood and another reminder of the transience of life. Lev wrote to Granny about Auntie:

She lived here for fifty years and not only was never evil but she never did anything unpleasant to anyone. But she was afraid of death. She did not say that she was afraid but I saw that she was. What does this mean?

After Auntie's death, Natalya Petrovna went to live in an old people's home which Turgenev had founded on his estate near Tula. The old ladies had been boring at times but even the children knew that something was lost when they were no longer at Yasnaya. Their gentle, formal and old-fashioned ways had been a reminder of bygone times.

In his letter to Granny about Auntie's death Lev mentioned that he would like to give up writing *Anna Karenina* because he disliked it so much. Lev might never have finished the book if it had not been for the nineteenth-century custom of serializing novels while they were being written—which, of course, committed the author to finishing the work. Perhaps Lev disliked this novel because its two stories symbolized a struggle within himself. While writing about Levin's search for truth and certainty he began to look askance at the society world of Anna and Vronsky, a world of which Lev himself had once been very much a part. All the same, 1875 was a productive year and three more installments of *Anna Karenina* appeared in *The Russian Messenger*.

In February 1875 Nikolai, the baby, contracted meningitis. Lev wrote about the illness to his friend Nikolai Nikolaevich Strakhov, a critic, essayist and writer on philosophical subjects who had called on the Tolstoys after the publication of *War and Peace* and struck up a lasting friendship with Lev. The friends corresponded regularly until Strakhov's death in 1896. About Nikolai, Lev wrote:

> The family grief is the cerebral illness of our nine-month-old nursing baby. It is now four weeks that he has been going through all the phases of this hopeless illness. My wife is feeding him herself and one moment despairs that he will die and one moment that he will live and be an idiot.

The dreadful threat of idiocy made the loss of this baby easier for Sonya to bear.[6] After another family summer on the Samaran steppe Lev wrote to Strakhov:

> 25 August
> . . . Now I am taking care of tiresome, commonplace A Karen [*Anna Karenina*] and I pray God that he give me

the strength to get her off my hands as quickly as I can
so that some time can be made free—leisure very necessary
for me—not for pedagological work but for other work
which occupies me more and more.

The other work to which Lev referred was his first attempt to
write down his tormenting questions about the meaning of life
and to consider them in moral and religious terms. These questions
were occupying him "more and more" and the anxieties of which
the Arsamas misery was a symptom remained. One midnight in
the autumn of 1875 the family was awakened by the sound of
Lev screaming, "Sonya, Sonya!" Grabbing a candle, Sonya ran
downstairs and found her husband groping in the dark hall.

"What happened to you, Levochka?"

"Nothing. I lost my way."

Sergei recalled this episode in his book about his father and could
not explain Lev's screams of terror except as due to an "abnormal
fit," i.e., a pathological condition. Sonya was well aware that once
more Lev was depressed. Not well herself—she was having a difficult pregnancy—she found her husband's depression contagious:

> *12 October 1875.* This lonely life in the country is finally
> becoming unbearable for me. Dismal apathy, indifference
> to everything and today, tomorrow, for months and
> years—always the same and the same. I wake in the morn-
> ing and I don't get up. Why should I rise, what is waiting
> for me? . . . And I am not alone; as the years pass I am
> tied closer and closer to Levochka and then I feel that it
> is mainly he who pulls me into this dreary, apathetic state.
> It hurts me to see him the way he is now; despondent,
> sunken, he sits without working, without effort, without
> energy, without joyful purpose for days and weeks as
> though he condoned this condition. Somehow, it's a moral
> death but I don't want this for him and he himself cannot
> live like this for long.

Sonya wrote dramatically and admitted that she might be overstat-
ing the situation:

> Perhaps my view is superficial and incorrect. . . . If people
> could not hope life would be impossible and I hope that
> God will once more give to Levochka the fire by which
> he lived and will live.

It was hard to hope, however, when Lev confessed to Sonya that he dared not look at the crossbeams in the ceiling of his study because they suggested a place from which he could hang himself. Lev came to Sonya with this horrible confession and it was to her that he cried out when groping in the dark in terror. The bond between husband and wife was still strong, although with uncanny prescience Sonya had noted the year before, "Something has come between us like a shadow." Lev's search for truth would not always bind them together.

3.

No matter how deep Lev's depression or how discouraged Sonya felt, the Tolstoys hid this dark side of life from their children. Outside of the confidences of the bedroom or the study, family life continued in its usual rhythm. The Tolstoy children remembered their childhoods with special fondness; Aleksandra, not yet born, was to be the only exception. Both Lev and Sonya had a good share of physical vitality and exuberance which they could summon for their children if for nothing else. Ilya recalled a favorite family romp, "The Numidian Cavalry," which was Lev's solution to bouts of temper or tears:

> All of a sudden Papa would jump up from his chair, raise one arm and run galloping headlong around the table. All of us would fly after him and, like him, we hopped and waved our arms. We would run around the table several times and, out of breath, sit down again at our places in an entirely different mood. There were many times that the Numidian Cavalry had a very good effect. After it, quarrels and hurt feelings were forgotten and tears dried up terribly fast.

Lev was now spending less time teaching his children their lessons, but he loved to tell them stories or to read aloud to them. When the Yasnaya library was exhausted of suitable books he went to Moscow and came home with the works of Jules Verne. Lev read aloud sitting at the table with the children around him. When the books were not illustrated, he provided pictures himself. He could draw no better than Sonya but his pictures were equally appreciated. While he worked on an illustration the children crawled onto the table to be able to watch him. His most successful effort was a goddess whose several heads were adorned with snakes. This was for *Around the World in Eighty Days*. Dumas' *The Three Musketeers* was another favorite, but Lev carefully skipped all the parts describing love affairs.

Sonya's depression that year may have been partly due to her physical condition. She was finally ill enough with her difficult pregnancy to take to her bed; Lev asked Zakharin, a prominent Moscow doctor, to send his assistant, who diagnosed peritonitis.[7] A sorrowful aftermath of the illness was the premature birth of a daughter, Varya, who lived only an hour. Sonya remained weak and Lev sent her to Moscow to be examined by Dr. Zakharin himself. A thorough going-over revealed that Sonya was in good health with no lingering problem. Her difficult pregnancy, illness and loss of her baby and her husband's depression had all exhausted Sonya, but the trip to Moscow and change of scene restored her and she came home with her usual vitality. She found Lev more interested in a philosophical correspondence with Strakhov than in finishing his novel.

On 30 November 1875 Lev wrote a long letter to Strakhov, almost an essay, in which he summarized his ideas concerning philosophy, science and religion. In this letter he included some paragraphs which showed his current thoughts about himself:

> I have lived through the period of childhood, youth and adolescence during which I rose higher and higher on that mysterious mountain of life, hoping to find on its summit an end worthy of the effort; I have then lived through the period of maturity, during which time I arrived at the summit, contented and peaceful. . . . I have lived through the little by little advancing bewilderment as to whether I have been mistaken to attribute an unusual significance to what I have achieved.

Lev wondered whether the discrepancy between his attainments and his satisfaction, or lack of it, was the general fate of mankind. He felt none of what he had expected to feel at the summit of life; all that remained was to descend the other side:

> And I have begun that descent. Not only do I no longer have those desires which involuntarily carried me upward, but I have an opposite, unworthy desire to stop and hold

on to something. I have moments of terror (even more
unworthy) before that which awaits me; and I slowly and
circumspectly go downward, remembering the way I have
come, examining the present and trying, from the present
path and from my observations of everything around me,
to penetrate the mystery of the life I have lived and the
even greater mystery that waits for me in that place toward
which I involuntarily speed.

Speculations such as these diverted Lev from *Anna Karenina*. Summer came and with it the Kuzminskys, now returned from the
Caucasus, who resumed in 1876 their summers at Yasnaya Polyana;
Sasha Kuzminsky had completed his service in Kutaisi and was
appointed a judge in St. Petersburg. Even when summer was over
Lev continued to avoid writing. He told Sonya, "My brain is
asleep." Then, on 21 November, Sonya returned to her notes and
recorded a conversation with Lev:

"How boring writing this is," he exclaimed to her.

"What?"

"Well, I've written here that Vronsky and Anna are stopping
in the same hotel room and that is impossible. At the very least
they definitely must stay on separate floors in Petersburg. So I
see that because of this change it follows that scenes, conversations
and various people's visits to them will have to be separate and
I must redo them."

A tedious task perhaps, but Lev was writing and Sonya was
copying every night. Not only did she make the fair copies of
Anna Karenina, but she had to copy out the galley proofs: Lev's
changes and additions made the proofs unintelligible to the printer.
Ilya recalled his mother going to his father when even she could
not decipher a scribble. Lev would read the passage impatiently
until he reached the part in question and then often he, too, stumbled and hesitated and finally had to guess at his own intention.
Besides this work, Sonya was putting together material in order
to write a short biography of her husband. In preparation she
went through all his papers and diaries and succeeded in upsetting
herself:

I avidly search every page of the diaries where there is
something about love and I torture myself with jealousy
and this obscures and confuses everything for me. But I
am trying.

Fourteen years of marriage had not blunted Sonya's jealousy nor decreased her need for her husband's company. When he went to Samara to buy more horses, she fretted so much missing him that she lost her temper with the children. She admitted to her diary:

> My God, how I am impatient, how I get cross with the children and today I screamed. I was distressed by Sergei's latest, poor composition on the Volga, his spelling mistakes and Ilya's laziness and at the end of class I burst into tears. The children were astonished but Sergei began to pity me.

A telegram from Lev, saying he would return in two days, turned the world around for her:

> And suddenly today everything begins to be happy, I teach the children easily and everything at home is so bright and good and the children are sweet.

Writing her husband's biography, however, proved to be too difficult and after five months of trying she gave up the project:

> His inner life is so complicated and reading his diaries agitates me so much that I confuse my thoughts and feelings and cannot look at everything reasonably.

She continued to keep her notes for another, future biographer. On 3 March 1877 she added to them:

> Yesterday L. N. went to his desk, indicated the exercise book in which he was writing and said, "Ah, would that I could quickly, quickly finish this novel (*Anna Karenina*) and start anew. Now my ideas have become clear to me. In order for a work to be good it is necessary to love its principal, fundamental idea. Thus in *Anna Karenina* I love the idea of the family, in *War and Peace*, because of the war of 1812, I loved the idea of the Russian nation and now I see that in my new work I shall love the idea of the Russian people in the sense of the strength of their [migrating] settlements.

For a moment it seemed clear and simple to him. Perhaps it was only Sonya who realized just how complicated his inner life was. Later the same day she returned to her notes:

> L. N. returned from his morning walk and said, "How happy I am." I asked him why and he replied, "In the

first place because of you and in the second place because of my religion."

Sonya was probably disappointed to hear him place religion above his writing. Neither she nor Lev had ever had a formal religious commitment and now she was puzzled to see her husband kneel each day like a child to say his prayers. But Lev had begun to wonder whether some of his depressions might not come from his lack of faith and he decided to find a faith by starting from the outside; that is, by strictly observing the practices of the Russian Orthodox Church. Sonya wrote in her notes:

> He goes to the celebration of mass. . . . On Wednesdays and Fridays he fasts and he talks constantly about the spirit of humility.. . . On the 26th of July [1877] he stayed at the Optina Monastery and was very pleased with the education, life and wisdom of the elders there.[8]

In the nineteenth century it was common for Russian intellectuals to visit monasteries and partake of the elders' wisdom. These churchmen were worlds apart from the average dirty and ignorant village priest. Gogol and Dostoevsky had stayed in Optina and other writers spent their lives in the monastery and were buried within its walls. When Lev made his first trip to Optina, the abbot was Ambrosius, who was famous for his intellect, holiness and the power of his faith. Lev was relieved that his own fragile belief was somewhat bolstered by his talks with Ambrosius.

Anna Karenina was finished "quickly, quickly" and appeared in book form in 1877. The critical acclaim was even more enthusiastic than for *War and Peace*. Both Tolstoys assumed that Lev would start at once on a new work, another major novel. Lev was, however, more concerned with his budding spiritual life. Sonya was tolerant of her husband's effort to find peace in religion but she was not optimistic. Lev's physical health, always her barometer of his mental state, worried her more than his spiritual quest. She wrote to her sister Tanya:

> He has constant headaches and his blood pressure is very high. He went to Zakharin who applied leeches but he is not better. . . . He shakes horribly in his sleep and I am afraid of a stroke. Zakharin's opinion is that this is not impossible.

Sonya believed that Lev's health would improve when he began writing a new novel. She was encouraged when he told her, "My mental valve is open." He added, however, that as a result he had a terrible headache. Another time he described the execution of the central idea of his new work as having "the same consistency." The same consistency as what, Sonya wondered in her notes, and how? Lev told her ideas for several beginnings. He based one plot on an old proverb; one son is no son, two sons are half a son and only three sons make a son. Sonya wrote down his summary:

> "I shall have an old man who has three sons. One is a soldier, one lives at home and is merely so-so and a third, dearly loved by the old man, has learned to read and write and has turned away from the peasant life which hurts the old father. So here it is for a start, a domestic drama in the soul of a prosperous peasant."

Sonya added:

> Then, I think, the educated peasant son will meet people from an educated circle and thus will start a series of events.

Lev said that in the second part of the novel he would introduce a migrant, a kind of Russian Robinson Crusoe, who settles on new land in the Samaran steppe. Sonya, who had witnessed twenty-five beginnings for the novel set in the time of Peter the Great, was not convinced that his mental valve was open. Then another son, Andrei (Andrusha), was born on 6 December and at the same time Lev settled down in his study. In a large, bound volume he began writing down some of his religious and philosophical thoughts. This was not the sort of writing that Sonya had hoped for, but she did her best to have a positive attitude. In December 1877 she earnestly described her husband's changing personality in the notes that she was keeping for posterity:

> The character of L. N. is changing more and more all the time. Although he has always been modest and undemanding in all of his habits, now he has become even more modest, meek and patient.

Reading between these lines, Sonya appears more wistful than admiring. Certainly she herself would have had to change to be in accord with a pious, meek husband. She felt a great relief when Lev told her that something was happening to him resembling the time when he was writing *War and Peace*. Then he had assembled material for a novel about the Decembrists but that had led him to writing about the war of 1812 instead. Now he was assembling material about the period of Nicholas I and he thought that this would lead to a novel about the Decembrists. Still intrigued with his idea of the migrating peasant, he told Sonya that he had thought of a plot in which a Decembrist would join a peasant migration and "thus the simple life will meet with that of the highest society." He added that the design of a novel must have a background; for his new novel the background would be his new religious spirit. Sonya's heart must have sunk. She did not observe that his religious spirit was inspiring his creative genius but she quietly asked him to explain what he was trying to say. Sonya recorded their conversation in her notes. At first Lev replied impatiently, "If I could know how it will be, I should not be thinking about it further." Sonya did not push him but recorded that he came back to the conversation, saying that he wanted to look at all sides of the Decembrist rebellion and condemn neither Nicholas I nor the conspirators. Sonya was pleased when he returned from Moscow with books on the history of the Decembrists. Sometimes he was moved to tears when he read these histories. His usual sensitivity and susceptibility to emotion was increased by the tensions that went with finding a theme for a major novel and finding a faith. Both Lev and Sonya realized that it was a time of great strain for him, but it does not seem to have occurred to either of them that the strain was anything more than the labor pains, perhaps more severe than usual, that preceded the birth of each of Lev's masterpieces.

Chapter Five

UNBEARABLE ANXIETY, FUTILITY AND SHAME, 1878–1884

1.

In the spring of 1878 a strange entry appeared in one of Lev's notebooks which, unlike his diaries, were usually kept for his eyes alone. The entry implied a new attitude toward Sonya and perhaps the shadow which she had feared was finally falling between them. On Easter they went to mass together and afterward Lev wrote:

> *16 April 1878.* At mass. Easter cake, pastry. "A good horse is rather lazy, doesn't charge forward and takes care not to fall." Butterflies around the candles in the sanctuary. *She* [Lev's underlining] in a white dress. She is waiting, is afraid, she desires, she defies and she mocks with kisses.

"She" was always Sonya and these impressionistic observations suggest more than casual feelings. Lev seemed to sense a change and admonished himself by the proverb to be cautious. He mentioned Sonya's white dress. He still found her beautiful but now she also disturbed him. She waited. Was it for him to start writing? A year had gone by since *Anna Karenina* was finished and there was still no new work. She was afraid. Was she afraid that he might fail? She desired. Sonya was young, thirty-four, and Lev knew that she still cared for him passionately. So far it is possible to guess at his thoughts. But what had Sonya done that Lev wrote, "she mocks with kisses"? Perhaps nothing and the answer lay in a change in Lev. Less than a year before, Sonya had written that her husband's character was changing "more and more all the time." Probably she meant Lev's behavior. Judging from his diary, his character was the same throughout his life; he remained sensitive, perfectionist and idealistic. He set too-high standards for himself and suffered guilt when he failed to meet them. At fifty Lev did not yet feel that he had paid his debt to posterity. He believed that he owed the world another sublime achievement, a third novel greater than *War and Peace* and *Anna Karenina*. The third novel, however, refused to be born in spite of agonizing effort and Lev was becoming increasingly frustrated and anxious. A sense of despair, which probably came from mental and physical stress, he believed to be guilt. Now, as is normal for a person under great stress, he looked outside himself for someone on whom to place his guilt. Who was more adequate to bear this burden than the one closest to him, the one he loved most, Sonya? Marriage to Sonya had created that special condition in which his genius flourished. Perhaps he feared that something had gone wrong with his marriage, since his genius seemed to falter.

Lev was too reasonable to fault Sonya as a wife and mother. She had been the faithful, loving companion of sixteen years, years warmed by a satisfying physical relationship, shared values and a sense of partnership in his work. Even from the strictest religious point of view, Sonya's conduct had been irreproachable. In desperation Lev chose to put the blame for his frustration on her sexuality. He could continue to love Sonya as a wife and criticize her as a sexual temptress. He did not reach this state of mind all at once, but the strange comment after the Easter mass was the first sign of a conviction that would grow in proportion to his frustration.

On the day after Easter Lev opened his diary for the first time in thirteen years. He returned to a habit of his bachelor life and listed each day's sins:

> Boasted of my ideas and got excited with Sonya. . . . Got angry at Alexei and the headman because they did a poor job digging around the apple trees.

A talk with Sergei's tutor revived childhood guilts. Sergei was fifteen at the time. Lev noted:

> I suffered serious and disturbing thoughts and sensations in consequence of a talk with Vassily Ivanovich [the tutor] about Sergei. [Here Sergei deleted three words.] Everything loathsome in my youth seared my heart with horror, sickness and remorse. I was tormented for a long time.

Lev, feeling better after a talk with Sergei, rose earlier than usual the next morning determined to write. He noted that he felt "full to the brim with good stuff," but there was no overflowing onto paper. Most of his jottings in diary and notebook concerned religion and his efforts to accept the Orthodox faith. Praying that the czar's enemies be defeated, however, disturbed him. The gospels taught that one should pray for one's enemies. Lev's head was spinning with questions and his nerves stretched taut. Outwardly he kept much of his composure. He noted in his diary:

> Ilya and Tanya told me their secrets, their loves. How terrible they are, bad [he wrote "nasty" first but crossed it out and substituted "bad"] and sweet. I began to write *My Life*.

Lev soon gave up the idea of an autobiography but he continued his debate on religion and the church, particularly in his notebook:

> *3 June 1878*. Yesterday I wrote at length in my little notebook—why, I don't know. About belief.

Summer brought the usual excuses for not writing: the arrival of the Kuzminskys, the pleasant, good-weather diversions, the annual trip to Samara. Sonya and the children went with Lev although now Sonya grumbled at having to leave her sister. She and Tanya had grown even closer since Tanya's return from the Caucasus; in the summer they shared the housekeeping, they confided in one another and they cared for each other's children. If one mother had to be away when both were nursing babies, the other would nurse her child.[1] Besides, Sonya no longer found it easy to rise to the rigors of primitive conditions and was relieved to return to Yasnaya. Autumn life was tranquil, the weather was warm and sunny, and the new baby, Andrusha, was a happy personality. Lev went hunting nearly every day and spent the evenings improvising at the piano. Sonya was busy making clothes for the children and her diary was full of small events attesting to domestic content:

> Levochka and Seryozha went hunting. . . . I stayed home to cut out the boys' jackets. . . . It is midnight, Levochka is having supper and soon we'll go to bed. . . . After dinner we danced a quadrille and to complete the set I took part with little Lev. . . . Levochka persuaded the children to go for a walk across the fields with the Borzois. . . . All the children crowded into Levochka's sitting room, chatting, laughing and scuffling with each other.

"All the children" in 1878 included Sergei and Tanya, then fifteen and fourteen, the younger boys Ilya and little Lev, twelve and nine, and seven-year-old Masha. The baby Andrusha was ten months old in October.

But neither the demands of all her children nor the pleasant family life diverted Sonya's awareness from what was going on in her husband's mind and heart. If she did not fathom his specific concerns, she at least guessed that he was troubled. "He's still unable to work," she wrote in her diary on 27 September, "and his back hurts." As always, she believed that Lev's physical problems signified mental stress and a glance at Lev's notebook on the same day suggests ample reason for stress: Several pages of annotations for *The Decembrists* indicate that he was contemplating a novel with a historical panorama and set of characters vaster than in *War and Peace*.[2] Nor was the novel his only challenge. On 30 September a series of statements and questions end his notebook for 1878:

> If there is a soul, then there are God's commandments.
> What should I do?
> The commandments.
>
> ---
>
> Here is the soul's question, the only one.
> How could there be others. How?

In spite of the punctuation, it is not absolutely certain which are questions in this entry and which are answers, as if Lev were still struggling to pose his soul's question.

Sonya's hopes for another major novel revived in October. She reported in her diary:

> This morning I went to Levochka who was sitting downstairs at his desk writing something. He said that he was starting his new book for the tenth time. This time it begins with a court trial involving peasants and a landowner. He had read about such an affair in actual documents and even plans to keep the same date. From the trial, as from a fountain, actions will flow out into the lives of the peasants and their landowner and to characters in St. Petersburg and other places. This *entrée en matière* [beginning] pleases me.

Once again Lev began a reading program for the background material but he complained of exhaustion and the feeling of a weight on his head. Then in mid-October he told Sonya, "All of a sudden, I think that it will be excellent." Alas, two days later he was dull and silent, his optimism vanished. Sonya took heart when she saw him reading *Martin Chuzzlewit*. Her diary expressed her hope:

> I know that when Levochka turns to reading English novels, then he will soon turn to writing.

On November first Lev came to Sonya with several pages which he read aloud to her. He said that they were the beginning of a major, serious work. Both Tolstoys tried to believe this.

During the dark autumn and winter evenings Sonya sat with Lev while he played the piano. She noted tenderly in her diary the joy she felt when, returning from Tula, she saw Lev's figure in his gray coat coming to meet her. She recorded all the good signs:

> He was reading *Dombey and Son* and suddenly he said to me, "Ah, what an idea has dawned on me." . . . Levochka said today that it was all beginning to be clear in his head, his characters are coming to life. He worked today and was happy, chained to his task. . . . I drank tea with Levochka. This happens so rarely. We ventured into long, philosophical discussions about life, death and religion and so forth. Talks like this with Levochka always have a soothing effect on me. . . . Levochka said, "All the ideas, characters, events—all are already in my head." But he does not feel well and he cannot work.

Traditional Christmas celebrations interrupted Lev's efforts. Sergei Tolstoy recalled in his memoirs the Christmas of 1878: the puddings cooking, the suppers at which the younger children were allowed to join the grownups and which lasted until one in the morning, theatricals, a visit from the Diakovs, dancing including a quadrille and a waltz, an outing to the circus in Tula, a Christmas dinner for twenty-two people after which everyone went sleigh-riding, three in each sleigh and no coachman, the tree decorated for New Year's Eve (Sonya wrote to her sister Tanya, "unusually well this year") and the Tolstoys welcoming 1879 by drinking champagne around the tree.

After these festivities Lev settled down to writing but not to literature. He had given up the Orthodox church and was writing his own interpretation of the gospels. Lev had sincerely tried to accept the church's teachings but in the end he came to despise its superstition, patriotic chauvinism and elaborate rituals. He decided to study the teachings of Jesus and find in them the true meaning of the gospel. At the same time he began work on *A Confession*, a long essay chronicling the growth of his belief. With hindsight and some poetic license he disparaged his literary achievement and described his life as a journey toward his present spiritual conversion. Lev often spoke of his conversion as spiritual or religious but it was always uniquely his own view. When he referred to God as father, a father who knew every hair that fell from a man's head, his language was not literal. From his youth, Lev had been skeptical of the supernatural—that is, a personal, omnipotent deity or the divinity of Jesus. Lev believed in the God that was pure truth and was within himself and within all mankind; and he believed that Jesus, a man inspired by truth, expressed the way to live by truth. He never meant, however, that God was accessible only through Jesus. He believed that people from all faiths could discover God within themselves and that it did not matter whether they called themselves Muslims or Jews, Hindus or Christians. God was universal. What Lev turned his back on was institutionalized faith, the churches and temples and the rites upon which they insisted.[3]

Now Lev applied his perfectionist standards to living the true Christianity—that is, not the teachings of the church but the teachings of Jesus. He avoided his worldly friends, he dreamed of giving away his property to the poor and he told his family that he was "beginning to know the light." There was no more mention of a novel. Sonya wrote to her sister Tanya:

> Levochka is always working, that is what he calls it, but alas! He is writing some sort of religious dissertations, he reads and thinks until his head aches, and all this in order to prove that the church is incompatible with the teachings of the gospels. There are hardly a dozen people to be found in Russia who will be interested in this. But one can do nothing; I only hope that he finishes it the soonest possible and that it passes, like an illness. To control him or to direct his intellectual work, whatever it is, no one in the world is able to do this, even he himself doesn't have the power.

Sonya would have been less annoyed and more concerned if she had read a *cri de coeur* that her husband wrote, probably in March 1879, but undated and on a loose sheet of paper:

> What am I doing here, abandoned in the midst of this
> world? To whom can I appeal? To whom to look for an
> answer? To people? They do not know. They laugh, they
> don't want to know—they say, it is trifling. Do not think
> about these things, they say.

Lev was isolated from the comfort he needed, and isolated twice
over. In his desperate search for certainty, he adopted such extreme
stands on moral issues that to others he seemed unreasonable,
even fanatic; to himself, his deepening depression clouded his view
of other people. His predicament was heartbreaking but it was a
predicament only to himself. "They," Sonya and his children, were
simply impatient with what they considered unrealistic standards.
Lev tried not to condemn them:

> They, just as I, are tormented and suffering terribly facing
> the thought of death, facing themselves and facing you,
> Lord, whom they do not want to name. And I have not
> called your name for a long time and for a long time I
> have been the same as they.

Sonya was actually more understanding of Lev's spiritual quan-
dary than her letter to her sister implied. Three years later she
summarized her husband's religious search, how he had been impressed by the faith of simple peasants and had tried to accept
the church as they did:

> L. N. soon saw that the source of goodness and patience
> and love in the peasants did not come from the teachings
> of the church. . . . Little by little, L. N. began to see with
> horror the disagreement between the church and Chris-
> tianity. . . . The church prays for and thanks God for the
> destruction of people, for useless victories while in the
> Old Testament it says, Do not kill. . . . The true teaching
> of the kingdom of God on earth has been hidden from
> the people who are strongly convinced that salvation is
> by means of christening, the Eucharist, fasting and so
> forth.[4]

Sonya agreed with her husband's opinion of the church; she knew
that her own attachment to religious conventions was sentimental
and not important to her. She could not understand, however,
Lev's need for a pure and literal Christianity. Sonya always remained very much a person of the day-to-day world. Even so,

she seemed to sense some of Lev's pain and vulnerability. To her sister Tanya she wrote in March 1879:

> Although you used to be angry with me, Tanechka, that I tried too much to keep peace around Levochka, I consider that men are constantly straining their minds and therefore this preservation of quiet for their nerves and brains is necessary above all else.

If Sonya could not be her husband's nursemaid of talent, she might still be his protector. Five months later she wrote some lines to Lev that their son Sergei found and treasured:

> You probably think that I am stubborn and persistent but I feel that a lot of the good in you is quietly passed on to me and makes it easier for me to live on earth.

In December 1879 another baby arrived, Mikhail (called Misha), and for the first time after giving birth Sonya did not rejoice in another child. Misha was her tenth and seven were alive. Just before the birth she wrote in her diary that Lev's conversation was full of the teachings of Christ. This must have been a trial for the family who for so many years had found in Papa the source of gaiety and amusement. Sadly Sonya wrote:

> He has put aside his novel on the Decembrists and all his literary work although he sometimes says, "If ever I write again then I shall write something entirely different. Everything that I have written so far has been only exercises."

Sonya's very last entry in her notes for a future biographer of Lev was made at the beginning of 1881:

> *January 1881*. . . . This winter his [Lev's] health has grown much weaker, his head aches, his hair turns gray and he is getting thin. . . . He grows gentler, more preoccupied and quiet. It hardly ever happens that he bursts into one of his gay, lively moods which used to carry us all along with him. I attribute this to fatigue from the terrible strain of work. It was not like this at all when he was describing the hunt or the ball in *War and Peace*. It seemed then that he was as gay and as excited as though he himself were there and taking part in those pleasant events.

Sonya recognized Lev's uncanny ability to live the fiction that he wrote, to get into the skin of the people he created. She appreciated this spontaneous identification Lev had with the people he created, an identification that assured that they would not act out of character, and she believed that Lev, sincere as he was, did not have the same joyful identification with his religious beliefs. She ended her last note:

> Personally he is certainly calm in his soul and in a peaceful state but the suffering of the peasants, of those who are poor, of those in prisons and the fact that there is injustice, wickedness, oppression, all of this has an effect on his sensitive personality and burns out his life.

Act One of the Tolstoy marriage was over, those years when Lev and Sonya shared the pains and the satisfactions that accompanied his greatest writing.

2.

In a letter to her sister Tanya, Sonya wrote in February 1881:

> Levochka overworks himself altogether, his head is always aching, but he cannot stop. The death of Dostoevsky hit us all. It made Levochka think of his own death and he has been preoccupied and silent.

Lev was now writing every day, formulating a religious philosophy in his essay on the gospels and in *A Confession*, which he finished in 1882. There had been times when writing his novels that Lev had worked with a similar intensity, but there was a difference in the relation of Sonya and the children to his new writing. The family had been able to revolve around Papa, the writer of great novels, and Sonya was born to be a novelist's helpmate. None of the same family enthusiasm was present for Lev's religious convictions. The older children were openly hostile to their father's ideas. They had been raised as the children of an aristocrat, not of a holy mystic preaching self-sacrifice and humility. Sonya, although in theory she believed in the abstract truth of Lev's beliefs, regretted the time and effort he devoted to ideals of impossible perfection. She regretted it especially since she did not see the ideals bringing him peace of mind. Again she wrote to her sister Tanya:

> Sasha [Sonya's brother] worried me by saying that he found Levochka changed for the worse, i.e., he is afraid

for his mind. You know how it is when Levochka is occupied with something, he devotes all his thoughts to it. So it is now. But this religious and philosophical mood is the most dangerous.

Sasha Bers was not the first to suggest that Lev Tolstoy might be out of his mind. The previous year Lev had excused himself from attending the unveiling of a statue commemorating Pushkin because he was too busy translating the gospels. The literary world was flabbergasted. Dostoevsky, shortly before his death, was dissuaded from making a visit to Yasnaya Polyana by Turgenev, who assured him that Tolstoy was much too absorbed in religious questions to be interested in anyone or anything else, and had written to his wife in May 1880:

> About Lev Tolstoy, Katkov [publisher of *The Russian Messenger* where *War and Peace* and *Anna Karenina* first appeared], too, has confirmed what one hears, that he has become entirely mad. Yuriev [President of the Friends of Russian Literature] urged me to visit him at Yasnaya Polyana. . . . But I shall not go, although it would be a very curious experience.

Lev had hardly lost his mind. *A Confession*, alone, was proof that his intellect was as sharp and original as ever. His diaries and notebooks, however, for the years 1881 through 1884 contain evidence of what in this age might be diagnosed as a severe depression. Among the symptoms of depression listed in medical literature today are anxieties, fears and irrational thoughts, particularly irrational thoughts concerning those close to the depressed person. Lev recorded anxieties, fears and irrational thoughts concerning his wife and family. It's impossible to say for certain what caused Lev's condition. Each person's depression has its own psychological roots, and hormonal changes might have had a contributing effect—Lev was in his fifties. The protracted stress of completing two masterpieces in less than a dozen years and the sense of failure (and guilt) at not having achieved a third work of equal or greater dimension would be enough to cause both mental and physical exhaustion. Lev's instinctive attachment to life, however, and his love for Sonya and his children staved off his final descent to the nadir of despair and confusion. Until 1884 his days of depression were often followed by periods of normal family life and intensive work.[5]

It was not in Lev's character to confine his new religious work to his writing. When he left his study he tried to put the gospel truths into daily practice. To achieve humility outwardly as well as inwardly, he dressed in a simple peasant blouse and asked visitors to drop the title Count and call him Lev Nikolaevich. He no longer approved of a privileged class that lived off the labors of others and so he made his own bed, cleaned his own room, emptied his chamber pot. In order to know his less fortunate brothers and to identify with them, he visited hospitals and prisons. He saw his faith not only as a standard for spiritual and philosophical decisions, but as a rule of life. Killing was a sin and so he gave up hunting and made sporadic attempts for the rest of his life to give up eating meat. He learned the cobbler's trade in order to have a useful and wholesome occupation in contrast to his way of life as a famous author. Lev made an all-out effort to renounce his former life. This meant that his position at home caused him guilt and anguish. More precisely, he could not live in what he believed to be "true Christian humility and poverty" without leaving his wife and family. To others it could seem that he ate his cake and had it, too; he preached impossible ideas and he enjoyed comfort. Lev saw this clearly and he saw his double bind. He wrote in his diary:

> *5 May. [1881]* The family is flesh. To give up the family—this is the second temptation—is to kill oneself. The family is one body. But do not succumb to the third temptation—serve not the family but God alone.

The first temptation of the family was flesh (sexual relations). Lev's strange reaction to Sonya at the Easter mass three years before was becoming an obsession that not only his wife's sexuality but all physical relations between men and women were sinful. The second temptation was to kill oneself in order not to give in to the flesh. This, too, was a sin because the family was one body and killing oneself killed the family. The third temptation was to put the family before God and this Lev struggled to avoid. For a man who had idolized family happiness this was a struggle against his whole nature. Sometimes his need for Sonya and the allure of domesticity was too much for him and he was his old self, the very heart of family conviviality. At other times he succeeded in withdrawing sanctimoniously or he raged angrily at the children and even more angrily at Sonya. The irony of his situation was that he had never needed Sonya more. If there had been occasion for some of those crucial talks between husband and wife that Sonya valued so much, then her practicality might have restored his perspective. But Sonya was too busy, with nearly all the responsibilities of both house and estate left to her, to see beyond Lev's critical preaching. Besides, she had seven children who ranged in age from two to eighteen and she was pregnant. For hours Lev stayed alone in his study, reading, writing and pondering.

Sometimes he found another kind of company. When the snows had thawed he made a habit of walking from Yasnaya to the main highway which led to Kiev. There he would meet and talk to the pilgrims who were walking from one shrine to another. He told Sonya that he was glad for the conversations because his speaking Russian was rusty. Much of the talk at home or with friends was in French. Lev was also glad to talk to other people who were seeking religious fulfillment, even though their quest was a far simpler one than his. On one of his walks he met an organ grinder with a fortune-telling bird. They fell into conversation and Lev asked,

"From where are you coming?"

"From Tula," the fellow replied. "Things are bad. Myself, I haven't eaten, my bird hasn't eaten and the czar was murdered." This was how the news of the assassination of Aleksander II on March 13, 1881, reached Yasnaya. Sonya and the children felt no punishment was too severe for the assassins but Lev brooded on their fate. He acknowledged that feelings of revenge were understandable after a barbarous killing but he could not accept the taking of human life under any circumstances. To Sonya's dismay he wrote the new czar and begged him to forgive his father's enemies and merely exile them. Lev's plea was not granted and the eventual execution of the assassins increased his despair. He decided on another trip to Optina Monastery. This time he went on foot like a peasant and traveled with only one servant and a teacher from the Yasnaya Polyana schools. Away from home he missed Sonya at once and worried that he had left her alone to cope with all the summer household. He wrote to her tenderly, praying that God would grant that they might meet again in good health and without misfortune. Sonya replied that she was lonely without him and that she worried about him, walking with the sun on his head. When separated the couple thought of one another with loving concern, but when Lev returned home refreshed from his trip he found that his wife was exhausted and short of patience. He noted in his diary that, "Sonya is angry but I bear it easily."

If Sonya read this smug remark it must have provoked her further. Lev's diary, however, showed that he felt more despair than smugness:

> 26, 27 June. There are so many poor people. I have been sick. Did not sleep or eat solid food for six days.

> 28 June. Conversation with Seryozha continuing one that we had yesterday about God. He and they [Lev's wife and family] think that to say, I do not know, it is impossible to prove, it isn't necessary, that this is an indication of intelligence and education. When it is an indication of ignorance. . . . Seryozha admits that he loves the carnal life and believes in it. I am glad that he raised the question clearly.

If Sergei was partly teasing his father when he said that he loved the carnal life, Lev was not amused.

June 30 was Petrovki, the Russian holiday that marked the passing from spring to summer. The Tolstoys celebrated with a feast at midday dinner and a picnic in the evening. Lev partook of both. Did he enjoy himself, was he once more the center of family fun? If so, his conscience caught up with him. That night he wrote in his diary:

> At home we had an enormous dinner with champagne. The Tanyas [the Tolstoys' daughter and Sonya's sister] in all their finery. All the children wore belts that cost five rubles. We ate and then left in a cart for a picnic, passing by peasant carts that carried people who were exhausted by labor.

Sonya was grateful for any sign of her husband's former good humor. When he lectured the family she told him that he was simply in a bad mood. When she became irritable, Lev said that she was having "an attack." He wrote in his diary:

> 11 July 1881. Sonya is having an attack. I stand it, but poorly. I must understand that she is ill and pity her but it is impossible not to turn aside from evil. This morning was occupied by a conversation with Tanya [his sister-in-law] on education. They are not human beings.

From the depths of his despair Lev saw illness in other people, not in himself. It was other people who threatened him with the evil of their lives. Tanya and Sonya, women who had inspired his creation of enchanting Natasha and beautiful, innocent Kitty, were not human beings.

Two days later Lev left for his kumys cure, taking only Sergei with him. His spirits did not improve on the steppe:

> Went on foot and on horseback to look at the horses. Unbearable anxiety, futility and shame.[6] . . . With Seryozha an argument about the soul. To try to prove, to explain.

Returned to Yasnaya, he found the house full of guests:

> At home. . . . A full house. . . . Empty people.

Turgenev was visiting and demonstrated the cancan as danced in Paris. This entertained the family, but not Lev:

> *22 August.* Turgenev, cancan. Sad.

It would be wrong to assume, however, that these melancholy diary entries told the whole story. Lev's attachment to life was strong, family life was still seductive and Lev's sense of fun was not entirely lost. He was always a ready participant in a game played in the summers with the Kuzminsky family. During the week each player wrote a description of one of the others and dropped it unsigned into a box. Once a week the contributions were read aloud. Lev confessed to writing one entitled "Inmates of the Yasnaya Polyana Insane Asylum." The first inmate described was Lev Nikolaevich:

> Of sanguine characteristics. Belongs in the peaceful section. The patient is afflicted with a mania called by a German psychiatrist *Weltverbesserungswahn.* The core of the madness is this; the patient considers that it is possible through words to change the lives of other people.

The next inmate was Sonya:

> Can be found among the quiet ones but from time to time must be isolated. The patient is afflicted with the mania, hurriuppica maxima. . . . Symptoms: Solutions to problems which have not been set, answers to questions before they have been asked, justification of herself against accusations which have not been made and the satisfaction of requirements not demanded.

Lev was accused of being the author of the following comparison between the two Yasnaya mothers, Aunt Sonya and Aunt Tanya, although it was suspected that Aunt Tanya herself had a hand in the composition:

> Aunt Sonya likes making underwear, *broderie anglaise* and all kinds of beautiful work. Aunt Tanya likes to make dresses and to knit. Aunt Sonya likes reading philosophy and having serious conversations and astonishing Aunt Tanya with frightfully big words. . . . Aunt Tanya likes reading novels and talking about love. . . . Aunt Sonya adores children, Aunt Tanya is far from adoring them. When the children hurt themselves Aunt Sonya caresses them saying, "Goodness me, my dear, just wait, we'll flatten this floor—take that and that!" And the children and Aunt Sonya beat the floor furiously. Aunt Tanya, when the children hurt themselves, is annoyed and begins rubbing the injured spot, saying, "Drat you and also the one who gave you birth."

Even in the worst year of his depression there were times when Lev indulged his nonsensical humor. In 1884 he wrote a short story about his sister-in-law Tanya's habit of shouting, "Oh, go to the devil" to anyone who provoked her. The story began with Susoichik, as assistant devil, receiving visitors; the first was Tanya's husband Sasha:

> The first visitor, Aleksandr Mikhailovich [Sasha] did not surprise Susoichik as he often appeared at his wife's request. "What, your wife has sent you again?" "Yes, she sent me," the Presiding Judge of the District Court [Sasha's position] said shyly, not knowing how exactly to explain the reason for his visit. "You are visiting here rather often. What do you want?" "Oh, nothing in particular," mumbled Aleksandr Mikhailovich, finding it difficult to deviate from the truth. "She bid me bring you her greetings."

Lev himself was a visitor, accompanied by Prince Urusov, an old friend from the Sevastopol campaign and probably a guest at Yasnaya when Lev wrote his story. Susoichik greeted them:

> "Ha, ha! The old man! Thanks to Tanya. It's a long time since I've seen you, old fellow. Your health is good? What may I do for you?" Lev Tolstoy shifted from one foot to the other in embarrassment. Prince Urusov, recalling diplomatic receptions, stepped forward and explained Tol-

stoy's appearance as due to his wish to make the acquaintance of Tatyana Andreevna's oldest and most faithful friend. *"Les amis de nos amis sont nos amis."* "Quite so, ha, ha, ha," said Susoichik. "She must be rewarded for today's work."

The tale ended with Susoichik awarding Tanya the "Insignia of the Order." It consisted of a necklace of imp's tails and two toads—one to be worn on the bosom and the other on the bustle.

Ilya preserved Lev's nonsensical story and recalled the hilarity it provoked. Living in the midst of two fun-loving and lively families, it is no wonder that Lev could not dwell all the time on his anxiety, futility and shame.

3.

In the autumn of 1881 Sergei was ready for the university, which meant a move to Moscow for the scholastic months. Neither Lev nor Sonya considered it possible for a son to live alone in the city. By the time the younger sons were of university age the parents took a less strict view. It was also time for Tanya to be presented to society. Without this formality there was little chance for her to meet an appropriate husband, an opportunity that even Lev did not want to deny his daughter. Perhaps because of the impending move from Yasnaya, Lev's spirits fell:

> *27 August.* August 24, 25, 26, 27. I remember nothing. Sonya is in Moscow. Shopping.

Sonya was shopping for a place to live in the city. Although seven months pregnant—a son, Alexei (Alyusha), was born on 31 October—the task of finding a house quite naturally fell upon her. In Sergei's recollections he wrote:

> Recalling today the years before our move to Moscow I understand better than I did then the importance of my mother in our family life and the great value of her care for us and for my father. At the time, it seemed to me that everything in our life went on of its own accord. We accepted Mother's care as a matter of course. I did not notice that beginning with our food and clothes to

our studies and the copying for father, everything was managed by her.

Now Sonya organized the move. Pressed for time, she rented a house owned by a distant Volkonsky relative and the family moved there in September. The house was not a great success, as Sonya wrote to her sister Tanya in September:

> Immediately we had arrived everyone became depressed and after three days this depression and melancholy became worse. The house turns out to be as if made of cardboard, so noisy that we have no peace, neither in our bedroom nor Levochka in his study. This reduced me to despair and I'm in a state of tension all day lest there be too much noise. Finally we [she and Lev] had a talk. L. said that if I loved him and cared about his state of mind, I would not have chosen these enormous rooms where there's not a minute's peace and where any armchair could make a peasant's happiness; that is, the 22 rubles it cost would buy a horse or a cow, that he is driven to tears and so forth. But now it is all beyond repair. Of course, he brought me to tears and despair. For four days I went around as if crazy.

Sonya felt that the family blamed her for the discomforts and began to sob hysterically. All nerves were taut but the most unhappy was Lev. He noted in his diary:

> *5 October 1881, Moscow.* A month has passed—the most tormenting of all my life. We have moved to Moscow. They are all the time getting settled. When will they begin to live? Nothing is for living but because it is the way it is done. Unfortunate people! And no life. Stench, stones, luxury and misery.

A stint as a volunteer for the census-taking increased Lev's awareness of the miserable conditions in which most of the city people lived. Early in 1882 he retreated to Yasnaya in search of the peace that he found more easily in the country. Sonya noted in her diary:

> *28 February 1882.* We have been in Moscow since the 15th of September 1881. . . . Seryozha goes to the university, Tanya to the Myachystkaya School of Drawing. . . . Our life in Moscow would be very good if Levochka were not so unhappy here. He is too sensitive to stand city life

and, besides, his Christian frame of mind does not mix with luxurious, idle conditions and the struggle of life in the city. He went to Yasnaya yesterday with Ilya to work and rest.

Because of an instance of Lev's refusal to compromise his principles, Ilya was not in school. He had prepared for the State Gymnasium and passed the qualifying examinations but it was necessary for Lev to sign a paper guaranteeing his son's loyalty to the czar. Lev was indignant. "How can I guarantee the conduct of another human being, even though my own son?" The warden of the gymnasium agreed that the formality was absurd but he did not admit Ilya, who finally went to a private school.

From the country Lev corresponded affectionately with Sonya. He confessed that Yasnaya had not cured his apathy and depression but that his unhappiness was perhaps similar to the pain felt by a frozen man returning to consciousness.[7] Sonya replied that he bewildered her. All the family was well and everything around him was happy. The first sad thing for her on waking that day had been his letter. She wrote to him on 3 March 1882:

> I begin to think that if a happy man suddenly sees in life only everything horrible and closes his eyes to the good, then this is from illness. You should be treated. This seems clear to me and I say it without any ulterior motive; I pity you awfully. . . . This dreary state has already existed for a long time. You said, "It's lack of faith" and you wanted to hang yourself. But now? You know, you do not live without faith, why are you still so unhappy? And really, didn't you know before that there were starving, suffering, unhappy and evil people? Look more carefully; there are gay, healthy, happy, good people as well. May God help you, but what can I do?

Lev did not agree to treatment but he missed Sonya and returned to Moscow. There he tried to publish *A Confession*. Even with Lev's reluctantly agreed-to changes, the censor would not pass ideas in such radical disagreement with the church. The censor's control was not absolute, however, and *A Confession* was copied by hand and widely distributed. This story of Lev's gradual change from the attitudes with which he had grown up (attitudes which he admitted were held by admirable people) and which he now saw as wrong was an indictment of the injustice of society and its unintentional ways of promoting immorality. Through the distribution of this article Lev began to acquire both among the poor and among the aristocracy a growing band of disciples or Tolstoyans. The knowledge that he had followers who admired his beliefs and looked to him for guidance intensified Lev's shame in taking part in the relatively simple comforts enjoyed by his family. In April he fled to Yasnaya where by June the others had joined him. There was not a Tolstoy who did not prefer the wonderful Yasnaya summers to life in the city.

The buoyancy of this life shared with the Kuzminsky family masked Lev's depression and Sonya was encouraged. Only one quarrel disturbed the summer and it began with a trifle. Sonya rebuked Lev for not helping her more with the children and he blurted out that his passionate desire was to escape from all of his family. He became so angry that he refused, for the first time in their married life, to share Sonya's bed. Sonya sat up all night nursing Ilya (he had typhus) and mourning what she thought was the end of her husband's love:

> *26 August.* . . . I shall not go to sleep tonight on the bed deserted by my husband. My God, help me. I want to take my life, my thoughts are so confused. It is four A.M. I have decided that if he does not come back it is because he loves another.

He did come back, they were reconciled, they wept in one another's arms and Sonya walked to the bathhouse on a cold, brilliant morning, marveling at the beautiful weather and rejoicing that the love for which she had mourned during her sleepless night had not been lost.

The rented house had been such a disaster that the Tolstoys decided to buy a house in Moscow. This time Lev took upon himself the responsibility of finding a place and preparing it for the family's arrival. He chose a house on the outskirts of town with a tree-filled park that gave the illusion of being in the country. The property had been a manor at one time; the main house was an attractive two-story building and there were other buildings on the grounds. All was surrounded by a gaily painted fence. Inside the house there was a large room for entertaining, a drawing room for Sonya and a study for Lev. Many renovations were necessary and Lev, for Sonya's sake, applied himself to these worldly tasks; he chose the wallpaper and had the kitchen redone, the stairs rebuilt and the floors repaired. Although he disapproved of extravagance he bought good furniture to please his wife. When the family arrived on 5 October the cellars were full of provisions, apples, vegetables, tubs of sauerkraut, jams and cucumbers, dinner was prepared and there was fruit on the table. But Sonya was so exhausted from a week of packing that she was irritable and nothing pleased her. It wasn't long, however, before she approved of the house.

In the spring of 1882 Lev met Nikolai Nikolaevich Gay, a famous Russian painter, who had been deeply moved by *A Confession*. He called on Tolstoy and offered to paint a picture of his daughter Tanya in gratitude for the inspiration he had received from Lev's article but Lev suggested, "Better my wife." Lev and Gay became friends at once, a friendship that lasted until Gay's death in 1904 and was shared by all the family. Sonya loved to pamper Gay and indulge his fondness for sweets, and the children affectionately called him "Grandpa Gay." When Gay was painting her Sonya wrote to her sister Tanya that he was depicting her "with an open mouth in a black velvet bodice with Alençon lace, my hair arranged simply." She wrote that she thought the portrait had a severe but beautiful style. Everyone was pleased with the finished product except the artist, who did not believe that he had caught Sonya's personality at all. "This is impossible," he said. "An aristocratic lady sits in a velvet dress and you have only to look at her to see that she has forty thousand in her pocket. I must paint a woman and a mother." Gay was actually so disappointed in his work that he destroyed the picture and in 1886 he painted another portrait of Sonya in a simple dress holding the two-year-old Aleksandra in her arms.[8] Lev loved this picture so much that he would not be parted from it. It was always taken along when the family moved from Yasnaya to Moscow and then back again to Yasnaya at the end of the winter. Today a copy has been made to be seen by visitors to the house in Moscow as well as those to Yasnaya Polyana. To the end of his life Lev clung to this picture of his wife who, in his heart of hearts, remained his ideal.

That heart of hearts, or soul as Lev would have said, was still disturbed. His only diary entry in 1882 referred to terrible mental suffering. He wrote of the need to love God and meet God's demands, of man's place in the universe and of man's duty to live well, to do good, to sow and let others reap. When his tensions mounted, or his shame at what he called his "carnal life," he resorted to the tonic of physical labor. In the Moscow woods he joined peasants cutting firewood and he returned from these excursions sweaty, dirty, tired and relaxed. At dinner he entertained the family with descriptions of the peasants' conversation and he needled them gently about the contrast between the Tolstoys' life and that of the simple people. Sonya was grateful that he was not scolding.

In 1882 Lev began a long short story, *The Death of Ivan Ilyich*, which he planned as a gift for Sonya. The story, finished in 1884, is compulsive reading and showed that Lev's creative powers were undiminished when he could find the inspiration to put them to use. At the same time Lev was working on *What I Believe*, a long summary of his new religious convictions. Of his religious writings, Sonya confessed lack of interest but she admitted, "Perhaps it is both God's will and necessary for great purposes." To her sister Tanya she wrote in January 1883 that Lev was

A man in the vanguard, going ahead of the crowd and showing the way that people should go. But I am in the crowd and live in the crowd's current.

Sonya wrote to Tanya that she admired Lev for his position, that she thought he carried the torch that every great man must carry; but she added that as far as her own self it was impossible for her to move any faster. A month later she noted in her diary:

Levochka is peaceful and kind, occasionally bursting out as formerly with rebukes and bitterness but rarely and briefly. He is becoming kinder and kinder.

Lev and Sonya were now living in two quite different worlds. Lev spent most of the day alone in his study reading and writing. There he received those visitors who shared his convictions or those old acquaintances with whom the bond of friendship was too strong to be broken by differences of opinion. He also received people from all classes of society who admired his religious writings and who had become disciples. When carriages came to the door, Lev would peer out of the window to identify the caller. If it was one whom he did not want to see, he climbed through a bedroom window and escaped to the woods where he walked until the carriage was gone. Daily walks were his habit; he also kept an exercise bicycle in his study and part of every day was spent on manual labor—working with a bootmaker, cleaning his room, chopping wood. Meanwhile Sonya directed the management of the house, paid the social calls, made the family's clothes and embroidered the household linens, crocheted coverlets for the beds and supervised the younger children's lessons. It was she who took the children to museums and concerts and she who received the visitors shunned by Lev.

Sonya was sought after in society, the young and beautiful wife of a famous author. Under increased pressure to offer reciprocal entertainment she ordered a large set of Wedgwood from England. Catherine the Great had ordered the court china from the first Josiah Wedgwood and the Russian aristocracy still followed her example. For parties, the table was set with the samovar, the Wedgwood, fruit, sweets and champagne. There was always someone who could play the piano for dancing. Lev did not avoid all the parties but he refused to dress up and came in his peasant blouse. Guests were received in the large living room which was reached by a flight of stairs at the top of which stood a stuffed bear holding a card tray. Between the stair landing and the living room there was a small anteroom where the younger children were permitted to stay and listen to the music. If they were noisy, it was their father's chore to reprimand them but the children remembered that his reprimands were gentle. A pleasant informality was present during Tolstoy parties. Although Lev complained of family "luxuries," the house was luxurious only relative to peasants' houses. The Tolstoys lived very simply in comparison with others of their class, a simplicity that often surprised visitors.

At the end of each day Lev and Sonya went to bed together. The bed linens were beautifully embroidered by Sonya, the coverlet was her crochet work and the bed itself was so narrow as hardly to qualify as a double bed by modern standards. There was no way to share it except by sleeping close together and close together was how the Tolstoys still thought of themselves in spite of diverging philosophies and sometimes bitter differences. Nor did their family and friends consider them an unhappy couple. If Lev could have changed his life, he would have converted Sonya to his new beliefs. "You can't imagine how alone I am," he wrote to a follower, "how much my true self is spurned by all those around me." [9] If Sonya could have changed anything she would have had her husband working once more on a great novel. She was not alone in her desire. In June 1883 the dying Turgenev sent an appeal to his old colleague:

Dear and treasured Lev Nikolaevich,
It has been a long time that I have not written to you
for I have been and am, frankly speaking, on my deathbed.
I cannot recover and there is no point in thinking about
it. But I am writing to you, actually, in order to tell you
how happy I have been to be your contemporary and in
order to express to you my final, sincere request. My friend,
return to your literary work! You have, you know, that
gift from which everything else comes. Ah, how happy I
should be if I could think that my request had an effect
on you.

Lev did not heed this moving appeal but devoted the summer to
making his position more in line with his new convictions. He
gave Sonya power of attorney over all his property so that he
would no longer have to involve himself in commercial gain and
he went alone to Samara where he sold most of his horses and
cattle and rented out the land. When Sonya returned to Moscow
in the autumn, he wrote to her affectionately from Yasnaya, but
confessed that he had refused a summons to jury duty because
of principle. Lev believed that by refusing to cooperate with a
government function he could protest the unfairness of many government laws. He has been called an anarchist but Lev never advocated violent revolution. He was against all violence, including
the government-supported violence of war and capital punishment.
The court accepted his refusal to serve but fined him two hundred
rubles. Lev wrote to Sonya begging her not to scold him for not
serving.[10] She replied gently, saying that she did not know what
she would have done in the same position, most likely she would
have thought about how to be the least disturbing. She added:

I am writing incoherently; I still haven't digested everything that was in your letter. . . . Misha has slobbered
all over this letter and crumpled it while I was giving
Andrusha a reading lesson. Good-bye, see you soon, I hope.
May everything end well.

I kiss you,
Sonya

Lev replied that he had never before thought of her with such
good feelings. He wrote to her that, "From every angle you are
dear to me."

4.

By a quirk of fate, a few days later Lev met a person whose eventual strong influence would prove detrimental to good feelings about Sonya and about himself. This person was Vladimir Grigorevich Chertkov, a former officer of the Horse Guards, an aristocrat who had the aristocratic habits of drink, gambling and womanizing. Recently this life had become repulsive to him. He had resigned from his regiment and had decided to devote himself to useful and unselfish activities. For a time, he tried good works on the Chertkov estate, established a clinic and a trade school, but only when he met Tolstoy and adopted Tolstoyan principles did Chertkov find a life that satisfied his two strongest needs: to exert influence and to feel morally superior to others.

Chertkov was handsome, self-righteous and moody. When gloomy he was often rude and unkind but in a good humor his manners were ingratiating and he could be entertaining. At the beginning of their acquaintance Sonya found him charming. Alas, Chertkov had no sense of humor or sense of proportion and no insight into human character—his own or that of others. Ultimately, it was disastrous that such a man became Lev's closest disciple. At the start of their friendship, however, Lev felt that he was now less spiritually lonely. Chertkov was a man from his own social class who had experienced somewhat the same kind of decision to alter his life for the better. This comfort was more than balanced by the shame that Lev felt in front of his new friend. Chertkov was a bachelor—he would shortly marry Anna Diterikhs, who became a Tolstoyan—without family obligations to interfere with his practice of strict Tolstoyan principles. Lev's guilt that he was not complying with the ideals he preached was reflected in his diary entries:

> Got up lazy and did not tidy my room. . . . I was ashamed
> to do that which I should have done, carry out the chamber
> pot. . . . Everyone works except me. I slept. Sins: Vanity,
> idleness.

Lev had excused his failure to produce a third masterpiece, the masterpiece he believed he owed to the world, on the grounds that the quest for spiritual perfection was a greater goal. Now he had the example of Chertkov before his eyes to remind him that he was not achieving his greater goal either and that it would be impossible to do so without giving up his wife, family and his entire world. This he either could not or would not do and Lev saw himself between two choices, either one of which was impossible: He could abandon all that he loved and needed or he could once again accept failure. This was his double bind and what he saw as his reason for despair. It was inevitable that Sonya became a target of the despair and resentment. She was inextricably bound up in his feelings about himself, first because she had been so aware of his artistic struggle (and thus of his failure) and now because he chose to believe that she was the block that prevented his living according to his ideals.

By the first months of 1884, Lev had shown many of the symptoms common to a major depression in the medical sense—loss of energy, loss of response to events that would normally be satisfying, insomnia, thoughts of suicide, complaints of diminished mental power, excessive guilt, feelings of worthlessness and the need to blame his condition on others:

> Got up late—listless. The same sadness. Now especially, watching everyone at home. The floor polishers are cleaning; it is we who have soiled ourselves. I am falling down and begin to be less strict with myself. I do not note my sins. . . . Dissatisfaction with my life and reproaches arise within me.

If Sonya had been reading Lev's diary she would surely have been alerted to what she had suspected two years before—that Lev's state of despair was an illness. But Sonya was too busy to write in her own diary and therefore probably too busy to even glance at Lev's. The dialogue between husband and wife came to a temporary pause. 1883–1884 was the winter of Tanya's official presentation to society. After the Christmas season Lev escaped to Yasnaya and Sonya was busy with the social whirl. Not all of it delighted her. After the Tolstoys had announced their At Home day and begun to receive callers, Sonya wrote to her sister Tanya that she did not derive much pleasure from it, that they sat in the house like "idiots" waiting for visitors while little Lev watched at the window to see who was coming. A ball given in January by the Governor General of Moscow, Prince Dolgorukov, was a different matter. For this grand occasion Sonya wore her favorite colors, lilac velvet trimmed with yellow pansies. Sonya was thirty-nine and still very young-looking for her age. The prince paid some flattering attention to her at his party and she bragged a little in a letter to Lev:

> Dolgorukov was more amiable than he has ever been. He had a chair brought so that he could sit beside me and we chatted a whole hour. . . . He said a lot of agreeable things about Tanya as well and yet we did not feel exactly gay yesterday. No doubt we were too tired.

Reading between these lines it seems that Sonya might have been gayer and less tired if her husband had escorted her to the ball.

Lev replied to Sonya that he, too, was tired. He was reading Montaigne, skiing, cobbling shoes, meditating and trying "not to offend anyone." When he returned to Moscow he lived in the midst of his busy family but he was moving on a separate track. He went for long walks, cleaned up his room, conscientiously emptied his chamber pot and sometimes those of his guests. He was not writing, having essentially given up intellectual work after finishing *What I Believe.* The winter season was keeping Sonya on the move without extra time for thoughts about Lev. She was six months pregnant and the very sight of her reminded Lev of his lapses from the total chastity that he was now openly advocating. In his diary he continued a chronicle of misery, resentment and self-disgust.

> I went downstairs and hectored my wife and Tanya about their evil way of living. . . . I felt boastful because I had taken out Orlov's chamber pot. I began lecturing Tanya with spite. And just then Misha stood in the big doorway and looked at me questioningly. [Misha was four years old.] If only he were always there in front of me! A big sin. . . . General weakness and decline of morals. Physical and mental illness. The conditions of life are insane and I indulge in them. Moving toward worse. Attempts at various works from which nothing had developed.

There was very little that could give him any pleasure at all. He found some comfort in his correspondence with Chertkov and in the times when he did clean his room or went to the bootmaker for lessons. He noted:

> After dinner I rode to the bootmaker. How bright it was and elegantly moral in his dirty, dark corner. . . . A letter from Chertkov. I love him and believe in him. . . . A beautiful letter from Chertkov.

Chertkov spent a three-day visit in the Moscow house and Lev admiringly noted in his diary that in Chertkov's own house the master ate with the servants. In April he wrote in his diary that he had not been able to sleep from sorrow and doubt—that he could only pray to God as never before to deliver him from his "horror." Lev's encounters with his family degenerated into angry confrontations and he saw that he was not blameless. He quarreled with his daughter Tanya but afterward he followed her around the house, longing to beg her forgiveness but somehow unable to.[11] He asked himself, was this good or bad? In his diary he called Sonya pitiful, without values and insane, but he admitted:

> It is frightful to say but . . . I see that I am spiteful. Spite rises in my heart but I try to keep this in mind. As I did yesterday in the conversation with Sonya about wealth. . . . Stayed alone with her. Conversation. I was unhappy and cruel and began to hurt her ego. I became silent. . . . She is very seriously mentally ill.

At the dinner table the family's talk of parties and their recent purchases enraged him:

> Their blindness is astonishing. . . . Sergei angry. He and Sonya both called me insane and I almost got angry. I went and bathed. . . . During tea she said she wanted to discuss something but I was afraid of her. The instant she started to speak it was impossible. It is a fact, to die soon would be happiness for me. . . . Poor thing, how she detests me.

Sonya's desperate talks with Lev were about family finances. She was not keeping her journal in 1884 but Lev referred to their quarrels about money. He dismissed the financial problem as Sonya's responsibility because of the way she and the children lived. His wife's very existence now became a burden to Lev and he described her as his cross. "If I must carry a cross, then a cross that crushes me." [12] The sin that tormented him the most was the sin that it was easiest for him to blame on Sonya—his inability to keep his vow of chastity. He confessed to quarreling with his wife and added, "and then a much greater, much greater sin." The quarrel had been made up in bed with natural consequences. The next morning he wrote that Sonya was "gentle and without spite" but two weeks later he was agonizing about having "fallen" again.

For the first time the return to Yasnaya and the summer reunion with the Kuzminskys did not restore Lev's spirits. He brooded on his resentments and the evil of his life. About this time Lev wrote on a loose sheet a plan of how he would like himself and his family to live. Chertkov dated the sheet June 1884, but it might have been written earlier, as in his 1896 diary Lev referred to "the plan made fifteen years ago." Either date, it was written during the early 1880s, the years of his depression. His plan was to

> Live at Yasnaya. The income from Samara to be given to the poor and to the schools in Samara. . . . The income from Nikolskoye [the estate Lev inherited from his brother Nikolai] the same, after returning the land to the peasants. Ourselves, i.e., my wife and children, to keep for now the income from Yasnaya Polyana, about two to three thousand. (To keep it for a while but with the sole desire to give it to others, i.e., to live on as little as possible for our bare necessities and to give away more than we keep.) . . . To live all together, men in one room and women and girls in another. One room would be a library for intellectual occupations and there would be a room for community labors. . . . One aim alone, happiness, true happiness, and that the family would see that happiness lies in this—that we be contented with very little and give generously to others.

It is almost inconceivable that Lev Tolstoy, the artist who sympathized with every kind of human nature and the philosopher who pursued truth, that this very Lev Tolstoy once seriously thought that a sterile commune would be a practical, even less a constructive, design for living for his or for any family or that it could have possibly satisfied his own intellectual demands. But Lev's depression had made him utterly rigid. Now even the children had to listen to his lectures on how they should live. Verochka, the youngest Kuzminsky, remarked, "Well, that's good for a week but, you see, it would be impossible to *always live that way.*" Lev copied her remark into his diary and added that he was horrified that a child had been raised to think in this manner.[13] Two days later he was pleased that another Kuzminsky daughter seemed to listen to him seriously. With some of his former insight he noted in his diary that the truth was, "I am softer, closer to loving my wife." Loving Sonya led to kindness and sanity.

Where was the Sonya who had always been so alert to signs of Lev's mental state and changes in his personality? Now she seemed to think that he was simply becoming crankier. Maybe her pregnancy, her twelfth, made her resentful and less sympathetic and aware. Life in the country also had its duties as demanding as those in Moscow. Each summer there were more visitors, and then there was her sister Tanya with whom to snatch precious moments of companionship. While Sonya huddled with Tanya, cared for the children, talked to the cook about meals, discussed the estate with the agent, planned for and entertained the guests, Lev was left alone with his "torturing struggle." On 26 May he wrote:

> I am not in possession of myself. I look for the reasons. Tobacco, lack of chastity, lack of creative work. All these are trifles. One cause alone—lack of a beloved and loving wife.

This cruel accusation seemed to jolt Lev's irrational thinking and he added:

> None of these are reasons. I must look for my wife within herself. And it must be, it has to be, that I find her. Lord, help me.

Lev knew that he was unanchored without Sonya and instead of blaming their separateness on her evil ways he decided that the fault was his own depravity. He resolved to improve his attitude toward Sonya. Unfortunately, an incident squelched his resolve. Sonya found out that he had sold more of his horses in Samara in order to have more money to give away. This to her was an act of wanton irresponsibility; they were already pressed financially maintaining a house in Moscow, and she reproached Lev. He controlled his anger but his refusal to reply and his cold silence hurt more than words. Sonya sobbed and Lev went to his room, packed a knapsack and announced on an angry impulse that he was leaving home forever. Tanya Tolstoy recalled later that her mother watched her father walking slowly down the beech drive:

> I can see my mother sitting outside the house under the trees, her face distorted with grief, her big, dark eyes quite lifeless as she stared unseeing in front of her.

Tanya remembered that her mother's labor pains began then but Lev's account, written in his diary at the time, is more likely the accurate one. Sonya was persuaded to play a game of croquet and halfway to Tula Lev, ashamed to leave home when a baby was due, turned around. He was still angry, however, when he returned. His sister-in-law Tanya told him:

"She is at croquet. Didn't you see her?"

"No, and I do not want to see her."

Lev went to his room and lay on the couch. He was soon overwhelmed with pity for Sonya. It was she who woke him from a nap. "Forgive me," she said, "I am about to have the baby. Perhaps I shall die." [14]

The baby was Aleksandra (Sasha), and after the birth Sonya's mood revived. She was relaxed and happy and Lev was amazed that she was unaware of what he termed their "total rupture." That a wet nurse was engaged was proof to him of Sonya's "speed toward ruin and terrible moral suffering." But during July he managed to keep up an outward calm. He gave up alcohol and meat and tried to cut down on his smoking. He adopted the peasant method of "biting tea," that is, sipping it through a piece of sugar held between his teeth. Sonya was still bleeding from Sasha's birth and the doctor had forbidden sexual relations. In her condition she could hardly have felt like resuming physical love at once, but she believed that she and Lev were close again. She was warm and affectionate and Lev saw her attitude as temptation. "She begins to tempt me carnally," he noted. He complained of suffering through "voluptuous nights." He rebuffed her gestures of affection and lectured her on the immorality of her life. Sonya replied that it was impossible to change their entire way of life and she began to weep. According to Lev she became hysterical; if so, her hysteria was understandable. Summer had always been the time of special family happiness but now Lev was gloomily finding fault with her character, with the very self that he had loved for so many years. On 7 June—and Sonya may have read this—he wrote the cruelest comment that he would ever make about her:

> Until I die she will remain a millstone around my neck and the children's.

And the next day:

> She came to me with spite. And I desire her. I did not sleep until five in the morning from suffering.

He longed for his wife and in his confusion he believed that his longing was simple lust. Finally, giving in to his physical desire, he went to her bed only to be reminded of the doctor's orders. Sonya's refusal tripped his last connection to reality and he raged in his diary:

> I called upon my wife and she, with cold malice and the wish to hurt me, refused me.

He went back to his study where he had been spending the nights but lay awake. In the middle of the night he once more prepared to leave home. Before his departure he went again to Sonya and wakened her. He wrote in his diary:

> I do not know what was in me, spite, lust, moral torment, but I suffered terribly. She got up and I told her everything. I told her that she had ceased to be my wife. A helpmate to her husband? For a long time she had been nothing but a hindrance. A mother to the children? She did not want to be that. A nurse? She did not want to be that. A companion of the night? Of this she made a temptation and a toy.[15]

Lev's account did not mention whether Sonya said a word. His insane tirade certainly alerted her to his disturbed condition. She could not have taken the accusations seriously. A wife who refused to help her husband, a woman who did not want to mother her children? She could not have believed that Lev himself was serious. Apparently she calmed him, because he did not leave home. In any event, a more permanent reconciliation was around the corner and eventually Sonya relented and disobeyed the doctor's orders. Lev's part in persuading her to relent remained on his conscience for the rest of his life. Many years later he remembered his selfishness and rebuked himself for delaying Sonya's recovery.

After their reconciliation Lev noted in his diary how very glad he was. Unfortunately, he sanctimoniously added, "Truly, if she would undertake to be good, she would be very good." His condition, however, began a gradual return to reasonableness although on two scores he remained difficult: For then and a good part of the rest of his life, when he had sexual relations with Sonya he treated it as a fall from virtue, and for the rest of the year he would not discuss family finances with Sonya. In September she pressed him about money matters and he refused to say a word. This sent Sonya into hysterics and she ran toward the pond shouting threats that she would drown herself. Hysterical she may have been but she succeeded in forcing Lev to speak to her. He ran after her and brought her back to the house, both of them exhausted from emotion. A few days later they were peacefully walking together in the woods. When Sonya returned to Moscow to put the children in school, she and Lev missed each other. Their letters were calm and affectionate. Before long he joined her in the city and soon the dreadful year was over. A decade later, 21 October 1894, Lev read through his diary for 1884. He was disgusted with himself when he saw his "cruel and wicked feelings toward Sonya" and the manner in which he had treated his wife during that troubled year.

Chapter Six

A NEGATIVE, MALICIOUS NOVEL, 1885–1891

1.

From 1862 through 1880 Lev and Sonya had lived together happily. Their quarrels and hurt feelings and their grief for the babies who died, all these normal problems had served to strengthen rather than weaken the ties of love and shared values that united them. This changed during the years 1881–1884 when Lev's periods of deep dejection and Sonya's increasingly hectic life put the Tolstoys out of step and out of communication with one another. Following 1884 much of their former rapport returned but resentments remained. The course of the marriage became one of constant ups and downs. Tanya Tolstoy described her mother and father after 1884 as living

> . . . side by side as good friends and total strangers, each filled with a great and sincere love for the other, but also increasingly aware of the gulf between them.

Tanya's brother Sergei wrote in his memoir that from 1885 on:

> The relations between my parents at times got better and at times got worse, but never were they entirely harmonious, in spite of the strong love between them.

Both Tanya and Sergei were away from home in the decade after Lev's seventieth birthday when the Tolstoys did bridge the gulf of their differences and find peace together. That mellow time was still over a dozen years hence in 1885. What made 1885 and the years following different from those immediately before was Lev's spontaneous recovery from his depression.[1] The fact that his depression lifted spontaneously supports the notion that he had been depressed in the medical sense. He was no longer isolated from Sonya by apathy and despair. The gulf that Tanya mentioned—the philosophical differences—remained. "I want him to return to me," Sonya wrote to her sister Tanya, "in the same way that he wants me to follow him." On this score both were intractable but in other ways they reached out to one another. In the spring of 1885 Lev made a trip to the Crimea with Prince Urusov and returned home eager to share his adventures with Sonya and she was eager to hear about them. The only time she opened her diary in 1885 was to describe an incident from Lev's journey:

> *25 March 1885.* Easter Sunday. Yesterday Levochka returned from the Crimea where he had gone with the ailing Urusov. While there he walked in the mountains, admired the sea and remembered the Crimean War. When he and Urusov were traveling on the road to Simigez they passed the place where Levochka had stood during the war with his artillery gun and the very spot where he had fired the gun the only time it had been fired. That was thirty years ago. . . . Suddenly, he [Lev] got out of the landau and went searching for something. It turned out that he had seen a mountain cannonball close to the road. Was it not the same cannonball that Levochka had fired in the Sevastopol campaign? There had been only one artillery gun and no one else could have fired it.

Lev, also, made only one entry that year and it was ten days after Sonya's. Refreshed from his trip, he applied himself to his religious writing and noted:

> *5 April 1885.* All that occupies me is the consciousness and expression of truth; I regret this because it is a dangerous and deceptive path.

As if to prove just how dangerous and deceptive the path could be, he continued:

> Today I thought about my unhappy family, my wife and sons and daughters who live alongside of me and try to put a screen between themselves and me so as not to see the truth and the good which would expose the lie of

their lives and could save them from suffering. If at least they could understand that idleness, a life supported by the labors of others, has not a single justification. If only they could use their leisure time to reflect on this. But they have assiduously filled their leisure with vain bustling so that they have even less time for thinking of those who are burdened with work.

A problem for Lev was that "all" that occupied him was his devotion to truth. He had recovered his mental health but not his literary inspiration and, entirely concentrated on his philosophical writing, he also concentrated on his frustration at not living according to the ideals that he promoted. In a further paragraph in the same diary entry Lev asked why it was that intelligent men, sometimes even good men, lived so stupidly and badly. It was

Because of the influence that women have on them. They give themselves up to the current of life because that is what their wives or their mistresses want. Everything is decided at night. They are guilty only in surrendering their wisdom to their weakness.

In blaming women for men's failures Lev was in accord with many men of his century and in accord with his own very human weaknesses. When he tried to abstain from sexual relations with Sonya, he chose a classic way in which to punish her for his own failures.

Sonya knew that Lev's love for her contained a seed of resentment but she put it down to his failure to write a third epic novel. She was not entirely wrong. There was nothing new in Lev's devotion to truth but this devotion had always been balanced with his literary activity. The balance was part of his genius. Lev's fiction was as true as any ever written, his characters true to life in a most literal sense and living in a real world. But between *The Death of Ivan Ilyich* in 1884 and *Master and Man*, finished ten years later, Lev's artistic work seems forced to a modern reader. An exception was *The Powers of Darkness*, a suspenseful and moving play about peasant life. Lev wrote one novel during these years, *The Kreutzer Sonata*, a work that grew from his seed of resentment.[2] Lev realized this himself and once referred to the book as both "negative and malicious."[3] *The Kreutzer Sonata*, which puts the blame for society's depravity on women and their sexuality, was written quickly in the summer of 1889, but it influenced the Tolstoys' relations before and afterward. While Lev's ideas for the novel germinated, so did his resentment.

In 1885 *The Kreutzer Sonata* was still a message that had not found its form and Lev applied his energy to finishing an essay started three years before, *What Then Must We Do?*, which suggests ways for society to correct injustice. Sonya never ceased to regret the time and effort that Lev put into these moral essays. She could go along with many of his ideas—the sham of churches, the unfairness of poverty, the evil of war and capital punishment—but the kind of spiritual perfection that Lev wanted his family to strive for Sonya thought not only impossible but an offense to her position. She saw herself as the guardian of her family's physical, financial and emotional welfare and on 6 March 1887 she complained to her diary:

> One thing seems to me impossible and unfair, that is that the personal life must be renounced for the love of the entire world. I think that we have unquestionable responsibilities, given by God, and no one has the right to renounce them; they are not an obstacle to the life of the spirit but a help.

Sonya would have most of the world on her side, but many of Lev's ideas have not been forgotten. He never organized his thoughts enough to construct from them a formal philosophy, but his thinking has influenced people as diverse as Mahatma Gandhi and Ludwig Wittgenstein. As Sonya wrote to her sister Tanya, Lev was the man with the torch in the vanguard; and there were even times when Sonya tried, in the words of her daughter Tanya

> . . . to find her way closer to him [Lev] in mind and heart, to take an interest in his work and to attempt to understand it.

It was easier for the Tolstoys to bridge their differences in Yasnaya than in Moscow. When Lev enlisted the children to help the peasants in the haymaking, he must have been surprised and pleased to see Sonya tie a scarf on her head, don a sarafan (a long, sleeveless coat worn by peasant women), take a rake and join the family in the fields. Like the peasants, all the Tolstoys sang and drank vodka while they worked at the haymaking. Sonya worked with such energy and enthusiasm that she actually made herself ill.

Sonya's cooperation in a project dear to Lev was one way in which she showed gratitude for his new reasonableness about family finances. Early in 1885 he made an agreement whereby Sonya could publish editions of all his works written before his conversion in 1881. Sonya borrowed the money to begin, set up an office in a building on the Moscow property, did the proofing herself and brought out new editions of all of Lev's important fiction. The idea of a publishing venture came from Anna Dostoevsky who, after her husband's death, supported herself with new editions of his work.[4] Sonya was so successful her first year that she earned 60,000 rubles, about $30,000 at the time.[5]

But, as Sergei Tolstoy remarked, there was no stability in Lev and Sonya's relations at this time. Just before Christmas 1885 Lev burst upon his wife with a tirade of complaints. Sonya described the scene in a letter to her sister Tanya and her account is borne out by Tanya Tolstoy in her recollections. Sonya wrote:

> He [Lev] came in one time when I was sitting and writing and I saw that his face was terrible. Up until this time we had been living beautifully with never a single unpleasant word spoken between us. "I have come to tell you that I want to separate from you, I cannot live like this, I shall go to Paris or to America." Believe me, Tanya, if the entire house had fallen on me I would not have been so surprised. I asked in amazement, "What has happened?" "Nothing, but if you put more and more into the cart, the horse stops and won't carry any more." "What is this unknown load?" But he began shouting reproaches, coarse words, everything worse and worse—When he said, "Wherever you are, the air is contaminated," I ordered a trunk brought to me and I began to pack. I decided to go to you, if only for a few days. The children came running, howling. Tanya said, "I shall go with you. But why?" He began to beg me to stay. I stayed. But suddenly he broke out in hysterical sobs, it was simply horrible. Just imagine, Levochka all shaking and convulsed with sobs. Then I began to pity him. The four children, Tanya, Ilya, little Lev and Masha, set up a howling clamor. I was stunned. I neither spoke nor cried. I wanted to speak but was afraid it would be all nonsense and I remained silent. So it came to an end.

It was not the end for Lev. For three days he worked on a long letter to Sonya telling her of the suffering he endured because of their different "moral attitudes." He told her how easy it would be for her to help him, that instead of stuffing their children with

rich food all of them should eat a vegetarian diet, that instead of
a life of parties and theaters the children should be home cleaning
their rooms and living serious lives:

> But you say no to this, stubbornly no, deliberately no. A
> struggle to the death goes on between us. For God or not
> for God. And as God is within you, you—

Lev broke off his letter here and, although he kept it, he did not
show it to Sonya. Instead he retreated to Yasnaya. In the peace
of the country he reflected and wrote to his wife on 27 December:

> I understand how wrong I have been and I am not saying
> this only to soothe you but I sincerely understand and I
> am taking from my heart especially all my fabricated re-
> proaches and putting back my love for you.

Soon afterward four-year-old Alyusha died of the croup and Lev
wrote to Chertkov that the death had united the family more lovingly and closely than ever before.

In 1886 Lev finished *What Then Must We Do?* and began *On
Life and Death*, a long article on the value of living unselfishly.
During the summer haymaking he cut his foot and picked the
hard scab that formed. The open wound became infected and Sonya
nursed him through a dangerous case of blood poisoning. She
noted:

> It was for me such a happy, obvious occupation, the only
> thing that I do well, that personal selflessness for the man
> I love. The more difficult it was for me, the happier I
> was.

Sonya was especially happy when, during Lev's convalescence,
he dropped his religious work and wrote a play. Once more she
was offering criticisms; at first she felt that the work lacked theatri-
cal impact, but she approved of the finished product. *The Powers
of Darkness* was published the next year and sold many copies
but the censor did not pass it for performance, fearing that it
would arouse too much sympathy for the peasant class.

Lev wrote the play without much effort and then went back to
What Then Must We Do? to add some final, angry paragraphs on
women who permit sexual relations without having children.
Sonya knew that such attacks were attacks on herself and she,
too, felt resentment:

> *25 October [1886]*. . . . My God, how I am tired of living,
> of struggling, and suffering. How great is the unconscious

ill will of those people closest to us, how great the selfishness! Why do I still keep doing everything? I don't know; I think that one must. I could never be able to fulfill that which my husband wants (or says he wants) without first dropping those family affairs to which I am bound by my heartstrings. But to get away . . . to get away from this unkindness, these backbreaking demands, this alone is on my mind day and night.

Sonya wrote that she was beginning to love darkness, when she could dream of former, happier times. She even found herself talking aloud in her dreams. "I terrified myself: am I going mad?"

Some of Sonya's fears came from the implicit threat to her marriage in Lev's attitude toward physical relations. She felt insulted when he slept with her and rejected when he abstained. A battle that would engage both Tolstoys was about to break out in their bedroom, but Sonya could still comment in her diary that the winter of 1887 was one when "We have lived together peacefully and happily." Those family affairs to which she was bound by her heartstrings continued to give her satisfaction and they included her care of her husband, doing his copying and fussing over his health. Lev complained of a constant pain in the pit of his stomach and Sonya made certain that he obeyed the doctor's orders—dressed warmly with flannel on his stomach, avoided butter and drank Ems water. In the spring she noted without other comment that her mother had died the previous November in Yalta and was buried there. She was pleased that Lev had not left Moscow for Yasnaya after Christmas. In March she wrote:

> Levochka sometimes says that he is going to the country
> but again he decides to stay.

She added that he was playing Vint, a card game, enjoying the piano and was not driven to despair by city life.

Moscow may have become more endurable to Lev because of his increasing involvement with Chertkov and this was an irritant to Sonya. She wrote in her diary on 6 March:

> There was a letter from Chertkov. I don't like him; he's clever, sly, narrow and not a good man. L. N. is partial to him because he [Chertkov] worships him. But I do respect the popular works which Chertkov began at L. N.'s suggestion and I cannot but give him credit for them.

The "popular works" were an idea of Chertkov's inspired by an article that Lev wrote on the importance of making good books, fiction and prose works, available to the masses at a price they could afford. For this purpose a publishing house, Intermediary, was founded and its sales were soon in the millions. Besides works by Russian authors, Intermediary published George Eliot, Charles Dickens, Matthew Arnold and Charles Kingsley. There were many works by Dickens—he was Lev's favorite. Lev once said that if all great literature were put through a sieve to select the finest, only Dickens would be left and if all of Dickens were treated in the same way, there would be only *David Copperfield*.

To Sonya's increasing annoyance, Intermediary was an excuse for Chertkov to be a frequent visitor to the Moscow house. She felt that the disciple undermined her position with her husband by stressing how wrong it was to earn money. Sonya described in her diary how Lev had spoken to Chertkov about the evil of wealth and money in front of her, as if he had purposely wanted to reproach her for her editions. Sonya described in her diary of 9 March how she

> . . . kept silent for a while but then I lost patience and said, "I sell twelve volumes for eight rubles but you sold one of *War and Peace* for ten rubles." He became angry but remained quiet. His so-called *friends*, the new Christians, try very hard to turn L. N. against me and are not always unsuccessful. I reread Chertkov's letter to him about the happy spiritual communication that he has with his wife and his condolences to L. N. that he, so deserving of this communication, is deprived of it—hinting at me. I read it over and it made me sick.

Sonya was angry and not only at Chertkov. She seemed to be venting her exasperation at Lev, too, for allowing the situation of Chertkov's influence to exist; probably Sonya's entry was poured out in the hope that Lev would read it. She continued:

> This character, a sly, dishonest man, winds L. N. around with flattery and wants (very likely this is *Christian*) to destroy the ties which for almost twenty-five years have bound us so closely in every possible way.. . . The relationship must stop. It is a lie and evil and we must get away from it.

Sonya was furiously angry but she was also right about Chertkov. This authoritarian ex-army officer did not shrink from playing

the role of Lev's conscience or inserting himself as a third person
in the Tolstoy marriage. He compared Lev's ideals to the worldly
ones of the Tolstoy family, flattered Lev and needled him about
the damage Sonya's "luxurious" living habits did to Lev's reputation. Although the disciple was much younger, Lev seemed to look
upon him almost as a father figure. Lev's father had also been
an army officer. Lev valued Chertkov's approval and thus was
vulnerable to his criticism. Besides, much of Chertkov's influence
sprang from the fact that he was the one person close to Lev who
agreed completely with all Tolstoyan beliefs.

Some relief from Chertkov came with the return to Yasnaya.
Sonya planned to spend the summer of 1887 copying and sorting
out Lev's manuscripts, but wrote in her diary 18 June:

> Here it is more than a month that I have been here and
> Lev Nikolaevich has had me entirely occupied copying
> for him his article "On Life and Death" on which he has
> labored intensely for so long. As soon as I have copied it
> all he scribbles over it again and then it has to be copied
> anew. What patience and attention to detail!

Lev eventually called this article *On Life*. As Sonya noted:

> He threw out the words *on death*. When he had finished
> the article he decided that *there is no death*.

But Sonya admired *On Life* and translated it for a French journal.
The ideal of unselfishness was one that she approved. Her diary
was more cheerful than it had been the year before:

> Levochka, without being surrounded by his apostles,
> Chertkov, Feinerman [Isaak Feinerman, a young disciple
> who almost starved himself to death because of his devo-
> tion to Tolstoyan poverty] and others, once again begins
> to be a sweet, happy family man. . . . When we arrived
> from Moscow on the eleventh of May, I insisted that he
> drink the water that Zakharin had prescribed and he
> obeyed. I would bring him the warm glass of Ems without
> speaking and he would drink it up silently. When his mood
> was not good, he would say, "If anyone says that it is
> necessary to pour something into you, you believe them.
> I am doing it because it won't harm me very much." But
> he drank it three times a week. . . . Yesterday evening
> the actor Andreev-Burlak [a Russian actor who specialized

in telling peasant stories] arrived for a visit so that he
and Lev Nikolaevich might become acquainted. . . . Lev
Nikolaevich, Lev and myself stayed up until two o'clock
in the morning [listening to Andreev-Burlak's stories]. The
stories were wonderfully good and Levochka laughed so
much that Lev and I began to be anxious for him.

Later in the summer Sonya's diary was even more contented:

In the evening Seryozha was playing a waltz and Levochka
came up to me and said, "Let's have a go at the waltz."
And we danced to the general delight of the young people.
. . . He [Lev] has been having long talks with Strakhov
on science, music, art; today they talked about photography because I have bought a camera and will work on
photography and take pictures of all the family. . . . On
the table I have roses and mignonette, soon we shall have
a wonderful dinner. . . . All around me the children are
so sweet—just now Andrusha has been earnestly upholster-
ing his chairs in the nursery and later my sweet Levochka
will come. This is my life in which I delight constantly
and for which I thank God.

Sonya would never "delight constantly" in her life but when she
did complain during that summer it was of some of Lev's scruffier
disciples, dubbed by Sonya and her sister "the dark people," a
term even Lev used at times, and there was some dry humor in
her account: [6]

Butkevich was here, a former revolutionary who was im-
prisoned, the first time for political activity and the second
time for being under suspicion. . . . I began to pity him
and invited him to tea. He then stayed here for two days
and was very unpleasant. . . . What unsympathetic characters, all these followers of Lev Nikolaevich's teachings!
Not a single normal person. Also the women, often the
more hysterical. Maria Aleksandra Schmidt has just left.
In the old days she would have been a nun. Now she is
an enthusiastic worshiper of Lev Nikolaevich's ideas. She
was a schoolteacher . . . and now she lives in the village,
just copying Lev Nikolaevich's banned writings. When
she meets or parts with L. N. she sobs hysterically.[7]

Sonya eventually became friendly with Maria Aleksandra.

One of the happy events that summer was the arrival of mail from America that excited both Tolstoys. Sonya noted in her diary:

> Today he [Lev] received several letters from America, an article of Kennan's in *The Century* about his visit to Yasnaya Polyana, his conversations with Lev Nikolaevich and a printed comment on the translated works of L. N., all very flattering and sympathetic.[8]

Kennan was more admiring of the character and personality of Tolstoy than of his philosophy, which he found sincere but inconsistent. At the beginning of his article he described Lev's appearance and the atmosphere at Yasnaya Polyana:

> Count Tolstoy's features may be best described in Tuscan phrase as "molded with the fist and polished with the pickax," and the impression they convey is that of independence, self-reliance and unconquerable strength. The face does not at first glance seem to be that of a student or a speculative thinker but rather that of a man of action accustomed to dealing promptly and decisively with perilous emergencies. . . . The rather small eyes, deeply set under shaggy brows, are of the peculiar gray which lights up in excitement with a flash like that of drawn steel.

Kennan met Sonya at lunch and described her as a "stately, dark-eyed, dark-haired lady who must have been extremely beautiful in her youth." He wrote about the "bright, spontaneous conversation" at the luncheon table "in which all joined without the least appearance of formality or restraint" and during which Kennan was surprised to see how boyish the formidable Tolstoy could be.

It did not offend Lev that Kennan did not accept his philosophy. Except where his own family or he himself were concerned, Lev was often disarmingly reasonable about his impossibly high ideals. In an authorized interview printed in Russia and quoted in Kennan's article, Lev admitted that he was often reproached for not living the life that he preached. His answer was:

> If I know the road home and go along it drunk and staggering from side to side, does this prove that the road is not the right one? If it is not the right one, show me another. If I stagger and wander, come to my aid and guide me to the right path.[9]

The article put Lev into a happy frame of mind and Sonya wrote in her diary that for some time afterward he would frequently exclaim, "How good life is!"

It was not until the end of summer that Sonya got to her task of sorting out and copying Lev's manuscripts. She planned to take them and his diaries and letters to the Ruminstsev Museum for safekeeping. She noted:

> I am acting wisely but somehow doing this makes me sad. Is it that I am going to die that I am putting everything in order?

Her fear of death arose from the fact that she was in her forties and pregnant again. She described the pregnancy as both physically and mentally tormenting. Her mental torment was due to anxiety as to what her husband's mood would be when yet another evidence of his lack of chastity appeared before the world. The summer had been happy but toward the end Sonya recorded that Lev's health was poor and that "family life gets complicated." Her intuition warned her that Lev's resentments had sunk beneath the surface but had not disappeared. And, indeed, they had not. One of Andreev-Burlak's stories had been about a man on a train telling his life history to a stranger. From this story Lev conceived the form in which he would write *The Kreutzer Sonata*.

2.

Lev could contradict expectations. Far from feeling unhappy about Sonya's pregnancy he wrote cheerfully to Gay in February 1888:

> All is well with us—very well in fact. My wife is expecting a baby in another month.

Ivan (called either Vanechka or Vanya), was born in March 1888, the Tolstoys' thirteenth child of whom nine were living. From the beginning a special aura surrounded him. Ilya recalled:

> This little boy . . . was the favorite of the entire family. Father loved him, as his youngest child, with all the strength of a parent's and an old man's heart. [Lev was barely sixty but no doubt seemed very old to the twenty-two-year-old Ilya.]

Vanechka bound his parents together by the special love for him they shared. Lev, who had taken little interest in the upbringing of his last three children, concerned himself with everything about Vanechka. He said that he looked upon the child as his spiritual successor. Sonya reveled in her husband's tenderness to the baby and said that she loved him for his resemblance to his father.[10]

For all the seven years of his short life Vanechka's health caused anxiety. In January 1889 illness swept the family and it was Vanechka who was sickest. Lev noted:

> In the night Vanya was ill. Sonya was frightened. So was I. . . . Vanechka is very sick. . . . At home all is good except the illness.

Lev felt a great sympathy for his wife. He noted that he was sleeping with the children. Perhaps he relieved Sonya from a nightly vigil. It seems that he did not leave her alone with her cares and fears because another entry ended:

> I doubt that I'll have time to write more today. I am going to Sonya.

When the rest of the family recovered and Vanechka was still seriously ill a doctor came to examine him. The doctor found symptoms of tuberculosis and prepared the parents for the worst. On 24 January Lev wrote in his diary:

> I pity Sonya so much. Around him [Vanechka] a strange feeling, ah, of reverence, terror before this soul, the embryo of a clean soul in this tiny, sick body. The soul has merely dipped into the flesh and blood. I think that he will die soon. For me it has recently become strange and very joyful—I begin to feel the possibility of eternal love.

Lev was trying to prepare himself for a great grief. He wished that there were a chloroform for the soul as there was for the body and he decided, yes, there was such a chloroform and that it was love.

Vanechka recovered and Lev was distressed by Sonya's resumption of everyday life:

> *30 January.* . . . Sonya loves her children passionately and painfully because they are the only reality in her life. From love, from care, from sacrifice for her child she can go in a straight line to Fet's jubilee, the ball that is not only empty but bad.

A month later he complained:

> Our house is a kingdom of depravity and women. The women are the moving force of everything. . . . Try and touch on this. There is no subject on which people become more embittered. But support it [the role of women] and you will be forgiven. . . . Everything would be good if only they, women, were in their place, i.e., humble.

He described his relations with Sonya as "terrible" but a few weeks later, after quarreling with Sonya about money, Lev regretted his anger and felt remorseful. He saw that he had hurt her and this hurt him:

> She was suffering and her hurt was like a toothache to me.

They made up their quarrel and Lev left to visit Prince Urusov at Spasskoe, his estate near Moscow, where Lev hoped to get some serious writing done. Nothing came of the serious writing. He worked unsuccessfully on the beginnings of several short stories, a play and on *The Kreutzer Sonata*. On 3 April he rose early in the morning resolved to write but he only managed to read through what he had done so far. A sad letter came from Sonya who was missing him and he decided to go back to Moscow. Once home he described his return journey in his diary for 8 April:

> I got up early, packed my bags, said good-bye to Urusov and left. In the station and on the way I propagandized for the Temperance Society. [Lev took the pledge for a short period.] From the station I went on foot alone and then used my skates. Near home I came across a young man, a seminarian from Ryazan who begged for money and pounced on me with all his force to tell me of his helplessness against masturbation. I was in a hurry to be home and was not able to help him in any way. I spoke with him and gave him what money I had.

His first morning home Lev wrote in his journal that he wanted to write *The Kreutzer Sonata*. As if to convince himself that this was true, Lev worked on the book for a short while before lunch and then abandoned his effort. At the same time he was also working on an essay on art and he read part of what he had completed to a Moscow acquaintance, Sergei Ivanovich Taneev. Taneev was an accomplished pianist and composer but Lev was not impressed by his comments and wrote in his diary:

> I am upset by Taneev. I read him *On Art*. He is an absolutely ignorant man who has mastered an aesthetic principle that was new thirty years ago and he imagines that he has discovered the last word of human wisdom.

Lev may have been more vulnerable to Taneev's remarks because Lev himself had doubts about *On Art*.

Finally during the summer in Yasnaya Lev settled down to writing *The Kreutzer Sonata*. Once really begun he wrote quite steadily until by autumn he had finished all but the revisions and corrections. Once more Sonya was his copyist and what she read as she copied did not contribute to domestic harmony. The story told by the stranger on the train in *The Kreutzer Sonata* seems absurd today and to Sonya it was insulting. The narrator described how he had married and seduced his wife to depravity. He then repented and made an effort to live a pure and chaste life. His wife, however, was unable to give up her corrupted ways and continued to tempt him. When he convinced himself that she was having an affair with a musician he killed her. *The Kreutzer Sonata* survives as a curiosity and because, in spite of its improbable plot, it was written by a master who never failed to bring his characters to life. Lev did not enjoy writing this short novel. "I do it for mankind," he explained in his diary, "and this makes it difficult." The blatantly contrived message was more important than the artistic integrity and this did not sit well with Lev the artist. Neither *The Kreutzer Sonata* nor *The Devil*, a long story that appeared the same year, was true in the sense that Lev's inspired fiction was true. In July he noted:

> Thought: I am writing *The Kreutzer Sonata* and *On Art* and both are negative and malicious, but I want to write good things. . . . Slept all day. Worked some on *The Kreutzer Sonata*. Finished a rough copy. I realize how I must change everything and bring in love and compassion for her [the wife].

No other work of Lev's produced such tension during the writing. He quarreled with Sonya, he quarreled with his son Lev and sometimes he quarreled with all the family at once. He described in his journal an argument that took place at the dinner table:

> They argued with stubbornness and insolence, saying, "It's impossible to talk to you, you immediately get angry and so forth." It hurt me very much. Of course, Sonya immedi-

ately pounced on me tearing my exhausted heart to pieces.
It was very sad. I stayed awake until one o'clock and slept
badly.

Time and again Lev referred to Sonya's bad mood. A situation
that should have amused them passed without smiles. Lev, coming
downstairs in the morning to empty his chamber pot, was con-
fronted by a young Polish lawyer who had come to see "the great
man." Lev described in his diary how he explained that the great
man was not available and at that moment the woman director
of a small Moscow theater arrived and greeted him as "Lev Nikolaevich." Lev admitted that it was awful to be holding his chamber
pot while talking to her and then they were joined by Sonya "in
a bad mood." [11]

Sonya's mood was not improved by copying *The Kreutzer Sonata*.
She objected hotly to the parts of the novel that attributed alternate
periods of passion and coldness to both husband and wife. She
felt that the habit of desire growing hot and then cold was a masculine trait and that women were not so variable. A young wife,
Sonya wrote in her diary, was not completely aroused to passion
but she accepted intercourse for her husband's sake:

> Nor does a mature woman feel these periods of love and
> coldness. A woman who has become spoiled only becomes
> more sensual as intercourse becomes more frequent—she
> never reaches the point of satiety; she calms down only
> when she is left alone for a long time. And when she grows
> irritable it is not because she is surfeited but because
> she is unsatisfied and ashamed of her perpetual passion.[12]

During her copying Sonya became more and more offended by
Lev's conviction that it was morally necessary to abstain from
sexual relations. Inevitably, she wondered whether there had been
nothing in her husband's love for her but sensuality, the same
sensuality that he deplored in his youthful diaries and which he
now struggled to reject. If physical relations were as Lev described
them, that is, lust without purity, then Sonya, too, wanted no
part of them. Thus with similar resolves, although for different
reasons, this vital, passionate, confused and loving couple retired
each night to the same small bed. There they played out a drama
of temptation and "sinning" or frustration, a drama that during
the day Lev parodied, or rather, caricatured, as he wrote *The
Kreutzer Sonata*.

The novel was not one that encouraged common sense or assured tranquility. Although Lev believed that his purpose in writing it was a moral and important one, some passages in the book are suggestive. When it was finally published it was banned in parts of the United States as pornographic. In Germany it appeared with a nude woman on the cover, touted by the publisher as a titillating novel. While he was writing the book Lev found that in dwelling on sexual temptations he increased his own physical desires. In August he wrote in his journal:

> Debauchery is not a curse but a condition . . . a condition of anxiety, curiosity and need for novelty coming from intercourse for the sake of pleasure not once but many times. Like a drunkard, one can abstain but a drunkard is a drunkard and a debaucher is a debaucher. At the first relaxation of attention he falls. I am a debaucher.

As unpleasant as Sonya found her task, she continued her copying and also corrected the spelling and grammar. Lev wrote in his diary:

> It [*The Kreutzer Sonata*] offends her and last night she spoke about the disillusionment of a young wife, about the sensuality of husbands so alien [to women] at first, and about the husband's lack of sympathy for children. She is unfair but she wishes to justify herself.

Could Lev have meant that Sonya was trying to justify her own sexuality which he found so irresistible?

By mid-summer 1889 *The Kreutzer Sonata* was ready for the first family reading. Lev noted that they found it "uplifting" but that he himself was agitated and disturbed during the reading. Tanya made some criticisms that impressed her father—mainly, that the character of the wife was such that she was not to be pitied nor was she a person to repent and ask forgiveness. And yet, Tanya added, her sin was so small compared to her punishment. Lev copied his daughter's remarks into his diary without comment.[13]

Besides the tensions brought on by *The Kreutzer Sonata*, the old argument about Sonya's earnings continued to simmer. Although Lev had given his wife the right to publish his works written before his conversion, it still rankled with him that family comforts were bought with profits from his writing. He wrote in a notebook that Sonya was afraid to listen to his arguments because to believe him would destroy her life; she could not give up her earnings and live as she wished. Sonya noticed this comment and crossed out "her life," substituting "the life of her children." Lev, in turn, crossed out Sonya's comment but it may have touched him notwithstanding because soon afterward he noted:

> To Sonya her mission. To the Army its mission. Whoever is not against us is for us. Each does his own work.[14]

Lev was relieved to finish *The Kreutzer Sonata* and put it aside. It did not disturb him that the book did not pass the censor. Like his religious essays, it was copied by hand and privately distributed. Even so, it soon caused a sensation. Was Tolstoy actually recommending total chastity? His cousin Granny asked whether he wanted to end the human race. Many of Lev's followers were confused by the book and he received mail begging for clarification of his meaning. He wrote in his diary that he should write an afterword but that he could not. Both he and Sonya tried to put *The Kreutzer Sonata* out of their minds. At the end of February 1890, Lev went for a third visit to the Optina Monastery but missed Sonya so much that he raced home, whipping the horses to make them go faster. "Sonya met me joyfully, happily," he noted. Soon afterward he admitted in his diary that he had been cross and rude to Sonya but for the most part his references to her had become warm and affectionate:

> Drank coffee with Sonya and for almost the first time in many years we had a heart-to-heart talk. She spoke about prayer sincerely and wisely, chiefly saying that for her prayer must be in doing something and not just saying Lord, Lord—this made me very happy. . . . Sonya is good.

When Ilya was rude to his mother Lev noted:

> Sonya controlled herself beautifully. She acted other than was necessary but with love and she tried to make the best of it. And how this was dear to me.

Writing *The Kreutzer Sonata* expiated much of Lev's resentment toward his wife but the book's picture of marriage hurt Sonya deeply. She knew that readers would see the portrait of the wife as a portrait of herself. The novel was an injury added to the insult implicit in Lev's opinion of sexual relations. But Sonya was able to swallow her hurt and postpone settling scores because of the numerous satisfactions of her daily life. The first time she opened her diary in 1890 was to paste a wildflower onto the page and note:

> Levochka brought me this flower in October 1890 at Yasnaya Polyana.

The same month Lev wrote in his diary:

> One thing alone makes me glad and that is that with Sonya I have the deepest love. Only now is her character clear to me.

3.

The Kreutzer Sonata was the topic of conversations in the drawing rooms of Moscow and St. Petersburg but at Yasnaya Polyana Lev and Sonya were immersed in domesticity. And, in spite of their philosophical differences, they were growing more alike as they grew older. Both of them had become excessively hospitable, although they would both complain from time to time about the intrusion of guests. Both had grown a little stuffy. They gasped audibly when Masha appeared in a family play dressed in boy's trousers described by Sonya as, "entirely too tight over her behind and she had not a drop of shame." But Lev and Sonya loved these family plays; theatricals were a holiday tradition, and both Tolstoys believed in traditions—a tree for the younger children, festive puddings and cakes and bonbons and toasts to the new year. They also believed in being with one another. During the winter they went together in the sleigh to fetch the mail from the village. (Sonya complained in her diary when Lev chose to go alone on horseback). When Lev smoked Sonya rolled his cigarettes, and when his beard needed trimming she was often the barber. Lev trimmed his beard once a month in the new moon, a habit he had learned from the Muslims. In the evenings the Tolstoys played piano duets or Lev sat beside Sonya while she sewed and he laid out a game of Patience. When she was knitting he amused himself by disentangling her balls of yarn or he read aloud to her and the children. Sonya described him playing horse for Sasha and Vanechka, putting them in a hamper and dragging them around the house. This pleased Sonya but she complained that Lev did not spend enough time with his younger children.

There were nine Tolstoy children in 1890 and six of them lived at home. All the children had strong and diverse personalities. Sergei, twenty-seven and still unsettled on a career, argued most with his father and tried at this time to be a moral support to his mother. Ilya was three years younger, the most sensitive son and the one closest to Lev. Once, while still in adolescence, Ilya ran to the screen behind which he dressed and noticed his father sitting at the bedroom desk.

"Ilya, is that you?" Lev asked.

"Yes."

"Are you alone? Shut the door. Now there is no one to hear us and we can't see one another so we shall not be ashamed. Tell me, did you ever have affairs with women?" After Ilya had replied "no" he heard his father burst into sobs of relief, sobs so touching to Ilya that he wept himself. In 1888 Ilya married his sweetheart of four years, Sonya Filosov, and moved with her to the ground floor of Yasnaya. Lev was happy with both young people and after they left for their own place he wrote to Ilya:

> There is a great deal of love in you and Sonya, above
> all, purity and love; preserve them with all your might.

Unlike Lev's relation to Ilya, there was little sympathy between him and his third son, Lev. When young Lev entered the university he enraged the older Lev by asking for his father's manservant to be sent to him. Young Lev tried to make a living as a writer but his father was generally cool to his efforts. The lack of sympathy between these two was echoed by the relationship between Sonya and Masha. Masha was nineteen in 1890, a serious young woman given to diets and homeopathic cures. She and her mother were always a bit of a trial to one another and Masha did not help matters by becoming one of her father's devoted disciples. In her late teens Masha fell in love with Biryukov, a Tolstoy disciple close to the family and known as Posha. Both of Masha's parents disapproved heartily. Lev liked Posha and Sonya certainly expected her daughters to marry, but neither she nor Lev felt that Biryukov was worthy to be a son-in-law. Only Sonya complained openly of Posha's courtship. Lev hid his dismay from the young people but moaned in his diary in July 1889:

> Why must they marry? I feel all of this deeply and I pity
> Masha.

When Masha was away from home Lev and Sonya read her diary shamelessly (there was no sense of privacy in the Tolstoy family) and commiserated at the indication of Masha's continued infatuation.

Sunny Tanya was the family peacemaker on whom Lev and Sonya, and sometimes her brothers and sisters, leaned emotionally. Tanya was able to balance her admiration for her father's ideas with warm respect for her mother. She had been born during the autumn of 1864 when her parents' happiness was especially radiant. Some of this radiance rubbed off onto Tanya and remained there all her life. In 1890 neither Lev nor Sonya was unduly concerned that Tanya was twenty-six with no prospect of a husband. A year later they were pleased when a young admirer of Lev, Mikhail Stackovich, confessed to them that he was in love with Tanya. If Stackovich proposed he was refused, as nothing came of the romance. Even at twenty-seven Tanya was not ready to leave her father for a lesser man.

Lev took little interest in the development of his younger sons, Andrusha and Misha, and they were raised by Sonya. Andrusha and Misha paired together and when Sasha grew into a quiet, sensitive little girl, they united in tormenting her. Sasha was a docile personality until she was four and then Vanechka's birth upset her equilibrium. Lev and Sonya were surprisingly insensitive to her needs at the time. The new baby was not only adored but his frail health made him the center of constant attention. Naturally, Sasha was jealous and her jealousy showed itself in frequent temper tantrums with governesses and servants. Later Sasha claimed that Sonya, when dying, begged her forgiveness for not having loved her. This is hard to believe. Sonya loved all her children fiercely and, at times, criticized all of them fiercely. Before her death she left a letter for them asking their forgiveness, as was the Russian custom before death or a long journey. She asked Sasha forgiveness for *unintentionally* not giving her *enough* love. Until Sasha was in her late teens Sonya's references to her were like those to her other young children—she was taking walks with Sasha, hunting mushrooms with her, reading aloud to her, praising her good school work and having her play on her mother's bed in the morning. When Sonya discovered Misha beating his little sister she was so furious that she made him go onto his knees before Sasha and the family. But Sonya, and also Lev, showed thoughtless neglect of Sasha at the time of Vanechka's birth.

By the age of three Vanechka already showed signs of his precocious sensitivity. Coming across his parents weeping together he asked, "What is it?" with pained concern and sighed with relief when Sonya explained that Mama had hurt Papa and they were making up their quarrel. Once Vanechka solemnly admonished Lev, "Papa, never hurt my Mama." When Sonya cut Vanechka's hair and stabbed him with her scissors, she suggested that he should punish her by hitting her hand that had been clumsy but Vanechka grabbed the hand and covered it with kisses. Sonya often said that he was so sweet and gentle that she feared he would not live for long. When Sonya was in Moscow, Lev and Vanechka had tea together and Lev wrote to Sonya that, "He is very sweet. He is more than sweet—he is good." Lev recounted for Sonya his conversation with Vanechka after Lev had told him that his mother did not feel well:

"And what if she were really ill, Papa?"

"Then we would go to her."

"We'd take Rudnev with us."

Rudnev was the family doctor in Tula.

Vanechka was sweet but not a goody-goody. When Lev scolded him for striking the cook's son, Vanechka was offended and said he would not have anything more to do with his father ever again and that Lev must not come into Vanechka's room. Acting rather like a three-year-old himself, Lev marched at once into the forbidden room but later felt ashamed and wrote in his diary:

Proud and spoiled as we are, it is hard to forgive an offense . . . even one from Vanechka, a sweet, three-year-old son.

Vanechka made friends with everyone he met, including the inmates of a lunatic asylum. The asylum bordered upon the garden of the Moscow house and one of the patients, a man who had lost his reason after the death of his small son, became particularly fond of Vanechka, chatting with him through the fence. Tanya Tolstoy recalled in her memoir:

After his [the inmate's] discharge he wrote to my mother a most touching letter. In it he told her that he had learned from Vanya that love and affection still existed in the world and he thanked her for having brought so enchanting a being into it.

The great love for the endearing Vanechka that Sonya shared with Lev helped her to control for the time being her rage at *The Kreutzer Sonata*, although the wound she had received from the novel remained raw. In 1890 and 1891 Sonya worked at the massive task of making legible copies of all of Lev's diaries. She wrote in her diary in December 1890:

I copy his diaries with the avidity of a drunkard and my drunkenness consists of jealous agitations wherever he describes women.

Her jealousy touched the *Kreutzer Sonata* wound and a month later she made a lugubrious comparison between Lev's diaries and the novel:

There seems to be a thread connecting Levochka's old diaries and *The Kreutzer Sonata*. And I am a buzzing fly sunk by accident into the spider's web and the spider sucks my blood.

Sonya refused to consider *The Kreutzer Sonata* an artistic work and she continued to complain that Lev was not doing creative writing. Lev himself was beginning to admit to a similar feeling. The same January he noted in his diary:

How happy I should be if I could write tomorrow that I had begun a great artistic work.

He added, "With Sonya, love. How good it is." Sonya described in her diary how she met her husband

Returning from his walk and looking happy and cheerful; it is always such a joy to see him anywhere, especially unexpectedly.

The next month their relations exploded. Lev reread some of his early diaries that Sonya was copying and was filled with self-disgust. Sonya recorded in her diary on 12 February 1891 that Lev accused her of preserving the evil of his past, an evil which could only hurt him when recalled. She added:

I replied to him that if I hurt him I did not pity him, that if he wanted he could burn his diaries, let him burn them, I did not value my work, but if he was considering the hurt done to someone, then he himself by his last book had given me such a hurt in the face of the whole world that it would be difficult for us to square accounts.

At last Sonya poured out to Lev all the pain he had caused her when he wrote *The Kreutzer Sonata*. She reminded him that people, from the czar to Lev's own brother Sergei, had expressed pity for her because the book was taken as an intentional blow at her. This was how she herself felt it was intended. They parted angrily but Lev reported in his diary that the anger lasted no more than an hour. They were affectionately reconciled. Lev noted, "We have been sinning." Both blamed their tensions on their inability to abstain from physical relations. The bedroom war was now at a peak of frenzy.

The Tolstoys' effort to abstain from physical love was ridiculous, but both were deeply serious. Lev's idea of purity was as longstanding as his ideal of truth. His early marital happiness had been blissful because Sonya had reconciled his ideal of purity with sexual relations. In his first year of marriage Lev wrote about his wife that she was "so impossibly pure and good and whole beside me." All that was gone now and the idea of sex as sin was so strongly established in Lev's mind that it remained there to the end of his life, not always a total obsession, but a recurring nightmare. Throughout these middle years of marriage Lev's diaries often began with the cryptic note, "Slept evilly." He seemed to have fallen back into a psychological snare left from childhood or youth from which he happily escaped during the first sixteen years of his married life.

For most of Sonya's life her mind and body remained in tune and she would hardly have had guilt feelings concerning sexual relations if her husband's problem had not existed. But now Sonya felt herself entangled in the spider's web that connected Lev's youthful diaries, so full of shame at his dissolute life, with his present attitude toward physical love and, contrary to her whole nature, she had moods of revulsion against their intimacy. Excerpts from her diary at this time show how similar to Lev's attitude her own was becoming:

> I am terribly displeased with myself. This morning Levochka woke me with passionate kisses. [Sonya put a series of dots here.] . . . All this unforgivable drunkenness which I give in to, and at my age! I feel that I am sinful, unhappy and I can do nothing about it however I try. . . . What a strange man my husband is. After we had that awful scene, the very next morning he spoke passionately of love for me and said that I had taken such possession of him that he could never have believed such attachment possible. But it is all *physical* and that is the secret of our discord. His passion takes possession of me but with all my moral being I do not want it nor have I ever wanted it. . . . Just now Tanya came to me and said that Levochka told

her to tell me that he is in bed and has put out the candle. Her innocent lips have carried a message that is far from innocent.[15] . . . Everyone has gone to bed and I am going. Save me, God, this night from those sinful dreams that awakened me this morning. . . . Happiness lasts only when soul and will overcome body and passion. . . . I want to think always of good things. But my dreams are sinful and I don't have much peace, particularly at certain times.

Sonya was forty-six, and her shame at feeling desire was made worse by fear of pregnancy. She began to see a connection between Lev's kind and affectionate manner and those times when he gave in to his physical desires:

Levochka is very loving and keeps thinking of me and all that I have to do. If only our relations could be like this without *that*.[16]

She wrote that if Lev's readers could know of the erotic life he led while preaching chastity they would tear him from his pedestal:

But I love him thus, normal in his habits, weak and kind. It is not necessary to be an animal but neither is it necessary to be under compulsion to advocate principles that are beyond oneself.

A similar current of good sense sometimes ran beneath Lev's attitude. A year earlier he had written in a notebook that, although the ideal married man was chaste, "I am not able to be chaste. . . . All the same, the ideal remains." If the Tolstoys' "ideal" had been more important to them than their mutual attraction, certainly they could have slept in separate beds. As it was, they continued to share the same narrow bed, subject themselves to temptation every night and to record their shame at their lapses. It is hard to believe that, in spite of all their intellectual somersaults, their intimate relations did not bind them closer to one another.

4.

If *The Kreutzer Sonata* could have been erased from their memories Lev and Sonya might have found peace in their marriage before

Lev's seventieth birthday. In 1891 Lev told Sonya of his desire to begin an artistic work; once again he was discussing his literary plans with her. In January he noted in his diary that with his deeper philosophical insights he would be able to surpass his two masterpieces, which he now called "accidental creations." He wrote:

> Now that I know *what is what* I could put all of it together and build on what I have already constructed.

But Lev was not able to follow up his desire to write fiction with any sustained effort. He had notes for a novel based on a true legal case told him by the jurist Koni and for a short story, *Father Sergius*, but most of his writing was not fiction but essays, the long essays on pacifism and nonresistance to evil that would be put together as *The Kingdom of God*. Sonya's words, however, on the hurt that she had received from *The Kreutzer Sonata* impressed Lev and soon after that conversation he began what he said would be a major novel, *The Story of a Mother*. This was written in the form of a diary kept by the heroine, the mother, and could have been Lev's effort to compensate for *The Kreutzer Sonata* with a true portrait of his wife. He never succeeded in getting very far with *The Story of a Mother* but for five years he returned to it from time to time.

And, unfortunately, *The Kreutzer Sonata* was not forgotten. This time it was Stackovich who brought it up. He wrote to Lev suggesting that Sonya should see the czar and ask that the ban on the book be lifted so that it could be part of her thirteenth edition of Lev's works, soon to appear. At first Lev had no objection to the suggestion but Sonya demurred and wrote in her diary:

> If I were able to be quite relaxed about [leaving] home and the children, if I liked *The Kreutzer Sonata*, if I believed in the future of Lev's artistic work, I would go.

After a dream in which she saw herself with the emperor and empress, Sonya admitted that her vanity was tickled by the idea but she still declared that she would not go to St. Petersburg. At the same time that Stackovich's proposal was in the air Lev was considering sending a letter to the newspapers renouncing all the rights to any of his works that had been published. In other words, he would take back from Sonya the exclusive rights to works written before 1881 and she would be forced to compete with anyone who chose to publish Tolstoy's writings. Such a situation would make a cut in her income but it was this income that tormented Lev. On 9 March he noted in his diary that he had brought the matter up with Sonya:

> This morning, with difficulty and with agitation, I told Sonya that I was announcing that everyone had the right to publish all my writings. I saw that she was grieved. Then . . . all red and irritated she came and said that she would go on publishing. . . .

Sonya even said that she would enclose a note with her edition begging others not to make use of her husband's announcement as he would be renouncing income needed for his children. This made Lev furious. He told her emotionally that if she really loved him she would renounce her copyrights herself. Sonya wrote in her diary:

> He left and I began to pity him; my financial interests appeared so insignificant compared to this hurt which strained our relations with one another. After dinner I told him that I would print nothing and that his pain hurt me above all else.

They fell into one another's arms and Lev wrote in his diary:

> After dinner she came to me and kissed me, saying that she would do nothing against my will and she began to cry. It was very, very joyful.

Sonya finally took Stackovich's suggestion and asked Granny to intercede with the czar for an appointment. Lev still felt no need to raise objections. Sonya admitted to being nervous about her possible audience with the emperor. Perhaps that was why she screamed at Andrusha and struck his hand during a piano lesson and why she fought with Ilya over his request for a loan of 35,000 rubles and even told him to go to the devil, slamming the door in his face. Or, her irritation may have come simply from the fact that once more she would have to think about *The Kreutzer Sonata*. Nevertheless, relations with her husband were warm. She and Lev both made diary notes of friendly talks and Sonya proudly recorded a heavy joke that pleased them. "Here is a stupid thing I thought of," Lev said to her, *"Quand est-ce que se porte bien?—Quand on a une bonne sans thé."* Sonya added the words *"bonne santé"* to make the pun quite clear.

Spring was in the air and Sonya had swept the winter snow

from the balcony when word finally came that the interview with
the czar was arranged. On 1 April Sonya left for St. Petersburg.
Perhaps Lev had never expected her to receive the appointment
because now he fretted about it. He had begun to despise *The
Kreutzer Sonata*. He wrote in his diary that Sonya's trip grieved
him. She was soon home. The czar had been courteous and easy
in conversation and he had agreed to her request. Sonya related
the details of her interview to Lev; he was embarrassed and one
point particularly annoyed him. One of his stories, banned in Russia
because it was unfavorable to Nicholas I, had been smuggled to
England and printed there. Sonya was pleased that she made it
clear to the czar that Lev had had no part in the smuggling. Lev
felt that this seemed as if Sonya were helping him avoid responsibility for what he had written. But he was not cross for long since
he was too glad to have her home again even after such a short
absence—the more so, he confessed to his diary, because of "a
sinful feeling for her." In April he wrote to Chertkov:

> He [the emperor] promised to allow *The Kreutzer Sonata*
> which does not please me at all. But any recollection of
> it has become terribly loathsome to me. There was some-
> thing bad in the motives which led me to write it, it has
> aroused such anger. Even I see it as bad.

Lev had second thoughts about his motives in writing his malicious
novel; as he labored over *The Story of a Mother*, his intent was
certainly to make amends to Sonya for his vindictive feelings.
Sonya herself wrote a vindictive story which she called her retaliation to the novel, but wisely did not try to publish it. This was
the story of a man who raped his bride in their wedding coach,
the story intended to show Lev how much untrue accusations could
hurt.

In May the ban on *The Kreutzer Sonata* was lifted and Sonya
wrote in her diary that she could not help but feel some inward
triumph that:

> I, a woman, dealt with the czar and got that which no
> one else had been able to obtain.

Sonya was glad to have her role in the ban lifting known to the
public. If the wife in *The Kreutzer Sonata* had really been based
upon Sonya and the book a picture of her marriage, she certainly
would not have made the effort herself to have the book published.
This reasoning helped to save her public face, but the unfortunate

book continued to plague the Tolstoy marriage. Sonya found that correcting the proofs for her edition was upsetting. It reminded her of her hurt and she was tense during Lev's periods of "satiety," haunted by the novel's descriptions of passion alternating with coldness and disgust. Sonya was at an age when a woman's sexual life is satisfying and important to her; much of her tension was probably due to simple frustration. This is evident in an angry diary entry complaining that Lev had kept her awake until two in the morning:

> At first he was downstairs washing for a long time—I began to think that for certain he was sick. Washing is a big thing for him. He told me that his feet perspired so much that he got sore between the toes. He nearly made me quite sick. . . . Then he lay down and read for a long time. I know I am in his way when he doesn't need me for his satisfaction.[17]

Reading between the lines in this entry, Sonya seems to say that she, too, had needs which Lev did not take into account.

Working on *The Kreutzer Sonata* aggravated Sonya's tensions and silly arguments erupted. In June 1891 Lev remarked to the family at large that there were some things that were simply impossible to do. Sonya commented lightly that one would do almost anything to save a life. "Why, then," Lev asked her, "could you kill a child?" The academic argument reached ridiculous proportions. Sonya described in her diary how

> He began to object in a frightfully angry voice, to shout hoarsely, Aye, aye, aye and he blew up at me in this tone of voice. I told him a lot of unpleasant things—that it was impossible to talk to him, that everyone had decided long ago that he only liked to sermonize, that I could not speak over the sound of his spiteful exclamations any more than I could talk to a barking dog.

At this point Sergei Tolstoy deleted more than forty words from his mother's diary. Sonya probably poured out her hurt and frustration in her relations with Lev. *The Kreutzer Sonata* was tormenting her rather more than less. And it was not her only worrisome concern; the same day she noted in her diary:

> I have been to Tula and talked a lot to the notary about the property division which is hateful to me.

Lev had decided to make his situation at home more compatible with his ideal of poverty and to give his property to his family. This was more in keeping with the letter rather than the spirit of the law as Lev remained living at home. He charged Sonya with the arrangements because of his distaste for dealing with government regulations, and here was another torment for Sonya. Besides having to involve herself in tiresome negotiations she saw Lev's act as a way of separating himself from her and their children. In June she wrote in her diary:

> Sometimes I long so for communication with Levochka, to have a talk with him. But this is impossible now. . . . I would be so glad to see him tender, sympathetic and friendly but, when he is not coarsely sensual, he is indifferent.

The property division took over a year to be resolved and much of Sonya's time and energy. She and Vanechka received Yasnaya Polyana which followed the tradition of leaving the family home to the youngest son. Besides, as Sonya noted in her diary:

> Yasnaya was given to me and Vanechka because it would be impossible to take his father from here and where I am, there must be both Lev Nikolaevich and Vanechka.

Lev added to the already highly charged atmosphere at home by bringing up once again his wish to renounce the copyrights of Volumes XII and XIII of Sonya's new edition since these were works written after 1881. Sonya wrote in her diary on 16 July how much she hated for their children to lose this income but she added:

> Nevertheless, the hurt to Levochka began to grieve me and yesterday I told him that I would let him do or print what he wanted and I would not remonstrate or reproach him. Up to now he has not spoken about it or done anything.

Five days later Lev told Sonya that he had composed his letter to the newspapers and, in spite of her resolve, Sonya's temper flared up. In the ensuing argument she called him a man thirsty for glory and he called her a greedy woman. When he began to shout, "Get out! Get out!" Sonya ran from the house, wanting to end her life. She eventually ran straight into her brother-in-law Sasha Kuzminsky, who calmed her and escorted her home. She went first to her room but then returned to the empty terrace:

> I lay outside in the hammock listening for him [Lev] to
> come back. Little by little everyone gathered on the terrace
> and Levochka returned. They all chatted, shouted and
> laughed. Levochka was animated as if nothing had hap-
> pened.

Sonya lay in the hammock, reflecting on the fact that Lev would
never know how near she had come to suicide. She admitted that
her behavior had been absurd, but still:

> Again and again the same, *The Kreutzer Sonata* haunts
> me. Today I announced again that I would live with him
> as wife no more. He assured me that this was his only
> wish but I did not believe him.

Could either of them have believed that such resolves were more
than empty words?

At the beginning of the school year Sonya took the younger
boys to Moscow. As a rule she returned to Yasnaya to spend most
of September and October with Lev. During this time Lev finally
sent his announcement to the newspapers, renouncing his rights
to any works written after 1881 including those in Sonya's new
edition. He made one exception, *The Death of Ivan Ilyich*, which
he had written as a gift for Sonya. Even though Lev had received
her reluctant permission, he was apprehensive as to how Sonya
would react to the fait accompli. It was a relief when she came
home without reproaches. The morning after her return Sonya
wrote in her diary:

> Yesterday I was again possessed by violent passion which
> my husband aroused in me; today everything is clear,
> holy, quiet and good.

After all the galley proofs for Sonya's edition of *The Kreutzer Sonata*
were corrected and sent off, the novel no longer occupied center
stage at home. Lev appeared to dismiss the book from his mind,
but Sonya's hurt continued to haunt her and she began to nourish
her own seed of resentment.

Chapter Seven

SONYA'S RETALIATION, 1891–1898

1.

In the autumn of 1891 a national disaster united the Tolstoys; large areas of central Russia were devastated by famine. Lev did not approve of organized charity, believing it to be self-justification on the part of the rich who did not otherwise concern themselves with the sufferings of the poor, but he could not ignore the plight of the starving. When the first news of the famine arrived Lev wrote to the Russian novelist, N. S. Leskov, that it was possible to feed others without loving them but impossible to love them and not to feed them. The agreement had been that Lev would spend the winter with Sonya in Moscow but instead he went to Begichevka, the village of an estate in Ryazan, a province on the eastern border of the province of Tula and a badly afflicted area. There, with the help of his daughters Tanya and Masha and their cousin Vera Kuzminsky, he organized soup kitchens. It was a blow to Sonya to stay alone with the little children in Moscow but her unhappiness did not last. She eventually approved warmly of what Lev was doing and the warmth that Lev felt for her in return eased her disappointment.[1] At the end of the year Lev spent a month in Moscow and wrote in his diary:

> Joyful relations with Sonya. Never have we been so loving.
> Father, I thank you.

Lev returned to Begichevka for ten days and then was back in Moscow. On 24 January 1892 Sonya accompanied him to Begichevka. The trip to Ryazan was arduous, first by ice-cold train and then by sleigh. In Begichevka Sonya's first task was to organize the soup kitchens to assure that only the neediest received food. She also worked with a tailor, making in all twenty-three boys' coats from donated cloth. She and Lev worked from dawn until nightfall, when they returned to their one room, traveling by horse-drawn sleigh along the River Don, a red sunset to one side of them and once a new moon on the other. For three years Lev's work for the famine relief brought him closer to Sonya and earned him the adoration of the Russian people. It was an era of good feeling for the Tolstoys although Lev still had his cantankerous moods when he raged in his diary about the frivolity of society or the domination of women. Women brought forth particular vitriol but Lev's references to the most important woman in his life were warm:

> With Sonya it is good. . . . Sonya arrived this morning.
> Our relations are beautiful. Something joyfully good. . . .
> Sonya is very cheerful and kind. Everything becomes bet-
> ter and better.

In October 1894 Lev repudiated the harsh words he had written about Sonya during the worst year of his depression:

> I have been reading my diary for the year 1884 and been
> disgusted with my cruelty and bad feelings toward Sonya
> and Sergei. May they know that I disavow all the bad
> things that I wrote about them. I love and value Sonya
> more and more.

As if to confirm that he was back to himself in every way, in January Lev finished one of his finest stories, *Master and Man*.

Lev's repentance and warm feelings, alas, came too late for Sonya. For several years her diary had been showing signs of stress and physical and mental exhaustion. She described unpleasant sensations of blood rushing to her head, palpitations of the heart, fits of weeping in which she could not stop, insomnia. A thunderstorm put her in a state of nervous excitement. More and more of her diary entries were critical and complaining:

> Today I spit blood from my throat—and a lot; and fever
> during the night, a pain in my chest, sweating. . . . My
> heart is so strained, so constantly aching with living this
> day to day life that I feel on the point of losing my strength.

. . . I am afraid that when I begin writing in my diary I fall into condemning Lev Nikolaevich. But I cannot but complain since everything that he advocates for mankind's happiness so complicates life in every way. . . . When the complications get really intense, then I get angry and say sharp words and this makes me unhappy and remorseful but it is too late.

For thirty years Sonya's birthright as a "black Bers," her enormous energy, had sustained her without rest. Her closest thing to a holiday had been a trip to Moscow to see the doctor. Fourteen pregnancies including her miscarriage took their toll on her body. Now she was in middle life, but nineteenth-century Russia offered little comfort to women of her age. The menopause was a never-never land where symptoms were supposedly psychological and nothing could be done for them. Even a fever or a sore throat was often shrugged off as due to a woman's "critical period." However ill or tired Sonya might feel she still remained responsible for everything—the finances, running the Moscow house and Yasnaya Polyana (both house and estate), raising the children and entertaining guests in the city and in the country. On 8 January she listed the following activities in her diary account of the day: She paid the laundry bill, gave instructions to repairmen, gave permission to the servants to attend a wedding and arranged for their absence, talked to the police about a theft at Yasnaya, paid the household wages, checked into family passports that were running out, read to Vanechka from Grimm's fairy tales, had a financial discussion with Ilya and, reluctantly, loaned him five hundred rubles, entertained four extra people for dinner, corrected Misha's schoolwork and finally received four more guests who called late in the evening.[2]

The important role Sonya played in family affairs was taken for granted and not the least by herself. What Sonya did not choose was her emotional stress. Besides her resentment of *The Kreutzer Sonata*, Sonya had been feeling for many years the gnawing hurt of intellectual separation from Lev. She longed for the days when her husband was writing his great novels and discussing his work with her. Did she matter as much to him since they no longer shared that common purpose? Once she had had what she referred to as "spiritual intimacy" with Lev; now Chertkov usurped this part of her marriage. Of all her anxieties, however, the one that

weighed on her most fiercely in January 1895 was Vanechka's
health. She wrote in her diary:

> I am terribly frightened of everything now and mostly
> of Vanechka's poor health. It is dangerous and wrong that
> I have tied my life so closely to his existence. But he is a
> frail, delicate child and so good!

Vanechka had not been able to go out of doors for three weeks.
He was thin, pale and had constant fever and indigestion. The
younger children, Andrusha, Misha and Sasha, had all gone to a
children's party, but Vanechka was too ill to leave the house. He
spent the evening with his head on Sonya's knee. She felt very
sorry for Vanechka, that he had missed the party fun, and sorry
for herself. After she had put Vanechka to bed she listed all her
cares in her diary: her husbandless daughters, Sergei's failure to
settle on a career, Ilya's poor organization and lack of success at
farming, and young Lev, whose efforts to become a writer found
little encouragement or sympathy from his father. For more than
a year young Lev had been ill off and on and Sonya suspected
psychological problems. A trip to Paris during the summer of 1894
had not improved his condition and on his return Sonya noted
that Dr. Zakharin found him in "a very poor way." Toward the
end of 1894 young Lev began a series of electrical treatments;
the new technique for treating nervous disorders had started in
Russia and was spreading to Europe and the United States. Sonya
noted in early January that young Lev seemed to be calmer but
soon afterward she wrote in her diary:

> I spent the evening with [young] Lev and I inadvertently
> mentioned his nerves and repeated Dr. Belogolov's words
> that everything was a case of nerves. He unexpectedly
> jumped up and began abusing me terribly: idiot, nasty
> old woman, you are always lying!

And ever tearing at Sonya's heart was her aching concern for "this
flickering flame of life in poor little Vanya." Tormented by fears
and despair, Sonya wrote in her diary that she was "not in possession of myself." Later, with some of her usual, practical, common
sense, she wondered whether the family worries were simply too
much for her now that she was debilitated by having her period
every three weeks.

Sonya had cared for Vanechka so constantly that she had not

been outside of the house for a month. She decided that shoveling snow would be good for her health, but when she glanced from the garden into Vanechka's window she saw him running naked around his room. Sonya hurried inside and had a row with his nurse. The next day, probably because of his naked foray, Vanechka was worse and his temperature rose. He had a hoarse cough and Sonya called for Dr. Filitov, their Moscow pediatrician. The doctor recommended large doses of quinine and Vanechka rallied. On 1 February Sonya was able to leave the house. She went for a drive and did some shopping—sheet music, toys, cheese and fresh eggs. That evening she sat at the piano with Lev and played duets. Four days later Sonya could note:

> Vanya hasn't had a temperature for three days. For four days I have been giving him arsenic, five or six drops two times a day after meals. I am feeling better. . . . With Levochka relations are good—and passionate.[3]

As for her own condition, Sonya knew that her reactions were out of control. She marveled in her diary at her sudden fits of sentimentality that quickly swung to the other extreme. When Lev gave her two beautiful apples she planted the pips to commemorate his gift, but minutes later she was complaining that he was a "selfish and pitiless man." In mid-February a storm broke out. Sonya asked for a copy of *Master and Man* for her edition and became distraught when Lev told her to wait until it had appeared in *The Northern Messenger*. She immediately remembered that someone had said that Gurevich, the woman publisher of the periodical, had "fascinated the Count" and Sonya jumped to the conclusion that Lev, because of infatuation for the publisher, was giving her priority. Sonya accused Lev of a preference for Gurevich and both Tolstoys got very excited. Lev charged upstairs shouting his old threat to leave home forever. Sonya ran into the snow-covered street wearing only her chemise and dressing gown with slippers over her bare feet. She screamed, "Let them take me to the police station, to the home for the insane." Lev, in similar dishabille, ran after his wife and managed to drag her back to the house while she sobbed hysterically.[4] Once home both were ashamed. Lev excused Sonya in his diary:

> She was feeling ill, weak, worn out after the illness of the gentle Vanechka.

This scene did not relieve Sonya of either her suspicions or her jealousy and the next day her resentment returned. As she remembered it later:

> The feeling of jealousy, vexation, pain that he never, ever did anything for me, the old feeling of grief at Levochka's little love in return for my great love—all of this rose up with a terrible despair.

Sonya put on her fur coat, cap and galoshes and took a cab to the Kursk station. Sergei and Masha were staying at the Moscow house and heard Sonya's instructions to the cabdriver. Frightened by her excited condition, they followed the cab to the station in time to prevent Sonya from throwing herself in front of a train. It is doubtful that Sonya would have carried out this drastic impulse and she may even have intentionally given her instructions to the driver in front of her children. That night she lay in bed weeping and Lev knelt at her bedside to beg forgiveness. Sonya wrote in her diary:

> If only a drop of the love which was in him then would remain all the time, I could still be happy.

Did Sonya truly want to be comforted? Years and years of rising to challenges and trying to make an orderly path through the tangle of her husband's and children's personalities and the recent years of "spiritual" isolation from Lev had worn her to the point where even her husband's obvious concern for her was not enough. She knew that her jealousy had been stupid and that neither it nor the family troubles cut so deeply as the knowledge that she and Lev did not have the communion that they had had when he wrote his masterpieces. During their courtship he had written that she was there, in his head and everywhere. Now she felt that he had put her out of his head and was blaming her unfairly.

Lev saw that his wife's needs were urgent and he sent for three different doctors. Sonya described them:

> It was comical. Each gave his own special medicine. The nerve doctor gave a bromide, the specialist in internal diseases gave Vichy water and some drops. Finally he [Lev] sent for the obstetrician Snegirev. This one gave me something of his own and spoke cynically of my "critical period." I did not take the medicines.

Sonya was ashamed and called her frenzy "inexcusable and irreparable." Lev's sister Maria Nikolaevna, now a nun in the Shamardino

Convent, was visiting the Tolstoys in Moscow and told Sonya that nevertheless she had said some very true things during her hysteria. But Lev understood only the surface reasons for Sonya's reaction to the priority he had given to *The Northern Messenger*. He wrote in his diary:

> *15 February.* . . . She was suffering terribly. It was a demon of jealousy, senseless, a jealousy based on nothing. I could only fall in love with her again and I understood her reasons and, understanding them, I did not forgive her as there was nothing to forgive.

About Vanechka he wrote:

> He is failing. He does not want to die. And he should not have to die.

On 22 February 1895 Vanechka was ill again, this time more seriously. He had a rash, sore throat and severe diarrhea. Dr. Filitov diagnosed scarlet fever, for which there was no cure. When Vanechka saw the tears run down his mother's face he said, "Don't, Mama. It is God's will." Dr. Filitov instructed Sonya to wrap Vanechka in blankets soaked in mustard water. The next day she noticed that his hands and feet were cold and that he hung his little head helplessly to one side. Lev and Sonya were at Vanechka's bedside at eleven o'clock that night when he opened his eyes for the last time with what Sonya described as a look "almost of surprise." Then he lay quite still. Sonya sat by Lev on the sofa resting her head on his chest. Their shock and pain was too great for tears. Before going to bed Sonya wrote in her diary:

> *23 February.* My sweet Vanechka died at eleven o'clock in the evening. My God, and I am still alive.

She did not open her diary again for two and a half years.

Vanechka was buried two days later in the Pokrovskoe cemetery. As the family drove along the road to the village, Lev reminded Sonya that during their courtship he had often taken the same road to come to see her. When he and their sons lowered the little coffin into the grave Sonya swayed and nearly lost consciousness. Her husband took her in his arms and she remained there in a kind of stupor until aroused by the joyful shouts of the village children. Sonya had remembered how Vanechka had liked to share his sweets and she had instructed that there should be candies and cakes distributed to the children from the village. At home again, the grieving mother and father wept together. "I always thought," Lev told Sonya, "that of my sons it would be Vanechka who would carry on my good work on earth." The next day he noted in his diary:

26 February. We buried Vanechka. It is horrible, no, not horrible but a great emotional event for my soul. I thank thee, father, I thank thee, father.

But with Sonya he sobbed and said, "I have lost heart for the first time in my life." [5]

2.

Lev kept trying to see Vanechka's death as joyful, a mercy from God. He wrote that it was "an event that untangled the lie of life, one which brought me nearer to Him." Sonya would have liked to have found comfort in religion but this was not to be. On 7 March she wrote to her sister Tanya:

I cry to God, Thy will be done, if this must be so that I pass to eternity. But, in spite of the constant exaltation of my soul or the sincere cry from my heart to give myself up to the will of God, I am not comforted, neither by this nor by anything.

Lev was disappointed that Sonya could not "expose herself to the universal wind of love." [6] He added:

But I love her. It is both sad and good to be with her. She is again physically frail; for two months without her period and she sometimes thinks she is pregnant. [This fear was unfounded.]

Immediately after Vanechka's death neither Tolstoy had the heart for physical relations and Lev had been pleased when Sonya attributed this to the purity of Vanechka. He wrote in his diary:

Sonya often says, "I am bad, of a gross nature, he [Vanechka] made me gentle by his love, he brought me nearer to God."

The Tolstoys did not maintain their abstinence nor could Sonya keep the feeling of being nearer to God. In an effort to understand her and sympathize with her suffering, Lev returned to *The Story of a Mother*. He worked on an introduction in which he spoke of the tragedy of "a good mother" who put all her heart and soul into her children. Such a mother could find a child's death a mortal blow. He noted:

> A mother suffers from the death of a child. . . . She cannot console herself until she can understand that her life is not in the vessel which was broken but in the contents which poured out; that all form is lost but that the contents have not disappeared.

Lev himself was not quite convinced by these lines and added:

> This was somehow fresh, clear and strong when I thought of it—now the meaning is lost.

He was floundering. He knew that in the months before Vanechka's death, Sonya had come close to a nervous breakdown. Now he was relieved to see that after the death Sonya had not gone entirely to pieces but rather had come together again. All her stresses were channeled into her one, hopeless sorrow. It seemed to Lev that the only problem was to relieve Sonya's sorrow. He confessed:

> But she amazed me. The pain of her loss released her from all that was hiding her soul. . . . The first days I was astonished by her wonderful loving kindness.

During this time of grieving Lev considered a new idea for a novel that would proselytize his spiritual convictions as *The Kreutzer Sonata* had attempted to but failed. The plot concerned a man who left his wife and took their small son with him that he and the child might together live a "pure, hardworking life." The wife remained corrupted by her luxurious surroundings. Lev noted:

> I could write this astonishingly well. At least it seems so to me now.

Fortunately, it did not continue to seem so. The novel might have been even more disrupting than *The Kreutzer Sonata* and hardly a comfort to Sonya. Lev longed to comfort Sonya but her despair was obstinate and finally he blamed it impatiently on the "animal nature" of a mother's love for her children.[7] Even a visit to the Kuzminskys could not restore Sonya's spirits, but before the family left for Yasnaya in June she found an opiate that calmed her raging grief and changed it to a gentle melancholy. Sonya described this time in her autobiography:

> After the death of my little son Vanechka I was in the most extreme despair of any time of my life. Such a grief often kills people, but if they remain alive, then the heart is no longer in a condition to suffer so terribly a second time. I remained alive and owed this chance to a strange remedy—music. . . . I was not able to live without it.

Sonya not only became addicted to music but to a particular musician, Sergei Ivanovich Taneev, the composer and pianist with whom Lev had discussed his essay *On Art*.

During the spring of 1895 Taneev called frequently at the Moscow house and played for the Tolstoys, perhaps his way of expressing sympathy for their grief. His playing, particularly of his own work, affected Sonya profoundly. Her musical taste was more sophisticated than her husband's and Taneev's compositions, combining a strong romantic spirit with technical virtuosity, were innovative in Russia at the time. Taneev was a pupil and lifelong friend of Tchaikovsky—the two very different musicians submitted their works to one another for criticism—and his own pupils included Scriabin, Rachmaninoff and Glière. Very soon Sonya was confusing Taneev's considerable art with the man himself. As she admitted in her autobiography, she was in "an abnormal state."

> Sometimes I needed only to meet Sergei Ivanovich, to listen to his passionless, peaceful voice and I became peaceful.

Sonya did not have a nervous breakdown; that is, her entire personality did not collapse, but she lost her judgment. The good sense that normally set her right after periods of emotional stress deserted her. Eager for Taneev's presence as well as his music, she invited him to spend the summer at Yasnaya Polyana.

The invitation was readily accepted. Taneev was an ardent admirer of Tolstoy and pleased to know the family. His only request was that he be allowed to pay board. A sum of 125 rubles was agreed upon and on 3 June Taneev moved into the annex at Yasnaya. The annex was usually occupied in the summer by the Kuzminskys, but an unpleasant incident had occurred. Misha Kuzminsky seduced the nurse of one of the Tolstoy children and bragged of his exploit to the younger Tolstoy boys. The families agreed not to spend the summer together for a while.

Taneev brought to Yasnaya his upright piano and his old nurse, Pelageya, who still looked after him. Once settled in he followed a regular routine of composing, writing and practicing and he amused himself with the young Tolstoys. He was thirty-nine at the time, just seven years older than Sergei. He played tennis with the young people, cycled and even shared Italian lessons with Tanya and Masha. He took his meals with the family and in the evening played for them or enjoyed a game of chess with Lev. Sometimes he and Lev discussed art. Apart from his music Taneev was not a colorful person. Sergei described him as kind, intelligent, extremely conscientious, truthful but a man who was naive in everyday life. Taneev's diary was a precise record of details, scrupulously factual (he recorded verbatim his conversations with Lev), but he made no mention of his own feelings or opinions. This was deliberate. When he reread passages that contained more than a bare factual account he found it unpleasant to imagine himself stirred by feelings he no longer experienced. For this outwardly dry and unexciting man Sonya developed a girlish crush. Taneev seemed to be the only person who saw nothing abnormal in her excessive admiration. He always remained more interested in Lev; he chose to play piano works that were Lev's favorites and when Lev praised a work of Schumann's, Taneev learned the piece in order to play it for him. As for Lev's feelings about the musician, Sergei recalled that his father was very polite to Taneev but his politeness sometimes seemed forced. Sergei noticed that when his father played chess with Taneev Lev would ask someone to read aloud to him during the game. Was this a not very subtle insult to his opponent?

In the meantime Sonya followed Taneev about the house, waited for him on the terrace and listened to his playing with an expression of rapture. Lev's diary for the summer made no direct reference to Sonya's obsession but he could not have enjoyed what he later called a "repulsive situation." He was ill a good part of the summer and the repulsive situation may have been partly to blame. Sonya attributed his bad health to his vegetarian diet. She did not look at her interest in Taneev as disloyalty to her husband. She was not in love with him nor was she sexually attracted to him. There was never so much as an improper handshake between them. Her older children believed that her schoolgirlish behavior was an escape from her great grief for Vanechka. Sergei wrote in his memoir:

Music had a soothing effect on her nerves, distracting her from her grief, and at the time she transferred to Taneev the effect of the music he played.

Taneev departed at the end of August. On 23 September 1895, the Tolstoys' wedding anniversary, Lev noted without other comment, "Thirty years of married life." Actually, it was thirty-three. In October he wrote in his diary:

It has been bad with Sonya. Admittedly, I have been at fault.

Soon after this he came across Sonya writing a letter which she hid from him, saying that she would talk about it later. When she delivered the letter to Lev he was stunned by what he read. Sonya wrote:

Why do all your references to me in your diaries treat me as if I were evil? Why do you want all future generations and our grandchildren to abuse my name as a frivolous, evil wife who made you unhappy. . . . After the death of Vanechka (recalling "Papa, never hurt my Mama") you promised me then to cross out the unkind words in your diaries referring to me. You have not done this but the opposite.

Sonya quoted the following remarks from Lev's diaries that had hurt her:

Sonya came from Moscow. She intruded into my conversation with Boll, pushing herself in. She has begun to be even more frivolous since the death of V. I must bear my cross to the end. Lord help me, and so forth.

Sonya reminded Lev how the "frivolous" could be interpreted by readers who did not know her. She begged:

I cannot ask you to love me, but spare my name. . . . One more time I try to speak to your heart. I write with pain and tears. Forgive me.[8]

Lev was touched and ashamed. He admitted that when writing exasperated comments about Sonya he had felt "in the depths of my soul" that it was wrong and he wrote in his diary:

And, poor thing, she suffered terribly and, my darling, instead of being resentful she wrote me this letter. Never have I felt so guilty or been so moved. . . . Now, I repeat again for everyone who comes across these diaries: I am often irritated at her for her hasty, thoughtless disposition but, like Fet said, each husband gets the wife who is for him. I see how much she has been the wife that I must have. She has been ideal in the pagan sense, faithful, domestic, selfless, with a pagan love for the family and within her lies the possibility for Christian companionship. . . . What happened today was actually joyful for me. She saw and she sees the power of love, of her love upon me.[9]

Lev's tone was patronizing but Sonya's letter cleared the air temporarily. Taneev was not mentioned between them, although he could not have been forgotten. Sonya went to St. Petersburg for the opening of *The Powers of Darkness*, which had finally passed the censor for performance. If Lev was disturbed that she also went to the opening of Taneev's opera *Orestes,* he did not mention it in his diary. When Sonya was home again Lev noted that their relations were better than excellent.

Sonya soon departed once more, this time for Moscow on 24 October, and when Lev helped her into the carriage he was overwhelmed with pity and sympathy for her. He wrote in his diary with discernment:

She has only me to hold on to and, at the bottom of her heart, she fears that I do not love her as I could with all my heart and that the reason for this is that she cannot follow my way.

He then addressed Sonya directly:

Do not think like this. I love you more than ever, I understand you and I know that you cannot follow my way and because of this you remain alone. But you are not alone. I am with you, as you are, I love you and I love you limitlessly—one cannot love more.

The same day he wrote a letter to Sonya:

I wanted to write to you, darling friend, on the very day of your departure, under the fresh impression of such a strong feeling I experienced but here it is that a day and a half has passed and I am not writing until the 25th. The feeling I experienced was of a strange tenderness, pity and a completely new love for you, such a love that

I transferred myself entirely to you and felt the same that you were feeling. This is such a holy, good feeling that one ought not to speak of it but I know that you will be glad to hear about it and I know that my telling you does not change anything. On the contrary, even as I write to you, I have the same feeling. This feeling of ours is strange, like an evening glow. Only now and then the little clouds of your differences from me and mine from you diminish the brightness. I am always hoping that they will disperse before night and that the sunset will be bright and clear.

Sonya replied at once:

26 October 1895

Darling friend, Levochka,

. . . Those little clouds which, it seems to you, still sometimes darken our good relations are not entirely terrible. They are purely outward, the result of life, habit, the inertia to change, weakness; but they do not come at all from inner causes. Inwardly, the base of our relationship remains serious, firm and harmonious. We both know what is good and what is bad, and we both love one another. Thank God for that! . . . I am a little envious that you don't have upholsterers, printers, governesses, the noise of carriages, policemen and the expenditure of money from morning to night. It is difficult in this mess to remain contemplating God or in a peaceful and prayerful mood. I shall try to get out from this earthly crust and thus not be entirely submerged. But it is difficult.

Sonya reassured her husband of the firm basis of their love for one another. Did she also mean to reproach him or was it unwittingly that she reminded him of the tasks that she was facing without having her husband at her side? Only ten months had passed since Vanechka's death. Sonya was not only alone in Moscow but she went to bed each night beside the door to Vanechka's room where his bed and toys remained as when he was alive. She was deeply hurt that Lev had called her love for her child an animal love. She had read this in Lev's diary and referred to it years later when she wrote her autobiography. One offense recalls another; *The Kreutzer Sonata* was not long past. Submerged in the earthly crust of tedious tasks, reminded of her grief and her resentments and alone without her husband, she found comfort in listening to Taneev's music and, perhaps, in imagining that it was played for her.

3.

All through the winter Taneev was a faithful visitor to the Tolstoys' house in Moscow. Perhaps beneath his placid exterior he enjoyed receiving rapt attention and flattering admiration from the wife of Lev Tolstoy. Openly he never indicated any regard for Sonya other than that due a person whom he respected both in her own right and as the wife of a remarkable man, but those present when he and Sonya were together clearly saw her exaggerated response to him. When, with reckless lack of concern for Lev and for appearances, Sonya invited Taneev for a second summer visit Lev let his jealousy and rage break out in his diary:

> *28 May 1896.* . . . Taneev, who repulses me by his smug, moral and, ridiculous to say, aesthetic stupidity (genuine, not superficial) and his *coq au village* position in my house.

This summer the cock of the village left earlier, the first of August, and Lev's torment was somewhat eased. In his diary he called his relations with Sonya "both good and bad." When she returned to Moscow Lev wrote her long letters which revealed his fears and his desire to woo her from her disturbing friendship. Discussing their marriage, he wrote:

> The past binds us together and the children and the awareness that we have been guilty toward one another and pity and an irresistible attraction. In a word, it [their marriage] is well tied up and knotted tightly. And I am glad.

Lev's anxiety brought about that which Sonya's entreaties over the years had not achieved; he decided to spend all the winter in Moscow. There he struggled with his unfinished essay, *On Art*, and in November contemplated an idea for a novel that he thought at first was "very good."

> The infidelity of a wife toward her passionate, jealous husband, his suffering, struggle and the joy of forgiveness.

He did not follow up on this idea.

Sonya remained innocently transparent about her obsession. She attended all of Taneev's concerts and visited houses where she could expect to meet him. In December Lev noted:

Sonya had a strange need to be concerned. Just now she came to me with the question, should we not call on P. V.? [Taneev's old nurse, Pelageya.]

By the end of January 1897 Lev could bear it no longer and he left with his daughter Tanya to stay with the Olsufevs, aristocratic friends whose estate was near Moscow. Sonya's final affront had been her determination not only to go to Taneev's St. Petersburg concert but also to attend the rehearsal. Lev wrote to her from the Olsufevs' on 1 February 1897, forgetting grammar and punctuation and letting his hurt and anger tumble onto the page:

It is terribly painful and shamefully humiliating that a complete stranger directs our life, and a man who is unnecessary and in no sense interesting, he poisons the last years of our life, it is humiliating and tormenting that it is necessary for you to ask when and where he is going, when he is playing and at what rehearsals. It is terribly, terribly disgusting and shameful. . . . Suddenly, instead of a natural, good, happy conclusion to thirty-five years of life together, this disgusting filth turns up and stamps its horror on everything. I know that it weighs on you and that you, too, are suffering because you love me and want to be good, but now you are not able to and for me everything is disgusting and shameful and I have a terrible pity for you because I love you with a good love, not carnal and not rational, but a heartfelt love. Forgive me and good-bye, darling friend. I kiss you. L. T.

A week later Lev felt slightly better. He and Sonya were staying at the Olsufevs' apartment in St. Petersburg. They had come to say good-bye to Chertkov, who had been exiled to England. The exile was the government's response to a letter signed by Chertkov and two other Tolstoyans on the subject of the Dukhobors, a religious sect harassed by the government because of their refusal to perform military service.[10] Lev did not sign the letter but added a supporting postscript. The three signers were exiled (Chertkov, because of his aristocratic connections, was allowed to choose England as his place of banishment) but the government did not dare move against Tolstoy, although he was followed by the secret police throughout his stay in St. Petersburg. After a visit with Chertkov Lev noted in his diary:

> *7 February.* Went to see Chertkov. He is joyful. . . . The evening at home with Sonya. We are fine.

Sonya returned with Lev to the Olsufevs' and their relations did not remain fine. After several heated quarrels she left for Moscow. From there she wrote to Lev:

> 16 February 1897
>
> If I could have yesterday I would have left everything to write to you what I think about you and about our relations so that you would completely understand what is going on in my heart. But now that life has suddenly enveloped me on all sides with practical demands, I am neither able to recall or say anything and this letter will be only a piece of paper from me to you and not, I am sorry, my thoughts and feelings.
>
> I am glad that you admit that I live only through feeling. You treat everything in me with reason but I know well that in this matter I could not have hit upon reason— the heart set everything right.—First, you tortured me with your latest disagreeable remark that now when you have lost so many friends we must be as close as possible and try to make their absence less painful for you, I wrote the children very warmly about this. It was the only time in my life that the more warmth I carried in my heartfelt attitude toward you, the more you pushed me aside coldly and painfully. Your words were never particularly insulting, but I felt in all of them a hostile, reproving tone, there was such a spiteful, bitter taste which hit me exactly in my heart's tenderness and straight off chilled me. And how this grieved me!

Sonya wrote no more on the subject of their quarrels but asked about Lev's health and gave him the family news. She ended her letter

> Good-bye, darling friend. I kiss you. I am awaiting your letter. Sonya

Sonya posted her letter with some apprehension and decided to follow it up with a telephone call.[11] Their conversation on the telephone was not satisfactory and two days later Sonya wrote that she was always feeling guilty because he was so melancholy, that she had received two letters from him and was amazed that even her telephone call had upset him. "If again my letter hurts you," she wrote, "forgive me. I am writing as I always do, not from deliberation but from my feelings."

Lev could not forgive Sonya but he joined her in Moscow and in April jotted a brief line in a notebook: "The physical sensation of jealousy." At the same time he wrote in his diary:

> In jealousy there is a physical sensation, related to lust, but it is painful.

For some reason he crossed this sentence out. In May Lev left for Yasnaya and soon afterward Sonya surprised him by making an impulsive short visit. After she left he wrote to her:

> My waking up and seeing you before me was one of the most powerful and joyful impressions that I have ever received; and this to a man of sixty-nine from a woman of fifty-three.

A letter from Sonya saying that Taneev would pay them a visit in June killed Lev's joy. For three nights he was not able to sleep and was so emotionally exhausted that the slightest effort made him sob. His despair was the worse because he had no one to turn to for sympathy and understanding. Chertkov was in England and both Tanya and Masha had deserted their father for other men. Masha, the spiritual, sensitive, humorless, serious Masha, had outgrown her feelings for Posha and was transformed by passionate love for a cousin two years her junior, Prince Nikolai Obolensky. Kolya (Obolensky) was an aristocrat, handsome, charming, intelligent but impoverished, and by Lev and Sonya's standards he was indolent. Tanya's situation was even worse. She was in love with Mikhail Sukhotin, a married man (his wife would die that summer) and the father of six children. Sukhotin had the reputation, perhaps not deserved, of being a rake and the Tolstoys were appalled that Tanya had meetings with him in which they professed their love for one another. Tanya was not the person to appeal to about the sanctity of marriage and Masha was, to use her father's words, "like a person drunk" and "made worthless." [12]

Lev attempted another letter to "My dear, my darling Sonya." He begged her to break off all relations with Taneev and to free both of them from the horrible nightmare which had oppressed them for a year. He appealed to her:

Sonya, darling, you are a good, kind, fair-minded woman.
Put yourself in my position and try to understand.

He never sent the letter. Sonya came home and Taneev's visit turned out to be for only three days, during which Lev accompanied him and Sonya on a walk in the garden, cheerfully expounding his theories on art. Publicly Lev kept face, but privately his agony continued. After Taneev left, Lev wrote another long letter to Sonya, a letter which he planned for her to discover after he had left home. He wrote that he was leaving her and his family to devote himself to God as the Hindus did when they reached the age of sixty. He mentioned neither Taneev nor his jealousy in the letter and he praised Sonya as an ideal mother. He recalled with love and gratitude the thirty-five years of their life together and, although he admitted that their paths had now diverged, he said that he did not blame her for not following his way. He ended the letter, "Good-bye, my dear Sonya. Your affectionate Lev Tolstoy." Once again Lev threatened to leave home forever and once again he did not carry out his threat. The letter was found among his papers after his death.

On the day of Taneev's arrival for his brief visit, Sonya picked up her long-neglected diary to record a family event; Masha and Kolya had just returned from their wedding, a ceremony attended only by Misha Tolstoy and one of Kolya's brothers. Masha was able to marry the impoverished Kolya because she had asked for the return of her share of her father's estate, which at the time of the distribution she had renounced because of her Tolstoyan principles.

The Sonya who opened her diary in June 1897 to write about Masha's marriage was quite a different person from the Sonya who had closed it sadly in February 1895. Now her thoughts were darting here and there in willful abandon. In one paragraph she contemplated suicide and in the next she was elaborating on domestic trivialities. Her emotions were in a grab-bag and blindly she reached for love for Lev, anger at Lev, obsession for Taneev, concern for her family, pleasure in her children, disillusionment in her children. When she had an emotional outburst it was not followed by calmer insights. She gave up the kind of good reading that had once given her so much pleasure and was absorbed by trash.

A visitor left a copy of *Aphrodite*, the erotic novel by Pierre Louÿs, and Sonya read through it to the end.[13] She noted in her diary:

> How depraved the French are! But on the other hand, reading this book does give one a way in which to appraise the beauty of the female body, and of my own.

She began reading Marcel Prévost's *Les Demi-Vierges* and admitted in another diary entry:

> I felt ashamed and somehow sick, almost physically, which happens to me when I read filthy books. The absence of purity in love is so terrible.

Sonya criticized the book for "titillating," coming almost to the final act but stopping short. Nevertheless, she noted a few days later that she had finished reading *Les Demi-Vierges*.

Sonya confessed in her diary that she often had feelings of impatience, excitement, temper and that she was bored with her household tasks, making beds for guests and choosing the daily menu. Instead of deciding upon menus she would have liked to be listening to a difficult fugue or to a symphony. In moods of poetic melancholy she brought herself to tears composing pathetic suicide notes to her husband and children. Like a young girl who is infatuated for the first time, Sonya became sentimental about nature:

> A lovely sunset, a fiery ball in the sky with only one, small black cloud. . . . The moon is shining as brightly as though it were competing with the early dawn in June. . . . Nature exultant to the supreme degree, rich and brilliant, in order to prove to us that before her we are poor fools with our passions and sorrows.

Yes, Sonya was making a fool of herself over Taneev. She seemed to realize that this was so but argued that her feelings toward him were harmless:

> 5 June. . . . The only reason for breaking off all relations with Sergei Ivanovich is the demand of Lev Nikolaevich's jealousy; Lev Nikolaevich is suffering. I should also suffer if I broke off this relationship. I feel that there is so little sin and such peace and warmth and joy and purity in my attitude toward this man that in the depth of my heart I am no more able to destroy our friendship than I am able to stop seeing or thinking or breathing.

Sonya wrote coolly of her husband's suffering. She did not add that she, too, had been suffering for a long time, suffering from Lev's criticism of her way of life, from *The Kreutzer Sonata*, from her husband's intellectual and spiritual remoteness, from his lack of understanding of her grief for Vanechka. These hurts underlay Sonya's need for Taneev as much as her grief for Vanechka. She invented Taneev's friendship and attributed to him all the understanding that Lev lacked. Because Taneev's feelings for Sonya were a fantasy of her own making she could continue to feel innocent of blame. She recorded in her diary that she had asked the spirit of Vanechka if her feelings for Sergei Ivanovich were wicked feelings. Sonya may have experienced a twinge of the guilt she denied, because she wrote:

> Vanechka turned from him [Taneev]. It seems it is just that he pities his father. But I know that he cannot condemn me. It was he who sent Sergei Ivanovich to me and he would not want to take him from me.

When Taneev departed after his short visit Sonya was affectionate with her husband. "What a warm, feminine voice you have today," he told her as they got into bed. "I do not like it when you shout." Sonya wrote in her diary that the remark made her happy until she realized that Lev's tenderness was due to sexual passion, although she still accepted her share of the responsibility. Soon afterward she wrote of her desire to

> . . . choke up that crater which is always erupting and bursting out of the volcano of my ungovernable nature.[14]

Sonya's diary was cruel reading for Lev that summer:

> I am necessary to him [Lev] at night but not during the day and this makes me sad and against my will I wish for the company of my recent, dear comrade. . . . Today Sergei Ivanovich left. These days were happy and peaceful. Sergei Ivanovich played several times: The first time, the evening of the 10th, Lev Nikolaevich had gone for a walk with Tanya to talk about Sukhotin and I asked Sergei Ivanovich to play Mozart's sonata for me. We were alone in the room, it was serene and happy. . . . There is something in him [Taneev] that everyone loves. . . . I think of him peacefully. It is always like this after seeing him. . . . In the evening I put in order and copied Lev Nikolae-

vich's article on art. Now I am entirely at his service and he is calm and happy. Again he takes up all my life. Does this make me happy? Alas, no, I do what I should and in that there is a share of happiness but often and sadly I pine for other things.

Sonya described Taneev as "calm, noble and kind." With complete disregard for Lev's feelings she recounted a dream:

Yesterday I saw Vanechka in a dream. He was lying down, his thin, pale arms stretching toward me. Today I dreamed of Sergei Ivanovich, smiling and also stretching his arms to me.

She described another dream, in which she was sleeping and was awakened by Taneev who entered her room and made many little notes on pieces of paper which he then crunched and threw onto the floor. When he left, Sonya leapt from bed to retrieve the papers and discover his thoughts but a knock on the door awakened Sonya from her dream and she wrote sadly that now she would never know Sergei Ivanovich's thoughts.

The older Tolstoy children suffered from their mother's behavior. In July 1897 Sonya wrote in her diary:

Masha told me that Ilya is very distressed because at my sister Tanya's in Kiev and at the Filisovs' [Ilya's in-laws] everyone talks of my affection for Sergei Ivanovich. How strangely public opinion becomes fixed! As though to *love* were wicked. But I am neither grieved nor embarrassed by any of this. I even feel glad and proud that my name is linked with one who is such an excellent, moral, kind and talented man.

A few days later Sergei commented in front of his mother, "Mama has fallen back into childhood. Very well, I shall give her a doll and a china tea set." [15] Sonya refused to be amused when she copied the remark into her diary:

His words were funny but my falling into childhood is not funny but very tragic. . . . They find fault with me because of Sergei Ivanovich. Let them! This man has given me such richness and joyfulness in my life—he opened the doors of the musical world for me. . . . And they all think that I am in love! How all of them have become vulgar! I am already an old woman and such words and thoughts are absurd.

Thirteen-year-old Sasha remained silent about her mother's friendship but she also suffered. For a second time she felt herself eased out of her mother's affections: The first time it had been for Vanechka, this time it was for Taneev. Since Vanechka had died, Sasha's only companion at home was her mother. Now when Sergei Ivanovich called at the Moscow house Sonya sent Sasha to her room. Sasha's temper tantrums became worse (she was known among the servants as impossible and prospective governesses turned down the position because of her reputation) but neither Lev nor Sonya took the pains to find the cause of Sasha's anger. Both were too caught up in their own difficult relations.

4.

Lev and Sonya could ignore Sasha's suffering because Sasha herself did not discuss it. It was a different matter when Tanya confessed that she had met Sukhotin (now a widower) at his hotel in Tula and taken a train trip with him. The Tolstoys were temporarily united in their dismay. This shock to their moral sense was followed by worry over Masha, who had come home for an August visit and soon after fallen ill with typhoid. Sonya took charge of the nursing and Lev, in his clumsy way, tried to help. When Sonya was making a poultice he volunteered to warm the napkins over a candle and managed to set his beard on fire. Sonya quickly put out the flame with her bare hands, a courageous act that made her husband furious.

A nurse was hired to care for Masha during her convalescence and in September Masha was sufficiently recovered that Sonya felt free to keep an appointment with a dentist in Moscow. To her chagrin she was getting false teeth, but preferred all the problems of adjustment to going almost toothless as her husband had done for all of their marriage. The first set of false teeth did not fit and Sonya made another trip to the dentist in October. During both of her stays in the Moscow house Taneev was among her visitors. Sonya's blinders where Taneev was concerned were finally coming loose and on 10 October she made a diary note:

Somehow there remains a dissatisfaction in our relations, even estrangement. I was not happy with him but unnatural and for a moment it was even painful. Was it because I had received a very kind letter from Lev Nikolaevich and my heart was carried away with thoughts of him and Yasnaya Polyana, or did my conscience torment me that the interference of Sergei Ivanovich into my life not only caused pain but perhaps even now still grieves Lev Nikolaevich?

But Sonya added a remark that showed how much her friendship for Taneev was a protest directed at her husband:

I still brave Lev Nikolaevich's displeasure and do not want to give up my freedom of action and emotion as long as I am not feeling guilty.

By November Sonya was settled in the Moscow house for the winter and waiting for Lev to keep his promise to join her. Lev kept postponing his time of arrival; he was contented alone in the country and even considering ideas for a novel. During the summer of 1896 he had been thinking about a Caucasian leader, Hadji Murat, an actual man whose story survived in legends. Lev experienced a sudden desire to write a novel about Hadji Murat and from that time his notebooks and diaries had jottings to remind him of ideas that came to him for the book. In October 1897 he noted:

14 October. . . . For H[adji] M[urat]: 1. On the mountain slope the shadow of an eagle flying 2. The tracks of wild beasts, horses and people on the sand by the river 3. The horses entering the forest, snorting cheerfully 4. A goat jumping out from a thicket.

A month later he wrote that he had been thinking a lot about Hadji Murat and had prepared some material. He added that it would be an effort to return to Moscow. Finally, on 25 November, Sonya ended a letter on a threatening note:

Well, good-bye now. I am not going to wait for you any longer. Making a sincere effort is becoming intolerable to me. I shall attend as many evening concerts as possible. I begin to love this solitude in a crowd very much, listening to music. It is good for my health and happiness.

S. Tolstoy

Her letter annoyed Lev but he packed himself for the winter and arrived at Moscow on 5 December. Sonya was not at home. Tanya explained that her mother had once more become jealous of the publisher of *The Northern Messenger*. Tanya had casually mentioned an article that Lev had sent the periodical and Sonya took umbrage and fled to the Trinity Monastery outside of Moscow where she stayed at the guest house. She told Tanya that she would remain there until Lev was home and a telegram summoned her. Lev wired at once:

> I want to come but feel too weak. Please come today.
> There is no reason for suffering. Reply.

Sonya's reply was to hurry to the station and take the first train to Moscow. Lev met her at the front door in tears and they threw themselves weeping into one another's arms. In the warm conversation that followed, Lev agreed not to publish the article in *The Northern Messenger* and Sonya promised not to see Taneev except by accident or in the normal course of events. Sonya added to her promise that she wanted to do her duty by her husband and to do everything for his happiness and peace of mind. That night she wrote cheerfully in her diary:

> We talked beautifully and it was easy for me to promise
> him everything and I loved him so strongly and dearly
> and I am ready to go on loving him.

Sonya kept the letter of her promise if not the spirit. She did not count attending Taneev's concerts as seeing him intentionally— ostensibly she went to them for the music, and she considered an occasional call on a "friend" as in the normal course of events. Lev stopped filling his diaries and notebooks with painful jealousy. His hurt went underground and emerged in a petty, carping misogyny. Snide remarks about women appeared regularly in his diary. He did not make any open connection between these remarks about the opposite sex and his tormenting experience of jealousy.

The jealousy exploded one more time. In July 1898 Sonya visited the Kuzminskys in Kiev and persuaded her sister to return with her to Yasnaya. Lev was delighted to have "darling Tanya Kuzminsky" with them once again. Tanya tried to be peacemaker during her visit. She talked to Lev about Sonya's attitude toward Taneev and insisted that it was no more than an innocent need for the comfort of music. To Sonya Tanya spoke in a different manner, scolding her and telling her that her behavior was scandalous. After Tanya left, the Tolstoys had a long and fruitless conversation which Lev wrote down in detail in his diary and titled "A Dialogue."

The conversation began when they had gone to bed for the night and Lev asked Sonya to admit that her feelings for Taneev were wicked and a sin against her husband. Sonya insisted that she had no feelings whatsoever for Taneev as a man and if she had any feeling toward him as a person it was so small that it was not worth considering. Lev stubbornly insisted that the feeling was not small and that she must face the sin of it. Sonya denied any sin but added, "I am sorry to have hurt you and I do repent of that."

This was not enough for Lev. Another man had exerted a spell on Sonya, a spell that had made her oblivious to his agonizing jealousy, and Lev believed that the only way to extirpate his jealousy with its acute physical sensation was for Sonya to open her eyes, see that she was sinning in word and act and remove her sin. To Sonya her peccadillo seemed so small that she thought it an unnecessary surrender to call it a sin. Alas, the very smallness of the sin now made it more painful for Lev. If Sonya could not do something so small as to give up Taneev's concerts for her husband's sake, how could he believe that she had no feeling for Taneev? Sonya wearily accused Lev of repeating the same thing over and over again; Lev accused her of being "one of those women who never miss a concert." His sneering tone hurt and Sonya began to weep. In the end, she cried hysterically and finally began to laugh and beg him to cut her throat. Lev calmed her by holding her hands and kissing her forehead. She finally became quiet and after several long sighs she fell asleep in his arms. The next day Lev wrote in his diary that he saw no way out of their absurd, shameful and sad situation. Sonya was actually physically ill after their quarrel. She stayed in bed and would not eat. She described in her diary how she had lost all ability to feel or take an interest in life. When she inadvertently knocked over Lev's photograph, which stood on her bedside table, she told herself that she had knocked him off the pedestal that he had occupied for so much of her life.

When it came to digesting such confrontations both Lev and Sonya had strong stomachs. A few weeks later Sonya was well and tranquility reigned at Yasnaya Polyana. Guests were arriving nearly every week. By 1898 four of the children were married and came home with their spouses. In July 1895 Sergei had married Maria (Manya) Rachinsky, the daughter of an academician, and young Lev was married the following May to Dora Westerlund, the daughter of a Swedish physician. In August family and friends gathered to celebrate Lev's seventieth birthday and Sonya's fifty-fourth. On the Tolstoys' wedding anniversary Sonya was in Moscow putting the younger boys in school. She wrote in her diary:

> Thirty-six years I have been married to Lev Nikolaevich and today we are apart. It is sad that we are not always together, how I should have liked it. And how much on my part I have strived for spiritual unity! The bond between us is solid but not on the basis that I would like. I do not complain, it is good as it is, it is good that he takes such care of me, that he guards me so jealously, that he is so afraid of losing me. His fear is for nothing. Whomever I might like there is no one on earth I could even *compare* with my husband. All of my life he has occupied too great a place in my heart.

Sonya had recovered from the worst of her foolishness without having anyone with whom to discuss her situation objectively. Her sister had scolded her but not urged her to take a holiday, a rest cure or have a change of scene. Sonya had had to invent her own opiate, her fantasy friendship, that both assuaged her grief for Vanechka and settled some old scores with Lev. The fantasy had alleviated her hurts without curing them entirely. Only one person had come near to understanding her emotional problems. Lev had written in his diary:

> She has only me to hold on to and at the bottom of her heart she fears that I do not love her as I could with all my heart and that the reason for this is that she cannot follow my way.

He had tried to reassure her:

> I am with you, as you are, I love you and I love you limitlessly.

But Lev could not be both the problem and the counselor. He understood Sonya in his moments of insight because he was sympathetic, sensitive and loved her. At the same time he resented her for reasons that he did not understand himself. What his love and understanding gave, his resentment would often take away.

After the Taneev crisis Lev tried to be more thoughtful of his wife. During an evening when the house was full of guests Sonya called to him to come and sit with her. "No," Lev replied shortly, "I want to be alone and to read." As soon as he had spoken, Lev saw that there was something wrong with his answer and he tried to make amends. Another time he met Sonya at the Moscow station (she had been to Yasnaya on estate affairs) and expressed satisfaction that she was home because he was ready to leave to visit the Olsufevs. Sonya replied tearfully, "What I should like is for us to stay home together." Lev canceled his visit and remained at home.

Sonya also was more careful and tactful and did not rave so often about music stirring her emotions. And she began to see that most of Taneev's virtues were her own invention. Years later she wrote about him in her autobiography:

> He was outwardly of little interest, always very flat, extremely reserved and, up to the end, a man completely incomprehensible to me.

But Sonya continued to attend concerts and was usually there when Taneev played. She found the kind of relaxation in music that some find in alcohol, drugs or mindless shopping. Finally even Taneev saw that there was something excessive about the amount of time that Countess Tolstoy spent at his concerts. If he happened to run into her he showed a marked coolness. This worried Sonya. Although she had separated her admiration for his music from the man himself, she wanted to keep at least the pretense of a friendship, perhaps as emotional ballast in her relationship with her husband. She wrote Sergei Ivanovich a letter which he referred to in his diary as "absurd" and apparently destroyed. He replied in a brief note that was even more distant than his manner. This was in 1904. Sonya did not mention Taneev in her diary that year but seemed to survive his rebuff without trauma. Perhaps her need for even the pretense of a friendship was less than she had thought. Her manner to Taneev after his note must have reassured him as he continued his visits to the Tolstoys. In 1905 he even asked for Sonya's help in writing to the head of the Conservatory and she noted in her engagement diary that they had spent two hours working on the letter.[16] (Beginning in 1905 Sonya kept a second diary in her engagement calendar in which she made notes more regularly but less extensively than in her diary.)

In 1907 Sonya was copying her husband's journals for the years 1895–1897 and this revived for her the period of her infatuation. Sonya noted:

What terrible recollections! There was nobody, except a strange, sick and hysterical lady.

Sonya usually referred to herself as a "woman" and it would seem that the "hysterical lady" was the only visitor that day. It could be, however, that Sonya was referring to herself. Lev's diary lists the visitors for the period and they were all men. Perhaps Sonya, after her terrible recollections, meant to say that there was no important "friendship" with Taneev, nobody else in her life but her husband, and that looking at herself at the time she sees a sick, hysterical person, a person now strange to her.

Chapter Eight

THE EVENING GLOW,
1898–1908

1.

In November 1898 Sonya wrote in her diary:

> I talked a lot with Levochka. About Misha, about me and
> about L. N.'s work. He said that not since the time of
> *War and Peace* has he been in such a creative mood and
> so contented with his work as he is with *Resurrection*.

Lev was writing a novel, *Resurrection*, to raise money for the
Dukhobors' emigration to Canada.[1] He had decided to compromise
his principles and to accept money for the book and it was hard
for Sonya to understand that he could earn money to give away
to strangers but not for his own children, particularly Ilya and
Masha who had less than the others. When the advance went entirely to the Dukhobors she complained to her diary:

> It is his *right*, and not mine, although it is a strange thing
> in any family that after thirty-six years of living together
> we must talk about *rights*. His children will be impover-
> ished. He did not educate them to work.

Sonya would always see Lev's generous gesture to the Dukhobors
as an unjustified betrayal of his family. Complaints, however, were
no longer the rule of her diary and more often than not her references to her husband were happy ones:

> Very friendly with Lev Nikolaevich. How I simply love
> it without fear on my side, without fault-finding and ulte-

rior motives on his side. . . . He [Lev] is relaxed and good willing. . . . Today we had a warm conversation. . . . We are happy together, without reproaches.

It was not in the nature of the sensitive and volatile Tolstoys to live together without reproaches but the bad feelings were less often and less bitter. The mood at home was a happy mood, like the "evening glow" that Lev had hoped for, the glow preceding the sunset that would be "bright and clear." When Sonya was about to join Lev in Yasnaya for Christmas, she wrote to him that

I never stop thinking of you, of how you are, if you are well, of how I shall soon be glad because I'll be with you.

Domesticity was filling Sonya's diary—family evenings when Lev read aloud, entertaining fourteen-year-old Sasha's young friends, the Tolstoys' many visitors, the spring cleaning at Yasnaya and the planting of the oats, shopping in Moscow for the grandchildren and enjoying the grandchildren's visits. "How I love it!" she exclaimed when there were grandchildren at home. Once when the grandchildren left, Lev admitted, "It is sad without children. Just now we had two perambulators but now there are none." (In 1898 Ilya had four children and Sergei and Lev one child each. Sergei was now unmarried; Manya had died a few years after the birth of their son. Before her death she had separated from Sergei.)

A family wedding took place in January 1899. Twenty-two-year-old Andrusha married Olga Diterikhs, a sister of Chertkov's wife and eight years Andrusha's senior. The Tolstoys were not enthusiastic about the match. Sonya described Andrusha at his wedding:

As if in a dream, very moved but not understanding why he is marrying and how it will be afterward. I still don't comprehend Olga.

But the marriage did not upset the Tolstoys unduly and the same month Lev noted in his diary:

I am living happily with Sonya. I am senilely tranquil.

Lev certainly smiled when he called his emotional peace senility; every day he was writing he proved that his intellectual powers and artistic skills were unimpaired. To be able to publish quickly because of the Dukhobors' need, Lev had turned to works that had been projected during the last six to ten years. In 1898 he finished *Father Sergius*, a short story about a worldly, egotistical man who repented of his selfishness, became a monk and resisted sexual temptation from a beautiful woman but finally sinned with a homely, retarded peasant girl. Originally this was to be a story like *The Kreutzer Sonata*, illustrating the evil of sexual passion, but in this case Lev's literary genius outweighed his message.

Once this short tale was out of the way, Lev concentrated on *Resurrection*, the plot of which came from a true legal case described to Lev by the jurist Koni. Lev's hero was Nekhuldov, a prince who had seduced and abandoned a peasant woman, Katyusha. Katyusha became pregnant and, because of her condition, was evicted from the household where she lived and worked. The baby died soon after birth and Katyusha earned her living as a prostitute. When Katyusha was accused of theft by a client, Nekhuldov sat on the jury trying her case and he recognized the woman he had deserted. This confrontation with his past was a confrontation with his conscience and the beginning of a new life. In the actual case the prince married the convicted woman, who died of typhus just after completing her sentence. Although true, Lev thought this ending unconvincing and for some time he debated Katyusha's fate. Finally, he decided that if a game of Patience came out, then his hero and heroine would marry. When the game did come out, Lev told his daughter Tanya, "The snag is that Katyusha can't marry Nekhuldov." Lev reminded Tanya of what Pushkin had said of the heroine of *Eugene Onegin*: "Do you know, that Tatyana of mine has shown Eugene the door? I simply would not have believed her capable of such a thing." [2]

Lev told Sonya that Katyusha and Nekhuldov would not marry and she replied, "Of course they won't marry. I have been telling you all along that it would be false if he married her." [3] Sonya respected the truth of Lev's story but she did not like *Resurrection* at first. She wrote in her diary, "It is an odious story. Perhaps he will make it better." The seduction of Katyusha reminded Sonya of the peasant women whom Lev had seduced in his bachelor days. She preferred *The Story of a Mother* and in November wrote about this projected novel:

> L. N. sent me a fragment from his beautiful, well-thought-out story, *The Story of a Mother*. The subject is that of a mother with eight children, a beautiful, tender, considerate mother who is alone in her old age and lives . . . with the dramatic awareness that all of her life has been

wasted on her children. Not only is she not happy with them, but they themselves are unhappy.

Perhaps Lev was never able to finish *The Story of a Mother* because once again he was writing a novel with a message that was more important than his artistic sincerity. But this time the message for Sonya, unlike the message in *The Kreutzer Sonata*, was positive and kind.

Sonya's confidence in her marriage faltered now only when she felt neglected by her husband and then she did complain:

> He does not talk to me anymore about his writing, his thoughts, he takes less and less part in my life. . . . No one is so lonely as I. In the morning alone, dining alone, in the evening alone. Against my will I go to concerts and wander among people who at least talk to me seriously.

When Lev was preoccupied and distant Sonya found solace in concerts and in Taneev's visits to the Moscow house. The musician had not let his Tolstoy connection drop but Sonya could observe that when he came Lev was less upset and sometimes even friendly. It was Sonya who, a year later, became annoyed when Sergei Ivanovich turned down her request to play for a benefit on the grounds that he did not have time to practice. She wrote in her diary:

> He was, as always, egotistical, logical and thoroughly correct in his reasons.

Much of Sonya's life was spent worrying about Lev's health, fussing over his stomach troubles and making poultices for his sore back. She noted wistfully that he was thin and showed signs of aging. It was Sonya, however, who was the first to be seriously ill. She fainted at a symphony concert and that night her fever was so high that Lev ran for the doctor at three in the morning. Sonya had influenza complicated by a lung infection. When she was well enough to write in her diary she described her pleasure that Lev worried about her, took care of her, and that Sasha was solicitous and pampered her. Lev's comment on Sonya's illness was written when they returned to Yasnaya for the summer:

> She was very sick and even now she is weak. It is still the time of her critical period.

It seemed that Lev could believe that Sonya's time of life, her critical period, was a contributing factor in influenza and threatened pneumonia.

All summer Lev worked steadily on *Resurrection,* sometimes writing for seven hours without interruption. Sonya often remarked on his concentration:

> He is always working on *Resurrection.* . . . [Lev] had a visit from . . . the superintendent of the Butirky Prison, who gave him a lot of instruction on the technical part of prison affairs, the prisoners, their lives and so on—all this for *Resurrection.* . . . We never see him. The cook catches him for a minute when he takes the Count his meals.

In December 1899 Lev completed the last chapter and briefly noted that the work was finished, "not good, not corrected, rushed"— but that it was done and no longer interested him.

Resurrection is not a vast novel (it is one-third the length of *War and Peace*) but it is still a masterpiece. This is so in spite of the central characters, who never totally enter the reader's life and remain there in the manner of Natasha, Pierre, Andrei, Anna, Vronsky, Levin, Kitty or even Karenin. Perhaps this was how Tolstoy wanted it to be; perhaps he saw his characters as incidental to his theme and the real protagonist of *Resurrection* is our flawed and unjust society.

Before *Resurrection* was finished, the final episode in Tanya's romance with Sukhotin again dismayed the Tolstoys. In October Sonya wrote in her diary:

> *4 October.* Tanya's birthday, she set off yesterday for Moscow, to where Sukhotin has gone, and again she wants to decide once and for all—to marry him or not to marry him. Poor thing! She has lived for thirty-five years, brilliant, wise, beloved by all, talented and gay—and she has not found happiness.

A week later Tanya wrote home that she was peaceful and happy and had put herself into good hands. Sonya noted bleakly that this meant that Tanya was going to marry Sukhotin. The wedding took place on 14 November in a funereal atmosphere. Lev and Sonya sobbed. The next day Tanya left with her husband for Italy. The Sukhotins would live abroad for part of each year and spend the rest of their time at Kochety, an estate near Yasnaya. Lev decided that Tanya's "irrational" behavior was simply more evidence of the essential baseness of women. He groaned in his diary:

> Tanya has left. I do not know why. With Sukhotin. It is
> terrible and insulting. I am seventy years old and always
> my opinion of women is lowered and lowered and I must
> again and again lower it further. The feminine question!
> How not to have a feminine question! It is not only that
> women have begun to direct life, but that they continue
> to ruin it.

Sonya wrote in her diary that Tanya's marriage was a heartbreak shared with Lev and that their grief had brought them close to one another as had their grief for Vanechka. On 31 December she noted, "The last day of the year! What will the new one bring?" The old year had already brought acceptance of Andrusha's marriage. He and Olga were living at Yasnaya and Sonya was worrying that Andrusha was "rude and despotic" to Olga, who was five months pregnant. Sonya felt that Andrusha was not himself because of liver trouble and that "his poor wife suffers from his unhappy liver." No matter what the initial aversion, the Tolstoys absorbed in-laws with remarkable speed. Kolya was now treated like another son and he assumed the family chores, copying manuscripts and taking dictation from Lev. But Tanya was a different matter. She had waited so long to marry that her mother and father had assumed she would always be there for themselves. Now Lev sneeringly and cruelly referred to the idea of a "thirty-five-year-old virgin" marrying. Even so, when the Sukhotins came for a visit in March the usual magic worked. Lev wrote in his diary:

> Tanya has arrived, contented, happy. And I am glad for
> her and with her.

Very soon Lev was happily playing chess with Mikhail Sukhotin. Not only was Tanya's husband embraced as a member of the family but so were his six children by his former marriage. Within a year Sonya had invited Misha Sukhotin, a school boy Sasha's age, to live with the Tolstoys.

Meanwhile, the first editions of *Resurrection* sold out at once in France, Germany, England, the United States and Japan. In Japan *Resurrection* was a greater success than any other Tolstoy work and a popular Japanese song in 1900 was called "Katyusha." In Russia the censor made nearly five hundred cuts; other countries also censored the novel where they found offensive remarks about sexual desire, the church, or the ownership of private property and the distribution of wealth. On the contrary, the French magazine *Illustration* invented passages when its readers complained that there were not enough love scenes.

1899 had ended with the pseudotragedy of Tanya's marriage; real sorrow was the Tolstoys' lot at the end of 1900. The young Lev's little son died the day before Christmas. Sonya went at once to Yasnaya to comfort the parents and then on to stay at Kochety with Tanya, who had given birth to a stillborn baby. On 3 January she returned to Moscow and wrote in her diary:

> Sasha and L. N. and all the servants were very glad to see me and it was good to be peacefully at home.

2.

Life was not peaceful for long. In January 1901 the Tolstoys' son Misha married his childhood sweetheart, Aleksandra Glebov. Sonya wrote in her diary that

> It was a very splendid, fashionable wedding. Grand Duke Sergei Aleksandrovich came from Petersburg for one day just for the wedding.

The wedding was barely over when the Holy Synod of the Russian Orthodox Church took a step against Lev that caused an international commotion: Ecclesiastical Registration No. 8, the excommunication of Lev Tolstoy, was published in all Russian newspapers. The chief architect of the excommunication was Konstantin Pobedonostsev, the powerful procurator (counsel) of the Holy Synod.[4] Pobedonostsev was a staunch believer in an autocratic monarchy and in his opinion Tolstoy's social and religious views, his pacificism and his outspoken support for oppressed peoples within Russia were a threat to the state. The decree read in part:

> Count Tolstoy, tempted by his proud intellect, has insolently rebelled against the Lord and his Christ and his holy property.. . . He has devoted his literary talent, given to him by God, to spreading among the people teachings contrary to Christ and the church.

The Holy Synod forbade the performance of any rites for Count Tolstoy so long as he was unrepentant. The public reaction was not what the synod had expected. Protesting crowds gathered in Kiev, St. Petersburg and Moscow. Lev was recognized on his afternoon walk and someone laughed and shouted, "There is the devil incarnate himself!" At once Lev was surrounded by a laughing, cheering crowd and forced to return home in a taxi. Sonya wrote an immediate protest to the metropolitans which was released to the press and published all over the world. On 6 March she pasted a newspaper clipping of the excommunication in her diary and wrote after it:

> They have given Lev Nikolaevich an ovation for three days running. They bring baskets with fresh flowers, send telegrams, letters and addresses. All the time, the expression of sympathy for Lev Nikolaevich continues and toward the synod and the metropolitans there is indignation.

On 26 March Lev sent his unrepentant reply, addressed not to the synod but to the "Czar and his Advisors." [5] Sonya remarked dryly, "What will come of this? I should not want us to be exiled from Russia in our old age." There was no danger of this; the synod, and the government that had backed it, knew that the excommunication had been an error, as worldwide it was being treated as a kind of honor. Aleksandra Tolstoy quotes, without naming the author, from one of the few letters that did not support Lev. It was addressed to "the beastlike Lev in human skin, offspring of hell, spirit of darkness, old fool," and prayed that henceforth Lev might be anathema and damned.

The mail and attention continued after the family returned to Yasnaya for the summer but Lev showed no further interest in his excommunication. He wrote in his diary:

> I am alone with Sonya. I am fine.

A month later Sonya exclaimed in her journal:

> My God, what a happy summer!

Her only worry was her husband's health; she noted in her diary that his face was pinched, his beard entirely white, he was thin and his digestion so poor that he could not eat as he should. In July while Sonya was attaching a compress to his stomach, Lev suddenly looked at her intently and then burst into tears. "Thank you, Sonya," he said. "Never think that I am not grateful to you and don't love you." That night Sonya wrote in her diary:

> And his voice broke from tears and I kissed his dear hands, so familiar to me, and told him that I wanted happiness for him, that I always felt myself guilty toward him if I did not give him enough happiness, that he must forgive me for what I was not able to give him and, both of us in tears, we embraced one another and it was something that I had wished for in my heart for a long time; it was a warm, profound admission of our close relationship through all of the thirty-nine years of our life together— everything that had temporarily disturbed us was somehow an outward delusion and had never changed the strong inner bonds of the beautiful love between us.

Lev and Sonya did not speak the words but clearly they were both aware that their life together could not be forever. The next day Lev told Sonya, "I am now at a crossroad. Ahead of me is a good death and behind me a good life. If I continue now it is only a postponement."

"A good death" was very much on Lev's mind. Years before, Turgenev, during a visit to Yasnaya, had suggested that everyone who was afraid of death put up his hand. Of all the people present Lev had been the only one other than Turgenev to raise his hand. The terror of Arsamas had been death. Death was the inevitable black void before which fame and genius and happiness were helpless. The only comfort that Lev had ever found against the black void was to embrace it. Pathetically he had tried to thank God for Vanechka's death, to believe that it was beautiful and God's will. Now, in his seventies, he tried to face and embrace the black void for himself. Death would be good and was not to be feared. But the fear Lev tried to deny was there and it became more and more necessary for him to reassure himself that he welcomed the final event of life.

Sonya did not even try to reconcile herself to the idea of losing her husband. She wrote in her diary:

> Now my Levochka is sleeping. He is still alive, I am able to see him, listen to him, hover over him—but what will happen next? My God, what an unbearable, horrible grief life without him would be; without his constant support

and love, the stimulation of his mind and, best of all, his interest in life.

Lev's doctor was often at Yasnaya throughout the summer. He found that Lev had a weak heart and malaria. On 14 July Sonya wrote that the doctor

> . . . prescribed quinine and suggested injections of arsenic which, I regret, he [Lev] stubbornly refuses. Right now he is very thin and weak but his appetite is excellent, he also is sleeping well, is not in pain and every morning is busy working on his article. [*The Only Means*, an attempt to show that through religion, workers could improve their position. Lev decided that his arguments were weak.] . . . Thank God, thank God, it [Lev's death] is postponed further! Just so we can live together longer! For the first time I clearly felt the possibility of separation from my beloved husband and I was seized with heart sickness. I could hardly go on if he were to die.

Masha, Kolya, young Lev and Dora came for the summer. Andrusha and Olga lived at Yasnaya with their new daughter, Sonya. When Lev was too weak to write he dictated to his daughters or to Kolya, most often to Masha. Many of Lev's diary entries concerned religion and morals but he was still obsessed with the question of women. He dictated to Masha:

> Only husbands know their wives. [The next statement, "when it is too late," was crossed out.] Only husbands see them from behind the scenes. That is why Lessing said that each husband declares that there is only one bad woman and it is his wife.[6] In front of others they [women] skillfully pretend and so artfully that no one sees them as they are, especially when they are young.

Lev dictated these words to a daughter whom he loved, soon after his tender moment with Sonya when, weeping, he thanked her for her care. Lev apparently deceived himself that he could keep his running rage against womankind separate from his feelings about the women in his family. If Sonya, who had lived with the rage for many years, read this entry she hardly felt a similar detachment, but at the time her concern was Lev's health. On 22 July she wrote:

> Lev Nikolaevich is getting well, he takes long walks in the woods, his appetite is excellent, also he sleeps well,

thank God. Yesterday evening we received the mail from
Tula and Kolya Obolensky read the letters aloud. [Lev's
illness had attracted worldwide sympathy.] All the letters
were sympathetic, rejoicing that L. N. had recovered. He
listened, then began to laugh and said, "Now if I start
to die, I must surely die without fail, it must not be fooling.
Yes, it would be a shame to go through this again from
the beginning. Everyone would swallow it as true, the
correspondents would come, letters, telegrams and suddenly, again it is for nothing. No, that would certainly
be indecent."

Sonya remarked that old age must be a dull business and that
she hoped that she would die quickly:

But L. N. suddenly came to life, as though bursting out
of himself, and protested warmly, "No, one must live,
life is so beautiful." This vitality at seventy-three years
is beautiful and it saves him and me.

Lev recovered from the malaria but his heart remained weak
and the doctors worried about his spending the winter in the north.
On 30 July Sonya noted in her diary:

I received a letter from Countess Panin [a wealthy woman
noted for her work among the poor in St. Petersburg]
offering us her dacha in Gaspra in the Crimea, and we
are going there but I do not want to go before September.

Lev's half-recovery—he was no longer sick enough to demand solicitous care nor was he well enough to live as usual—left Sonya
restless. She worried about leaving their normal activities for so
long a time as winter in the south:

L. N. and I have lived together one broad stretch of life—
thirty-nine years. And now begin changes: we shall go
together to the Crimea. L. N. is growing weaker and despondent although, it is true that he keeps to his regular
schedule: in the morning he writes, walks a little in the
garden or the nearby wood, sits with me in the evening.
Will this go on for long? And what will my life be made
up of? No one can foretell, I know. Thy will be done,
Lord.

Departure was set for 5 September and just before that time
Sonya went to Moscow on errands. While her mother was away,

Masha seized an opportunity to reinstate herself as a devout Tolstoyan in her father's eyes. Until she had fallen in love with Kolya
Masha had been a faithful follower of her father's principles even
to the point of renouncing her share of his estate in favor of poverty.
It must have been a difficult moment for Masha when, in order
to marry Kolya, she asked for the return of her portion—and humiliating as well, because she discovered that her mother had never
taken her renunciation seriously. Instead of dividing Masha's share
among the others, Sonya kept it in trust for Masha and even added
a codicil to her own will ensuring that this portion would go to
Masha in the event that she had not asked for it before her mother's
death.[7]

Now Masha presented her father with a paper of several pages
that she had copied from his 1895 diary, in which Lev had stated
his requests to his family concerning his death and burial. In this
diary Lev asked for the cheapest coffin possible, no service unless
that were disagreeable to his family and in that case the simplest
service possible, no obituaries or speeches and no notices to the
newspapers. He asked that his papers go to Sonya, Chertkov and
Strakhov and he left instructions for their disposal. It was the
final request that interested Masha; Lev begged his heirs to give
all his copyrights to the public but he stressed that this was his
"wish" and not a "demand." Masha now urged that he sign her
papers to give his wishes the status of a will. She was naive if
she believed that his signature could change the sense of the text,
but Masha's motive was to make another renunciation in front
of her father. When he was reluctant to sign even such a harmless
document Masha assured him that if he did not sign her paper
his heirs would earn money from his works. Lev gave in to her
demand.

When Sonya returned from Moscow she found out about the
document. She was hurt and annoyed that the matter had taken
place behind her back but she was too busy preparing for the
family's departure to pursue the subject at the time. On the evening
of 5 September 1901 Sonya and Lev, accompanied by Masha, Kolya,
Sasha and Lev's disciple P. A. Boulanger, left for the Crimea. The
beginning of their journey, the carriage ride to Tula over rough
country roads, was the most arduous part of the entire trip. Lev
was feverish and uncomfortable but when the train for Sevastopol
pulled out of the Tula station at three in the morning he had
revived and was dictating to Masha.

The Tolstoys' quarters were luxurious, as Boulanger was a former worker for the Moscow-Kursk railroad and had persuaded the company to give the family a private car. The first morning was already sunny and warm and the Tolstoys decided that they would dine in the station restaurant at the stop in Kharkov. This was not to be—when the train arrived at the platform it was impossible to leave the rail car. A sea of humanity milled around and there was a great roar: "Tolstoy! Lev Nikolaevich! Are you there? A delegation! Let us on! Hurrah! Tolstoy!" One by one delegations with tributes were brought into the rail car and when the train started to leave the crowd called for Lev to show himself at the window. Boulanger and Sonya supported him while, sweating and trembling, he waved to the crowd. When they finally got him, weeping, into bed he had an attack of angina. There was a similar crowd in Sevastopol but by now the police were alerted to what a Tolstoy progress involved and Lev and his family were whisked into carriages and taken to their hotel. The next day they traveled by carriage to Gaspra. When they went through the gates of Countess Panin's imposing driveway the fountain was playing in the garden and the steward stood at the door with the offering of bread and salt.

Lev's children gathered in the Crimea, some staying in the villa and some nearby in Yalta. A multitude of friends, including the Obolensky in-laws and the pianist A. B. Goldenweizer, came for short visits. Goldenweizer had met Lev in 1896. He became a close friend and eventually a disciple. Anton Chekov lived in Yalta, Maxim Gorky near Gaspra; both writers made frequent calls. Lev's health was good enough so that he and Sonya could go out once a day but his mood was apathetic and Sonya found it exasperating that he was either dictating religious articles or brooding on death. She missed the northern winter, the snow and sleighs and invigorating air. Gaspra was a tiny village and she had little to do besides shopping in Yalta and running the house. Her eyes were failing and she had put off getting stronger glasses, so could not do much reading. Tanya gave birth to another stillborn baby in November which further depressed the family. Sonya began to brood on death herself:

> *2 December.* . . . I think more and more about death with peaceful joy, about that place where I shall be with my children, where it seems that there will be peace.

Peaceful resignation was not Sonya's strong point and the next lines she wrote were more in character:

In this life one cannot have tranquility; if one seeks it in life, if one acts wisely, has an even attitude toward everything, has religious humility and understanding, then life its very self ceases. Life has energy, constantly changing emotion, struggle, climbing, falling, good and evil; life is life.

It was this turbulent life that Sonya longed to share with Lev but he was tired of being ill, exasperated at his inability to do good work and he turned the brunt of his impatience onto his wife. Cheerful and patient with visitors, he was rude to Sonya; he snarled and snapped at her and her spirits fell. On 7 December she wrote:

> The news from Moscow does not make me particularly glad, nor from Yasnaya. Little by little, [household] affairs are being neglected. Wonderful music—symphonies and friends and concerts beckon and entice but I sit here bored and powerless. Duty, duty, and all my energy goes into fulfilling it.

This was not the atmosphere of evening glow. She was further upset when Lev moved out of the room next to hers:

> He did not like the stairs. His room next to mine is deserted and the lifeless silence upstairs is ominous and painful.

Her mood hung upon Lev's:

> *15 December.* . . . Today Levochka is better and all of us cheered up. He is cheerful, his heart is good. . . . He dined with us and went to the gates of the estate and back.

A week later Lev walked in the meadow and gathered a bouquet for Sonya:

> Wonderful! I begin to love the Crimea. Thank God, my melancholy is gone, chiefly because Lev Nikolaevich's health begins to improve.

Lev continued to get better and Sonya was briefly tempted by a trip to Yasnaya and Moscow, but when she thought of abandoning her husband she was overcome with pity for him. And then, suddenly, she was no longer restless but frightened. Lev's heart stopped momentarily:

> *4 January.* For three nights I have slept on the leather couch in the drawing room or, rather, I have not slept

all night but listened to Lev Nikolaevich next door, fearing for his heart.

Sonya wanted to do all the nursing herself but admitted that her patient was tyrannical, fault-finding and that it was hard to care for someone who thought he knew everything about medicine and hygiene. When Lev's temperature began a rapid rise Sonya was so alarmed that she sent for doctors from St. Petersburg and Moscow. (She was later embarrassed as none of the doctors would accept pay.) She rarely left the sickroom and while Lev slept she sat at the table and wrote in her diary. The Russian newspapers carried daily bulletins on Lev's condition; nevertheless, Sonya received a note from Taneev suggesting that she should come north for a concert by a "remarkable singer." Sonya was not tempted:

> I feel somehow indifferent to and tired of everything in the world! Oh, how I have become tired of living in general. Today I did exactly *nothing* except take care of Lev Nikolaevich. My eyes are very poor, I cannot read. But only one thing is important and only one thing can make me happy—to be near L. N.!

The doctors could not diagnose Lev's condition beyond the fact that it was complicated by pneumonia and that they feared that he would not recover. Sonya sat at the table in his room and wrote in her diary. She asked herself why:

> It is my conversation with my heart. My Levochka is dying and I realize that my life cannot go on without him. For forty years I have lived with him. To others he is a famous man—to me he is my existence. Our lives have bound us to one another and, my God, how much guilt I have accumulated, how much repentance. All is over. I cannot make restitution. Help me, Lord. How much love I gave him, how many kind words, but how I have hurt him with my weaknesses. Forgive me, Lord! Forgive me, my darling, darling, dear husband!

The next day she confessed:

> I should like to write down everything about my darling Levochka but I cannot because of tears and my tormenting pain.

Still, she managed to keep long accounts of each day. She rarely left the sickroom.

Sonya watched a doctor give camphor while Lev said calmly, "Wait, one minute it is camphor, now it is oxygen, then it will be a coffin and the grave." Sonya kissed him and asked if he suffered. "No," he replied, "it is peaceful." To Masha he said that physically he felt very bad, but spiritually "good, very good." Once in his sleep Lev suddenly cried out, "Sonya!" She leaned over him and he told her that he had seen her in a dream. He believed that he was dying and was gentle and tender with Sonya. Was she ever lying down? Did she eat? He told her to rest more and not stay by his bed but when he woke he would cry out, "Sonya, are you there? Are you writing?" or "Why are you so quiet? Are you lying down?" Sonya leaned over him and he studied her face intently. "You are tired, sweetheart," he said. Sonya lifted him to turn him and he stroked her hand and said, "I am grateful to you, sweetheart." [8] Lev's gentle mood did not last; he became depressed and withdrawn and would neither speak nor eat, except to take a little coffee or champagne. It seemed to Sonya that nothing could interest him; he stared at her glumly and she admitted that her strained emotions pined for an outlet. On 10 February she wrote:

> Announcements of concerts, especially those full of the music of Sergei Ivanovich, stir my small soul and I, like a person hungry for food, suddenly want music passionately, and the music of Taneev which with its profundity acts so powerfully upon me.

But Sonya no longer considered a trip north nor did she leave the villa. In mid-February the doctors announced the crisis, the turning point in pneumonia when the patient either recovered or died, and the family stayed near the sickroom. Death was postponed. For all of his professed eagerness to submit to dying, Lev held on to life. He said to the doctor, "It seems that life must go on." Sonya asked him if he found that boring. "No, no. How could it bore me? It is good."

Once more Lev was interested in the world. He wanted to sit in the sunshine on the terrace but Sonya was afraid to allow this. For most of the day Lev sat in his armchair with Sonya beside him sewing. She wrote in her diary:

> I determinedly sit at home all the day long and sew, getting up only to care for Lev Nikolaevich. In the morning I always give him his bath, fix his hair and feed him breakfast.

As Lev recovered his health he recovered his irritability. When Sonya dressed him he scolded her for being clumsy. Sonya was emotionally exhausted after weeks of anxiety for her husband and found Lev's impatience hard to bear. In a burst of biting sarcasm she reflected in her diary on what it meant to be the wife of a genius:

> Geniuses must create in peaceful, enjoyable, comfortable conditions; a genius must eat, wash, dress, he must rewrite his work a countless number of times; one must love him, give him no cause for jealousy so that he has peace, one must raise and educate the innumerable children who are born to a genius but for whom he has no time.

It was forty years now, Sonya noted, that she had cared for her genius and given to him all her intellectual and artistic life. Others might ask, she wrote, "But for what would you, an insignificant woman, need an intellectual and artistic life?" Sonya replied to her rhetorical question:

> And to this question I can only answer, I do not know, but always suppressing my needs to care for the material needs of a genius is a great hardship.

Sonya admitted that she was tired of what she had to endure, the bearing and raising of the children, the management of the household, all the material services for others for which she received "absolutely nothing even close to gratitude" but instead "always more reproaches." [9] And as Lev became annoyed at the slow return of his strength, he demanded ever more understanding from Sonya. He was quick to anger and shouted at her, prompting her daughters to take her place and send her away. Sonya wrote in April:

> I am often alone. My children are more despotic and persistently harsh than their father.

Finally Masha persuaded Sonya to take the trip north that had tempted her once but no longer. Masha and Sasha promised a daily telegram on their father's condition and Sonya agreed that a change of scene would do her good. She left on 22 April but began to worry at once. She sent her husband and daughters a note from nearby Balaklava the very day she left:

> I am going through everything that is happening in Gaspra and worrying. But I am trying not to become unraveled

because of this. I kiss everyone. Sasha, have you sent my telegram?

The telegrams from Gaspra were reassuring and both in Yasnaya and in Moscow Sonya was happily affected by her warm welcome from friends and from tradespeople. She spent a whole day at Yasnaya in Andrusha's company and then went to Moscow for two nights. One evening she went to the opera and the next night stayed at home. Friends called, including Taneev, and, although he played several pieces Sonya did not comment in her diary that they affected her "powerfully." Her tonic had been the change of scene and after the three days in the north she was glad to return to Gaspra. A shock awaited her there. The telegrams had not informed her that Lev had typhoid.

Sonya took over the nursing and stayed by Lev's bed day and night, wiping his forehead and giving him spoonfuls of coffee mixed with brandy. Lev was tearful and confessed, "I am tired and I want death." Nevertheless, once more life triumphed and he rallied quickly. In May he was writing in his diary and in June walking with a cane although still very weak. Sonya wrote in her diary:

> It is often painful to watch him, it hurts me especially when he is submissively gentle, as lately he is all the time. Yesterday when I washed and cut his hair was the only time he became irritated with me.

A few days later the doctors approved the trip to Yasnaya and on 27 June 1902 the Tolstoys arrived home. Sonya wrote in her diary:

> We are very glad to be in Yasnaya but again a dark cloud. Masha went into labor and in the evening gave birth to a stillborn baby.

3.

The Tolstoys were frightened by the Crimea illness and decided to have a doctor live at Yasnaya. Several medical men filled this position until Dushan Makovitsky came and remained until the end of Lev's life. The doctor slept in the room next to Lev's in order to be on constant call; this practical necessity resulted in a lack of privacy at night. The Tolstoys remained permanently in separate bedrooms. Their separation at night meant less time when they were alone together, just the two of them without the demands and intrusions of others, and both knew that these were their best times. "I am alone with Sonya—I am fine." "L. N. and I are very affectionate now, yes, and we always are when we are alone together."

The doctor's presence was not the only reason for less privacy; an ever-increasing number of family and friends came to stay, Sasha lived at home and Masha and Kolya spent months at a time at Yasnaya. The two daughters competed for their father's attention and both were eager to step into their mother's place in his affections. Had not all of Masha's pregnancies resulted in stillborn babies, perhaps motherhood might have claimed some of the intense devotion she gave her father. Sasha had grown into an overweight, coarse-featured young woman of eighteen, rough in manners and without the Tolstoy charm. From the beginning of her life shadows had fallen on Sasha. Born during the year of her father's severest depression, neglected for an angelic younger brother, jealous of him and also adoring him and hurt by his death, jealous again when she was only thirteen of her mother's interest in Taneev, Sasha chose to make Sonya the object of her revenge against her own fate. Toward her father she became doggedly attentive and toward her mother critical and unsympathetic. Sasha and Masha both reminded their father that if it had not been for his wife he could have chosen a life according to his principles. The young women's inconsistency did not seem apparent to them. Both partook of the comfortable life their mother made possible for them and both complained of the "luxuries" at home and the money Sonya was earning through her editions.

Actually, Sonya gave this income less priority than her daughters credited her. In July 1902 N. S. Tsetlin, the owner and publisher of the periodical *Enlightenment*, came to Sonya with an offer to buy, for one million rubles (about $500,000), the permanent rights to those works which she published.[10] Sonya flatly refused, although if she had accepted Tsetlin's offer she would have solved her financial problems, and had money to leave to her children and saved herself from work that she was beginning to find exhausting. Sonya, however, was loath to have the family lose control of Lev's writings and Tsetlin's offer reminded her of the paper that Masha had persuaded her father to sign during the previous summer. A few months after turning down the offer of a million rubles,

Sonya asked her husband if she could have the document he had signed for Masha. Lev readily agreed but a terrible row broke out between Masha and Sonya. Sonya's account of the quarrel, written at the time (10 October 1902) with the knowledge that Lev would read it, is probably accurate:

> Something happened that I in no way expected. Masha went into a rage, her husband shouted God knows what and said that he and Masha would collect and publish the document after Lev Nikolaevich's death in order to make known to the greatest number of people possible that which they themselves have known all the time— that L. N. did not want to sell his works but that his wife sold them. And the result of this story is that the Obolenskys, Masha and Kolya, are leaving Yasnaya.

But neither Sonya nor Masha wanted to quarrel so finally. Less than two weeks later Sonya wrote:

> 23 October. I was reconciled with Masha, she has remained living in the wing of Yasnaya and I am very glad about this. Again everything is peaceful and good.

Masha and Sasha were not alone in needling Lev about the style of his life at home and the royalties from his work that made it possible; a host of people who, for political, social or religious reasons, sought changes in society looked to Tolstoy as their adopted leader. These people wanted more than words from him and begged Lev to free himself from his social and domestic bonds and leave his home for a life closer to his beliefs. Some letters taunted him with inconsistency, reminding him that at home he ate at a table laid with silver and was waited on by servants in white gloves. Aylmer Maude, Tolstoy's biographer and translator, wrote that the luxury that made Lev so uncomfortable was luxury only in comparison with the frugal existence of the peasants and that Yasnaya Polyana would have seemed very modest and simple next to life in a similar English country house. But the mail upset Lev and over and over he thrashed out the implications for Tolstoyans of the manner of his life at home. At the same time Lev certainly realized that if Sonya lived as he advocated, this would deprive him of many of the home comforts on which he was becoming more and more dependent. The doctor who attended him, the many visits from children and grandchildren—not to mention those from friends and disciples—none of this life would be possible in a peasant's hut. In the Crimea the Tolstoys lived free of charge in Countess Panin's palatial villa, but without her offer of hospitality Sonya's earnings would have had to pay for their lodging. Lev and his family believed that the winter in the south had saved his life. In 1908 Lev wrote in his notebook that he had come to realize with joy *"vaut mieux tard que jamais"* that Sonya and others who did not agree with his ideas, did not disagree because they disapproved of his convictions but because they could not see the importance of religion.[11] This was a way of exonerating Sonya for making the life he needed possible. During these years Lev made an accommodation with his ideals and the reality of his family life. More important than his material needs, however, was Lev's belief that it was right to remain with his wife and also his wish. He therefore wrote to his correspondents explaining that it was God's will for him to bear the cross of a life of which he disapproved.

Lev's stay in the Crimea and his long hours facing death had been a natural preparation for returning to his book about Hadji Murat, first conceived in 1896. *Hadji Murat* was Lev's last novel. Although he revised and corrected it until 1904, most of it was written on his return from Gaspra. *Hadji Murat* is a short but complete and moving book, the story of a Caucasian chieftain who deserted to the Russians, regretted his desertion and was killed by his own people when he tried to return to them. Lev took great pains with this novel and often noted that he had simply been thinking about *Hadji Murat*. In August 1902 he wrote in his diary:

> For four days I have not written. [In his diary.] Entangled in thoughts about *Hadji Murat*. Now, it seems it is clearer.

Sonya noted in October 1902 that Lev had finished *Hadji Murat* but this was only the first writing. Lev revised and corrected the novel for nearly two years until he was satisfied with the final version. While he was working on *Hadji Murat* Lev had ambivalent emotions. All his artistic, creative being was satisfied but sometimes he was ashamed to take so much satisfaction in producing something that did not contribute directly to the betterment of mankind. In 1903 he began a project that he believed met this test; a compilation of great thoughts throughout the centuries, eventually called *The Circle of Reading*. The quotations came from both eastern and western cultures and were put in the form of a calendar with a different subject assigned to each day. Lev interrupted this work to finish a short story, *The False Coupon*, and noted in April of 1904, "I want to write *The Decembrists*." Nothing came of this; his health would never again be strong enough for such a task, but in 1905 he finished a very short tale, the touching and appealing story of *Alyosha the Pot*.

Meanwhile momentous events swept Russia—the Russo-Japanese War, 1904–1905, and the Revolution of 1905—events which the Tolstoys followed with concern but which did not disturb the rhythm of life at Yasnaya, a life still brightened by that special Tolstoy mixture of vitality, creativity and fun. When in good health Lev took walks, rode, played cards and chess, enjoyed the talk around the dinner table and participated in the family teasing. He once greeted his daughter Tanya with the warning, "Take care! Mama has bought the most enormous quantity of glossy paint and is busy painting everything she can lay her hands on, although in all justice, I must admit that so far she has spared the living." Sonya was so amused that she laughed until she was almost out of control and Lev stood gazing at her with gentle approval. He provoked her to another laughing fit when he found her caring for a village baby. "I am going to have a rubber baby made for you," he said, "one with constant diarrhea. And then you will be completely happy." [12]

Sonya, as her sister Tanya had remarked forty years before, did not know how to be idle. Besides running the household and working on her editions, she kept up her hobby of photography and, since returning from Gaspra, was writing her autobiography. She did not find this an easy task and mentions of it in her engagement diary were often followed by exclamations such as, "Difficult!" "Very hard!" "It is too difficult!" When she read aloud chapters to Lev he suggested changes and additions and generally approved. Sonya wrote:

> Today I read my autobiography for the years 1877 and
> '78 to Lev Nikolaevich. He added something and praised
> it and this was delightful for me.

Because of Sonya's writing Yasnaya now had two secretaries, one for Lev and one for Sonya, and a Remington typewriter. Lev's secretary beginning in 1907 was a disciple, N. N. Gusev, and Sonya's Varvara Mikhailovna Feokritov. In 1910 Valentin Bulgakov became Lev's secretary. The secretaries were busy, as replying to his mail was Lev's major chore. His diary and notebook no longer contained much mention of family life—Lev was devoting his journal to trying to sort out his religious and philosophical ideas. Sonya was doing some sorting, too, arranging Lev's diaries to give them to the Historical Museum. In 1905 Sonya also handed over to the museum all her own diaries up to that year. She edited nothing. After Lev's death she made comments in the margins of both his and her diaries, but there is no reason to believe she erased any material.

Lev's health continued to be a concern to his family. Sonya wrote on 29 December 1902:

> Lev Nikolaevich gets better and then worse. Today he said to me, "I'm afraid I shall be worrying you for a long time."

She took this to mean that he believed he would not get well and she was frightened and lived with "pain in my heart." She noted in her diary:

> In Gaspra I did not feel such profound suffering and such tenderness toward Levochka as I do here.

Lev's health improved in the new year and she wrote:

> My heart leaps up with joy that he is going out; that he goes driving, taking the reins; how many times I have thought it the end of his life and he is again restored!

Sonya's relief was intense but the fact remained that, although she had not lost her husband, they slept apart and there was little chance that he would be her lover again. Sonya was fifty-eight and vigorous. The last flare-up of her fantasy relationship with Taneev came in January 1903 and was probably a romantic sublimation of her wish for physical love. Copying *Anna Karenina* in March of that year she compared her infatuation for Taneev with Anna's love affair. She wrote in her diary that even her happiness that Lev was getting well did not cure her "sick heart":

> I want to cry, I want to see that man who now is the center of my shameful, inopportune folly. But let no one raise a hand against me because I have worn myself out with agonizing and am afraid for myself. But one must live, I must care for my husband and children and I must not show or betray my folly or see him whom I painfully need.

Sonya's need seems to have been less for Taneev and more for romantic escape from her cares; the need passed and she did not identify herself with Anna again nor did she indulge her fantasy further in her diary. The next time she mentioned Taneev was two years later (after his rebuff) when she wrote that his article on Rimsky-Korsakov was "dryly logical."

When Lev was well and cheerful her life was good:

> We, L. N. and I, are very friendly. . . . A good and happy day. . . . He tenderly stroked my cheek, like a child's, and his fatherly love made me rejoice. . . . We live peacefully, quietly, even happily.

When Lev was preoccupied or apathetic she was resentful:

> My passionate husband is dead, my loving friend never existed.

But the evening glow was there and sometimes shimmered with tears. On the first day of 1905 Sonya went to Lev's room to kiss him and give her new year greeting. Lev referred at once to a misunderstanding of the previous evening and Sonya tried to explain that she had not neglected him. Later she wrote:

> And suddenly L. N. burst into tears and began to caress me and say how much he loved me, how happy he had been in his life with me. I also wept and told him that if ever I had been unhappy, then I myself had been to blame and I asked him to forgive me my unstable moods.

A few months later Lev noted in his diary that his relations with Sonya were "very good," and this in spite of a concert at Yasnaya in which both Goldenweizer and Taneev played. The Tolstoys still quarreled, but quarrels soon ended in reconciliations. Sonya's editions of Lev's works remained an irritant; both Lev and Sonya noted an unpleasant conversation on this subject in August of 1905, but following their quarrel Sonya brought a book of family photographs to Lev and they sat together looking at the pictures and recalling the past. The following summer, tensions rose when Sonya complained to the authorities that the peasants' pilfering was draining Yasnaya of significant income. Guards were posted and, although the stealing was not stopped, some peasants were tried and found guilty. Sonya knew how much this upset her husband but found herself powerless once she had asked the authorities to intervene. Lev continued to rant about the question of women in his diary and notebooks but he confessed that he could not solve the question by putting all the blame on the female sex and wrote in his notebook in April 1905:

> Woman does a great work. She gives birth to children,
> but she does not give birth to ideas. This is done by men.

In August 1906 it was Lev's turn to be frightened for Sonya's life. For some weeks she had had severe pains in her abdomen and often she was too uncomfortable to leave her bed. When the pains became agonizing, Lev summoned the gynecologist, Dr. Snegirov, from Moscow and the family gathered at Yasnaya, swept with emotion for the person whom they had always taken for granted. Even Sasha dropped her critical attitude. Lev noted on 1 September:

> I have not written for six days. Sonya's illness is worse. Today I felt especial sympathy for her. She is touchingly reasonable; honest and good.

Sonya asked for a priest and Lev complied, explaining in his diary that some people choose simple ways to express their spiritual feelings but that their simplicity in no way made their experience less spiritual. Ilya observed his father's agony as Lev tried to face Sonya's death as he had Vanechka's, by embracing the black void. He told his family, "The great and solemn moment of death draws near; we must submit to the will of God and any intervention by the doctors violates the grandeur and solemnity of the great act of death." But Dr. Snegirov diagnosed a ruptured tumor and asked Lev point blank to consent to an operation. Lev could not decide and said that the decision must be Sonya's and the children's. When an operation was agreed upon, Lev retreated to the woods to walk alone and pray. He told the children, "If the operation is successful, ring the bell for me two times, if not, then—no, it is better not to ring at all, I'll come myself."

Lev walked slowly into the woods. The operation took half an hour. Ilya and Masha went to look for their father and met him coming toward them, pale and frightened. "Successful, successful," they cried. Lev replied in a voice breaking with emotion, "Good. Go, I shall come presently." When he went to Sonya's room he was enraged. "My God, what a terrible thing," he cried. "They do not let a person die in peace. A woman lies with her abdomen split, tied to the bed, without pillows, and moaning more than before the operation." Ilya noticed that as soon as his mother showed signs that she would get well, Lev no longer blamed the doctor.

Sonya's calmness in the face of death convinced Lev that she had accepted his religious convictions and that they were now truly united. Alas, Sonya did not remain on the spiritual mountaintop, but rapidly returned to life and its prosaic routines. Lev regretted that her terrible suffering had been for nothing. But it was not until he was assured that she would get well, that he could settle down to his work. Once the agonizing fear for her was over, he resumed his grumbling comments. Was there, he asked in his diary, a more disgusting act than that of sexual intercourse? If Sonya read this, she did not react to it in her diary.

Sonya had barely convalesced from her operation when she noted in her engagement diary:

> *19 November.* Masha was very ill in the evening with a high fever and I am very alarmed for her.

The next day she wrote:

> It is a weight on my heart. She [Masha] is pitiful and it is awful for her. At home all is quiet and sorrowful.

Lev, too, was frightened. He wrote in his diary that he loved Masha "very, very much."

Masha was nursed in her brief illness by her mother, Sasha and Kolya. Sonya sat at her bedside long hours without sleeping, watched over her daughter's restless movements and tried to comfort her during the delirium of high fever. When Masha's thrashing ceased, it was the peace of approaching death. She sat up in her bed, propped up by pillows, surrounded by her mother, father and husband. Lev held on to both of her arms and just after midnight on 27 November Masha died peacefully. Sonya recorded:

> I kissed her forehead and stayed near to L. N. Kolya wept from time to time and kissed her arms when she was gone. A bitter wind howled and tore at everything. It is very painful and I can hardly believe that Masha is no more.

Masha died in the vaulted room where Sonya had spent the night on her first visit to Yasnaya Polyana forty-four years before.

Lev was determined to see Masha's death as a beautiful event. Two years earlier when his beloved Granny had died he wrote in his diary:

> How simple and fine this is.

He wanted to see Masha's death as simple and fine and to believe that in dying she had opened herself to God. He found the letters and telegrams offering sympathy offensive. When he met Kenya, a half-witted woman from the village, he asked her if she had heard of the family's grief. "I heard," Kenya answered. "Give me a kopek." Lev wrote in his diary, "How much better and simpler this was."

Sonya grieved for the daughter whom she had loved throughout their differences and at first her only comfort was her one-year-old granddaughter. Tanya had finally given birth to a healthy baby girl, a third Tanya (called Tanushka). In the spring of 1907 Sonya had another sorrow to bear; her brother Vyacheslav, an engineer, was killed by an unemployed workman during the excavation of a harbor near St. Petersburg. (Ironically, Vyacheslav, just before he was killed, had been working in the interests of the unemployed workmen.) But two tragedies in one year and her own near brush with death did not stifle Sonya's formidable energy. She continued her work for the Historical Museum, putting Lev's papers in order, and she completed her autobiography through the year 1884. In the autumn one of the foremost Russian painters of the period, Ilya Repin, came to Yasnaya. He had done portraits of Lev and now planned to paint both Tolstoys. Sonya liked Repin and read parts of her autobiography aloud to him.

Lev's eightieth birthday fell in August 1908 and during spring and summer there were rumblings of a vast celebration in his honor. When Lev heard that a committee had been formed to organize the events he became so upset that he wrote to beg that the plans be canceled.[13] The committee bowed to his wishes and the birthday was celebrated privately at Yasnaya Polyana. On 7 September Sonya described the day in her diary:

> The following crowd gathered to face him around the table: Four of our sons, Seryozha, Ilya, Misha and Andrusha. [The year before Andrusha distressed his parents by divorcing Olga to marry a woman who left her husband and six children to be his wife.] [Young] Lev was in Sweden with his wife who is expecting. Of his daughters, just Sasha.

Tanya had come for Sonya's birthday and did not want to leave her little girl so soon again. Sonya mentioned fourteen other guests, including Chertkov, whose exile was over. She continued:

> The mood was warm, peaceful and touching. . . . There was such a feeling of love from all over the world and

from each of those present that day. When Lev Nikolaevich lay down to go to sleep in the evening and I covered him as I always do with my warm, crocheted blanket, he said to me, "How wonderful! How everything is wonderful!"

Sonya got up early on 8 September and went to check on her husband, who had been troubled with heartburn during the night. When she reached the netting that covered his balcony door she found him awake. "Ah, Sonya," he sighed happily when he saw her. Later in the day she wrote in her diary that this had made her very content. Her mood was mellow and she described wistfully the conversations Lev had had with their visitors during the day. She added:

Days somehow are flying by to no avail and this makes me sad; as though something precious is being lost and this something precious is time, the last years of my life and of the life close to mine.

Chapter Nine

CONSPIRACY AND TRAGEDY, 1908–1910

1.

Lev had two more years at the crossroads, the place he had described to Sonya where a good life stretched out behind him and a good death was for a short while postponed. There were times when illnesses, attacks of angina, fainting spells, even convulsions, all implied that the postponement was not for long. At other times Lev felt well enough to ride, go for walks, enjoy his guests and work. His working hours were spent answering his mail, writing in his diary and searching for appropriate quotations for *The Circle of Reading*. When he found one that pleased him he would go at once to share it with Sonya. She marveled at how much he loved this work.

Lev's diary writing had become a long dialogue with his spiritual self, that is, with the God within him. "Does God love tête-à-tête?" he asked, adding in English, "Two is company." God was the pure truth that could make mankind good, but now a personal note crept into Lev's speculations. Could one know and love God face to face? While Lev's diary was full of thoughts about God, Sonya's was full of thoughts about her husband. In September 1908 she compared her life to his, he who had always been able to do as he pleased, who wrote when he wanted to write, made boots when he wanted to make boots, plowed or taught, whatever his impulse. What ceased to interest him he flung aside. How different her options had been:

How could I have attempted such a life? What would
have happened to the children or to L. N. himself?

Looking back at her long life with Lev, Sonya wrote:

No one knows him and understands him as I do. . . . He
is a man with enormous intelligence and talent, a man
with imagination, perception and extraordinary sensitivity.

She noticed that there had been a change in his spontaneity. He
seemed to be kind "on principle" and not from "genuine kindness."
She observed that there were two sides to his life:

He likes to go riding, he loves good food and a glass of
wine. . . . He likes to play vint and chess but it is as if
his body is living a separate life and his soul remains
indifferent to earthly life, existing independent of and really beyond his body. This somehow happened after his
illness: he became more of a stranger. One felt further
from L. N. and sometimes he is unbearably sad and pitiful
to me, lost in his life and in his relation to me and to all
his surroundings. Do others see this?

Sonya's chief worry at the moment was, as so often it had been,
his physical health. She saw his energies drained by the constant
visitors to Yasnaya Polyana and by the demands of his disciples.
She asked:

Is it illness . . . or is it this wall of Tolstoyans, chiefly
Chertkov, who plant themselves in the house, influence
Lev Nikolaevich and never leave him alone?

Chertkov planted himself at Yasnaya nearly every day. He assumed that his years of exile for Tolstoyan principles had earned
him special rights including the right to be officious and imperti-
nent toward Lev. To the horror of the family, Chertkov strode
unannounced into Lev's study. He criticized Lev for killing a mos-
quito (a living creature!) or for inadvertently making the sign of
the cross (might not someone think that he had returned to the
orthodox religion?). "What a narrow-minded creature Chertkov
is," Sonya wrote in her diary after hearing him rebuke Lev for
the sign of the cross.

Chertkov's narrow-mindedness was not disinterested. A literal devotion to Tolstoyan principles suited him very well, particularly to the notion that Lev's works should be given freely to the public. Behind high-minded concern Chertkov hid his real purpose, which was to wrest from Sonya all control of her husband's work. Chertkov saw his own place in history as editor and distributor of Tolstoy's work after Lev's death. With this in mind he built a large house on the grounds of Telyatinki, an estate bordering Yasnaya.[1] Besides an apartment for himself and family, there were offices for thirty employees. From here Chertkov directed the editing and distribution of those works written after 1881 whose copyrights had not been given to Sonya. This work took up only a small part of Chertkov's time, the rest being devoted to schemes by which he hoped to gain control of those works, written before 1881, that Sonya published.

Chertkov soon found a considerable ally in Aleksandra Tolstoy. Sasha saw clearly that Chertkov was humorless, self-righteous and scheming but she never admitted this to her father, preferring to take the side of her mother's enemy. Sasha's anger at her mother had grown and she justified it as anger at Sonya for thwarting Lev's wish to live according to his ideals. Later Sasha regretted that her anger had been distressing to her father. She then blamed her feelings in 1909 and 1910 on her old resentment that her mother had preferred Vanechka, but the wasting hurt that blighted Sasha's relation to Sonya had a wider base than jealousy of Vanechka. She had also felt rejected for Taneev and perhaps Sonya's constant care of Lev during his illness reminded Sasha of the kind of devotion that she believed her mother had withheld from her. Now she was twenty-six, unmarried, without particular grace or talent and without that special place near her father's heart that Tanya could always claim and that Masha had had. It was natural for Sasha to seek revenge against the most important person in her life and she seized the opportunity to hurt her mother.

Chertkov and Sasha recognized that they were natural allies and together they conspired against Sonya.[2] At first the conspiracy was emotional; they informed disciples and friends of the family of the "true" picture of the Tolstoys' relationship; that is, that Sonya was the obstacle between Lev and the fulfillment of his life's work. The pianist Goldenweizer and his wife and Dr. Makovitsky were among those they converted to this belief. Chertkov's manner toward Lev combined arrogant domination with obsequious flattery. He carried a small notebook in which he recorded

Lev's remarks for posterity. He also made note of any criticism or sharpness Lev showed toward his wife. Chertkov and Sasha always spoke to Lev in lowered voices and stopped their conversation if Sonya came near. The conspirators would stare at Sonya without expression, Sasha with tightly pursed lips.

Sonya saw clearly what Chertkov was about and she was ready to fight to keep her publishing rights in order to leave them to her children and grandchildren for their future income. In this she was not mercenary but practical. She pointed out to Lev that if he gave up all his copyrights, as he frequently threatened to do, he would be indulging a whim to absolve himself from earning money. The only real beneficiaries would be the publishers, who would then have access to Tolstoy's work without paying royalties. The small number of books that Chertkov could print and distribute free of charge was nothing compared to the number that the publishers sold for profit. Sonya also wanted to keep her rights to works prior to 1881 as evidence of her husband's loyalty to her and she did not want to lose to adversaries whose antagonism was fueled by a spite they did not try to conceal.

Two of the Tolstoy sons, Andrusha and young Lev, tried to support their mother but they had little influence with their father. Sergei, Ilya and Misha were seldom home; Tanya, nearby in Kochety, adored her father to such an extent that, much as she tried to be compassionate toward Sonya, she was not objective. In the 1920s, when Tanya's parents and husband were dead and she lived with her daughter in Paris, she saw the situation differently. She and her daughter did not have the price of admission to see the film version of *Anna Karenina* with Greta Garbo and Tanya wondered aloud, "What would Papa have said if he had seen that? Or the sight of me sweeping the floor, doing my shopping, not knowing if I'll have enough left to pay the rent?" Even then Tanya hastily added, "Though he was quite right." [3]

For all Chertkov's interference and the black cloud of emotional conspiracy, much of the evening glow remained in the Tolstoy household; Lev and Sonya might have resisted all the evil scheming if they had been physically and mentally stronger. Their love was very much alive. In the spring of 1909 Lev, alone with Sonya, suddenly burst into tears. "I am so happy, so happy," he said. Sonya asked him, "Why? Is it because so many people love you?" "No," Lev replied. "It is you. I am happy because of you." This was the truth that should have brightened the Tolstoys' last years together so that the sunset could, indeed, have been bright and clear but this was the truth against which Chertkov and Sasha launched their assault. The battle was not evenly matched. Lev's health was frail and he was averse to arguments. He felt an enormous debt to those disciples who had suffered exile for his principles and he was troubled by guilt about not having shared their trials. To Sonya he was bound by nearly fifty years of marriage and a love and intimacy that he had known with no one else. When Chertkov's demands conflicted with Sonya's Lev tried to maintain a neutral position but in the matter of the copyrights neither Chertkov nor Sonya would accept neutrality. Lev was once more in a double bind and he was tired, confused and longed for peace.

Sonya was also tired but she was not confused. She held her copyrights by verbal agreement and uneasy questions tormented her. Without a formal document outlining her rights what would happen when Lev died? Would her enemies deprive her and thus her children and grandchildren of everything? What agreements had Chertkov succeeded in wresting from Lev? But Lev and Sonya, who had valued and practiced openness throughout their marriage, could no longer talk to one another.

When Sonya questioned her husband he refused to answer. When she asked him for a formal document stating the copyrights that were hers, he refused emphatically. He wished to leave the matter as it stood in his 1895 diary in which he begged, but did not insist, that his works be made free to the public.[4] This paper made no mention of the copyrights held by Sonya and thus was ambiguous but, similarly, Lev's life was ambiguous. He preached austere poverty and lived in relative comfort. Since his return from the Crimea Lev had become tolerant of this ambiguity and referred to it as a special role given him by God.

Sonya had also been content to leave matters as they stood in Lev's 1895 diary until she began to fear that Chertkov was bent on altering the situation to his own purposes. In June of 1909 Sonya was not only suffering the subtle tortures of the emotional conspiracy but she was terrified that there was a specific plot afoot to take all her rights from her. On top of this anxiety she had a high fever and neuralgia in her arm and shoulder. She described herself as crazy with worries and wrote in her journal that all her nervous system was completely shaken. Faced with Lev's implacable refusal to give her a document that would reassure her, she became more and more agitated and tried to reach her husband through hysterical behavior. Then she would regret her histrionics and drop them. Her enemies' sharpest weapon against Sonya was their ability to provoke her hysteria, which then further eroded her self-respect. Her hysterical behavior also gave Lev a way out of his double bind. He could not admit that Sonya's requests were reasonable because that put him in conflict with Chertkov; therefore he ignored them on the grounds that she was "mentally ill."

The situation appeared to improve when Yasnaya Polyana was relieved of Chertkov's company in the spring of 1909. The government of the province of Tula banned him for distributing Lev's censored works. Sonya recognized the banishment as an act of harassment against her husband and wrote an outraged letter to the newspaper. Nevertheless, she was relieved to have Chertkov's relationship with Lev limited to letters and Lev's occasional visits to a house that Chertkov rented outside the province.

Chertkov was not deterred by banishment. He left behind a camp of supporters to carry on his schemes under his direction: his wife Anna Konstantinova, his son Vladimir and the staff at Telyatinki, the most important of whom were A. P. Sergeenko and F. A. Strakhov (no relation to Lev's deceased friend, the philosopher and critic N. N. Strakhov). Sergeenko and Strakhov were in and out of Yasnaya Polyana nearly every day seeing Lev on matters not shared with Sonya. She realized that something important, something secret, was under discussion and she was certain that it had to do with her copyrights. On 8 July she recorded another blow:

> My nervousness increases with the staggering news that
> Lev Nikolaevich has suddenly decided to attend the World
> Peace Conference in Stockholm.

Sonya feared that Lev would not survive the physical hardship and emotional excitement of the trip. She became so agitated that Lev promised her he would not go and Sonya at once moved to take advantage of his conciliatory mood. She begged him to give her formally the rights to his work that she held by verbal agreement. When Lev refused she flung herself at his feet, clung to his knees and pleaded with him not to deny her "this comfort." Neither husband nor wife was pleased with the violent argument that ensued and Lev dropped his harsh manner. They were reconciled and Lev described in his diary a "conversation full of tender emotion."

Not long after Lev gave up the Stockholm trip for Sonya's sake, his son Sergei and Buturlin, a family friend, visited Yasnaya and urged him to reconsider attending the peace conference. Without much thought Lev agreed and began work on his talk; Sonya learned he had not kept his promise and, sobbing, took to her bed. When Lev went to her she told him that Dr. Makovitsky, who had given her a sedative, had tried to poison her. It took a visit from the Tolstoys' daughter Tanya to restore peace. "My sweet Tanya," Sonya said feebly from her bed, "you know, I suppose, I thought that they wanted to poison me." Tanya comforted her mother but told her that she was being obstructive about the trip to Sweden and Sonya relented, deciding that Lev could go if she went along to look after his health. The drama came to a sudden end when the conference was postponed indefinitely because of a strike in Sweden.

Chertkov received from Sasha an account of all the domestic strife surrounding the proposed trip and wrote a presumptuous letter to Lev regretting "the horrors which for so many years already have been going on around you." Sonya's behavior was playing into Chertkov's hands. She knew this herself but she could hardly have changed. Sonya would have been able to communicate rationally but part of her husband's mind was closed to her, that part Lev allowed Chertkov to dominate. Hurt and angry because she could not discuss with Lev any demand that conflicted with Chertkov, Sonya took the only course available to her—hysterical behavior to provoke her husband's attention. She documented her behavior in her diary and, worse, she paraded it openly. Chertkov's influence on Lev became her obsession. Thirty-eight years before, Sonya had spotted the first signs of Lev's depression and had written in her diary:

> Something has come between us like a shadow that divides us.

At that time Lev had said it was his age but Sonya had insisted it was illness. Whereas she had believed then that the illness was due to psychological stress, now she believed that the illness was due to Chertkov.

Outwardly Lev maintained control but inwardly he was as distraught as Sonya, torn with division and shame. All his life he had been too prone to guilt and now he suffered two agonizing guilts—guilt concerning Sonya and guilt concerning his disciples. Both sides demanded allegiance and neither side could he deny.

Eventually his diary began to contain confessions of anxiety, futility and shame similar to his 1884 entries.

In September Lev accepted an invitation to visit Chertkov and on the third departed with Sasha. Several days later Sonya decided to visit Chertkov herself while her husband was with him. She was happily surprised by her welcome:

> Everyone met me, including Lev Nikolaevich, very affectionately. It was very good, friendly, beautiful.

Sonya was pathetically eager for acceptance among those close to Lev—a little warmth and civility and she forgave all, willing to believe only the best. She became agitated, however, when Lev decided to return to Yasnaya directly and not stop in Moscow with her. Lev went to her and afterward wrote in his journal:

> She was so pathetic, the poor thing, sick and weak. She wasn't calm at once but then she was so kind and she spoke beautifully, she was sorry, she said: Forgive me.

A few weeks later in Yasnaya Sonya noted that Sasha had begun to be kind and sweet to her and Sonya thanked God for this.[5] She was grateful to be included in the circle around her husband and she did not suspect ulterior motives.

2.

Sonya's thinking was wishful; scheming lay behind Chertkov's and Sasha's civility. It was expedient to relax the emotional conspiracy in order to divert Sonya's suspicions from more serious betrayal. Lev had refused to sign a document outlining Sonya's copyrights but, during his visit to Chertkov, he had signed a paper which authorized the free publication of all his works written after 1881 and had appointed Chertkov as their editor. This paper was not adequate for Chertkov's purposes nor was it legally binding, but it was the most to which Lev would consent. Chertkov knew that it was Lev's loyalty to Sonya that stood between Chertkov and the legal document he wanted. In October he began a campaign against Lev's reluctance to a formal document assigning the rights to part or all of his works. There were two prongs to his attack— the undermining of Sonya and the aggravating of Lev's guilt. On 1 October 1909 Chertkov wrote Lev:

> I am collecting separately all your letters about your [private] life in order to, in due course, put together from them an explanation of your position for the benefit of those who are actually tempted by . . . general rumors.

Chertkov instigated a series of visits from A. F. Strakhov to Yasnaya, the aim of which was to extract a legal will from Lev. At the same time Sasha cooperated by planting suspicions in her father's mind about the cupidity of his wife and children. She told him that she had heard his family discussing ways in which to make more money from his writing. Lev wrote in his diary on 21 October:

> Just now a conversation with Sasha. She talked about the greed of the children and their calculations on my writings which will come to them after my death.

If there had been no Chertkov, Sasha's efforts to come between her parents could not have succeeded because, in spite of Lev's enjoyment of Sasha's unqualified support, he remained clear-eyed about her animosity toward her mother and he was hurt by Sasha's rudeness to Sonya. After an explosion in November between Sonya and Sasha, Lev noted:

> To be sure, Sasha was guilty. I am grieved for her because she was guilty. I am tired of life.

He wearied of the strife around him. He wrote in his diary that he had spent an evening playing piano four hands with Sonya; that was how he wanted his last days to be, in peaceful rapport with the one whom he referred to as "my dear old wife."

Events were moving inexorably against this rapport. On 26 October Strakhov arrived at Yasnaya, believing that Sonya was in Moscow for a stay of several weeks. In his own account Strakhov explained that Sonya's presence would be "extremely undesirable" for his business. To his consternation Sonya decided to return home early and also arrived on the twenty-sixth. Strakhov waited to catch Lev alone and then presented him with a document drafted by Chertkov which he referred to as a will. Although the paper covered only the rights to Lev's works it could be considered his will since he owned no other property. Lev read the draft and said, "All of this business is painful for me. And what is more, it is unnecessary to guarantee the spread of my ideas by means of all kinds of measures." He added that a will actually expressed lack of confidence in the ideas and he strode out of his study.

Lev wrote in his diary that it seemed to him that he had decided everything in the simplest and most natural manner: He wanted to leave all his works to Sasha's care to be freely distributed, with the verbal understanding that during her life Sonya retained her rights to publish all works written before 1881. Lev did not want to take these rights formally from Sonya any more than he wanted to give them to her formally. He did not want to sign a legal document.

In the evening Strakhov found Lev alone again and told him that by refusing to sign a will he was transferring the copyrights of his works to his family. Lev promised that he would think about Strakhov's words, but once again he broke off the conversation and strode out of his study. In his diary he regretted that he had promised to even consider signing a document:

> I consented. I wanted to say, but I didn't, that all of this
> is very distressing for me and it were better not to do it.

Strakhov's account of his visit showed that he believed his mission was conspiratorial. He noted that at dinner "Sofia Andreevna was far from any suspicions." When Sonya asked him why he had come, he told her "with an easy conscience" that he had come about one thing or another.[6]

The next time Strakhov came to Yasnaya he brought Goldenweizer with him for support and presented Lev with the draft of another will. Lev noted in his diary:

> They brought papers from Chertkov. I changed it all.
> Enough of this boring thing!

Lev thought that he had disposed of the matter. The fact that it eventually took Chertkov ten months to get the complete will he wanted testifies to Lev's aversion to a will. The paper Lev had signed in September did not purport to be a legal document. In November Strakhov was more successful; Lev gave in and signed a formal will giving away all his copyrights to works written after 1881. These were not Sonya's copyrights but they were copyrights that she hoped would one day belong to their children and grandchildren. For the first time in his life Lev had an important secret that he kept from his wife and this did not make him happy. When he returned to Yasnaya just before Christmas he was despondent and silent. There were the usual holiday festivities, decorated trees, masquerades and Sonya dressed up as a witch and did a song and dance for the grandchildren. Lev wrote in his diary that he felt alienated from all around him. He knew that in signing a secret will he had betrayed his wife but he had agreed in order to please Chertkov, the authoritarian figure who made rigorous demands in the name of right and whose approval was not easily won. This time Lev knew that he had bought approval at a terrible price. In his diary he described his constant shame and asked:

> Shall I really end my life in this shameful situation? Lord, help me.

As in 1884, he transferred his shame to his wife and children and to those among whom he lived who were without his beliefs; he wrote that he must treat them as animals, with love and pity, but with no effort to have spiritual communion. In 1884 he had written that Sonya and her sister Tanya were "not human beings." His inner struggle exhausted his health. On 21 January 1910 Sonya noted in her diary:

> This morning Lev Nikolaevich slept late and when he woke he could not remember anything and didn't recognize Ilyushka [a grandson]. He came to my room to say that he could not remember if I were in Moscow or at home.

Lev never lost sight of Sonya's importance in his life and in his angriest moods still recorded her comings and goings. When he woke in confusion he went to her room to be sure that she, his magnetic north when he was lost, was there.

In January Chertkov sent a young university student, Valentin Bulgakov, to help Lev with his correspondence. This served both to increase Lev's indebtedness to Chertkov and to give him another witness besides Sasha to daily events at Yasnaya. Bulgakov, an intelligent and sympathetic youth, did not perform his spying function but was eager to serve Tolstoy, whom he worshipped. Both Lev and Sonya took to him immediately and it was Sonya who persuaded him to give up his daily trip to and from Chertkov's residence at Telyatinki and live at Yasnaya. Bulgakov's journal during his stay, a day-by-day account of the last ten months of Lev's life, eventually reads like an indictment of Chertkov and Sasha.

In spite of the struggles that crisscrossed between Chertkov and Sonya, Lev and Sonya, Sonya and Sasha and Lev and Chertkov, the family life of the Tolstoys was still alluring to others. Bulgakov enthusiastically described a puppet show that Sonya wrote for the grandchildren. Sonya made the puppets and stage herself and spoke all the female roles, giving the male characters to her son-in-law Sukhotin, the former "rake" now thoroughly domesticated by marriage to a Tolstoy. Lev sat in the rear of the audience, watched the performance through binoculars and was entranced to the end, slapping his knee and laughing loudly. Bulgakov was impressed by Lev's lively enthusiasm and interest and by his mental and physical energy. He wrote in his diary:

> He sits on his horse beautifully—erect, holding the reins in his left hand and his right hand on his hip. But when he flies into the wind, then it is beautiful: his horse leaves tracks in the powdered snow and his gray beard glitters in the sun.

Bulgakov told Sonya and Sukhotin how much he admired Lev's horsemanship, but both laughed and agreed that no doubt Lev Nikolaevich had been showing off to impress his secretary.

The underlying tensions were not keeping Sonya from her usual occupations. The previous winter she had taken up again the task, started earlier, of making a bibliography of Lev's works and she had copied *Hadji Murat*. She wrote in her diary:

> I have done positively nothing but copy *Hadji Murat*. Excellent! I cannot tear myself away.

Sonya continued writing her autobiography and kept up her work on her editions. But even in her good moods she was nervous, easily agitated and sensitive to Lev's grumblings. He complained about the second cake at dessert, the flowers on the table (if the land had been given to the peasants there would be no flower beds) and when the warm weather came and Sonya set the dinner table on the terrace he asked why she made a shameful spectacle that passersby would see. Sonya remarked quietly, "I thought you would say: Ah, how wonderful, nature is so—" Her voice trailed off.[7]

It was not always so tense at home. Once when Sonya was playing Beethoven, Lev came in to tea and told her that he had been listening to her with pleasure. Sonya blushed and said that he was surely joking, but Bulgakov saw how pleased she was. In the same kind mood Lev talked to Sonya about his moral qualms when he considered the way they lived and she listened without disagreeing. That night he wrote in his diary:

> I kissed her silently—she completely understands this language.

In Bulgakov's presence Lev told Chertkov about his conversation with his wife. "I spoke warmly," he said, "although calmly and, it seemed, she understood." Long afterward Tanya Tolstoy mused to her daughter, "If only that old couple had been left to live in peace and resolve their problems, if only no one had interfered." [8] But Lev and Sonya were not left alone. These friendly moments came when Sasha was in the Crimea recovering from possible tuberculosis. Lev wept with pleasure when she returned but he made a curious note in his diary:

> She [Sasha] is too cheerful. I am afraid.[9]

Lev seemed to realize that Sasha's cheerfulness did not presage peaceful relations at home.

Meanwhile Chertkov had not relaxed his campaign against Sonya. He borrowed Lev's diaries to copy and quoted freely to others any unfriendly or critical comments about Sonya. He wrote to Dosev, a Rumanian disciple, that Sofya Andreevna was:

> A woman who does not love him [her husband] and hates his soul, and who has lost her mind from egoism, malice and cupidity.[10]

Chertkov's access to Lev's diaries was a painful humiliation to Sonya. She had been their custodian, had copied them and had been the one to give them to the Historical Museum. She feared that Chertkov would not only repeat unkind remarks about her out of context but that he would delete favorable ones. Late in May 1910 she went to Lev with another anxiety—the management of the estate was becoming too much for her. She was nearly sixty-six, increasingly nervous, troubled with neuralgia and no longer the efficient organizer she had been. Even by putting out new editions of Lev's works she could not keep up with the household expenses. Sonya put it up to Lev: What should she do? Her question made him uncomfortable; it touched too closely on the home life of which he took advantage and then complained. He replied that the fault was hers for insisting on an aristocratic way of life and he said that if she did not like her situation she could live elsewhere, perhaps Odoeveo (a small village) or even Paris. This cruel reaction to a request for help sent Sonya running from the house. She lay down in a ditch where the family found her and brought her home. Lev had been frightened and thanked God for her return. The two were so happy to fall into one another's arms that they both dropped the problem that had caused their quarrel. In this friendly mood Lev departed on 12 June for a visit to Chertkov. He took with him what Sonya described as:

> The whole retinue—Sasha, Dr. Makovitsky, the secretary Bulgakov, and the manservant, Ilya Vasilevich.

It was Sonya's earnings that made it possible for Lev to travel in this style but she did not seem to intend any irony; they had parted affectionately. When Lev wrote he asked kindly about her editing and the household affairs and told her:

> However good it is to be a guest it is better to be at home.

He promised to be back before 23 June and ended his letter:

> Good-bye, my dear old wife. I kiss you. Until we meet again—I hope.

Sonya was pleased, but as time went by Lev made no further mention of returning. She worried that at Chertkov's, surrounded by flattering adoration and reminders of his "problem" at home, he would enjoy himself and want to stay longer. Sonya was alone at Yasnaya with only her secretary, Varvara Mikhailovna, for company. Varvara was a close friend of Sasha and unsympathetic to Sonya. With no one to distract her from her fears, Sonya finally insisted that Varvara telegraph to Lev that his wife was nervously ill and that he should come home. Sonya, still afraid that Lev might postpone his return, also telegraphed, "Implore you to come on the twenty-third." An unfortunate reply arrived on that morning:

> More convenient to come tomorrow. Send telegram if absolutely necessary and will come tonight.

Sonya recognized Chertkov's influence in the cold words "more convenient" and she broke down. Sitting at her writing table she composed what she called a "Memorandum before death" and subtitled "A sick woman's ravings." [11] Sonya called herself mad, her enemies called her mad, even her husband referred to her insanity—but her behavior was more like that of a person courting insanity than one actually insane. In the most dramatic manner that she could summon she tried to call attention to her deep emotional needs and to point to the person who had come between herself and her husband after nearly half a century of marriage. Between writing paragraphs she got up and paced the house. She compared the rumbling of the hay carts with a rumbling in her head, she fetched a bottle of opium and read in a medical book the results of opium poisoning. She pictured herself lying under the train on which her husband was returning to her "more conveniently." How big her nose would appear, sticking up straight as she lay in her coffin! Sonya recorded all her wild imaginings, her hysterical effort to go mad, but one can't lose one's mind at will. Sonya's world remained a world of cruel reality.

As for the heartless telegram that provoked Sonya's despair, it had not been sent by Lev. He denied all knowledge of it and suggested it was Bulgakov who wired—but Bulgakov also knew nothing. Sonya's suspicions of Chertkov were probably correct. Either he or Sasha sent the telegram without consulting Lev. In Lev's diary written on the morning of the twenty-third he described his reaction to Sonya's pathetic plea for his return:

> Last night I had only just lain down but was not yet asleep when a telegram came saying, "Implore you to come on the twenty-third." I shall go and am glad of a chance to do my duty.

3.

When Lev came home on the twenty-third he was cold and distant. Sonya at once poured out all her fears concerning Chertkov. For one instant, seeing her husband sitting on a stool, hunched over and silent, she suddenly pitied him—then he looked at her with eyes flashing anger and she spoke roughly. They separated for the night without making peace, but Sonya could not sleep and went to Lev's room to continue the quarrel. In the morning she was frightened and flung her arms around Lev's neck, begging him to pity and caress her. This was what they both wanted; weeping, they held one another and promised to make a fresh start.[12] There might have been a fresh start if there had been no Chertkov, no Sasha and no alterations in Lev and Sonya. Both Tolstoys had changed. Sonya was more aware of her isolation and helplessness (when she and Lev differed Sasha, Chertkov, Goldenweizer, Strakhov and Sergeenko all stood with Lev against her) and thus more desperate and more easily agitated. Lev's change had occurred at Chertkov's, where, injected with Chertkov's poison of suspicion and resentment of Sonya, he wrote a will in his own hand specifying that all his works should eventually go to the public domain. Sonya would not be able to will even her own copyrights to her children. Chertkov had also persuaded Lev to give him all his diaries from 1900 on; that is, all except those written before 1900 that Sonya had turned over to the Historical Museum. Lev was seduced into these actions by a combination of flattery, bullying and reproaches, tactics which he found hard to resist, torn as he was by his inner divisions and guilt.

Lev's diary showed that he was not happy betraying Sonya. At Chertkov's he had written in his diary that he was weak, depressed and

> However much one may wish to live in all things for the spirit, for God, one does remain in doubt and unsettled before many, many questions. The only salvation: Do not allow questions, do for the present that which one thinks at the time better for God, for the spirit. To believe that one is able to live without making mistakes, without sinning, is a great and harmful error.

This was Lev's rationalization for giving in to Chertkov. Even so, the action he had taken made him so unacceptable to himself that he turned away from the truth and chose to play the role of a persecuted, long-suffering, patient husband who tolerated a mercenary, insane wife as part of his service to God. What was left for Sonya? She, too, played a role when she used her facetious madness to try to shock her husband into looking at her and thus at himself. As it was, courting madness, Sonya came close to self-destruction. She complained of heart spasms, pains in her head, intolerable despair, fits of trembling, teeth that chattered, uncontrollable sobbing and a nervous contraction in her throat. Once her former good sense returned, she went quietly to Lev and said that she was ready and eager to change to the life he wanted. Let them start over again somewhere else; she asked him to tell her where he would like to go. "To the south," Lev replied, quickly. "To the Crimea or the Caucasus." For a moment it seemed possible to him. Sonya urged that they leave at once; Lev demurred then and said that before such a change they must try to establish "kindliness" between themselves. Sonya was too late. Three weeks earlier Lev could have accepted her offer; now, however, he was bound to Chertkov by the guilty secret of the will and the awful knowledge that he dared not make plans without Chertkov's approval. Something probably whispered to Lev that Chertkov was not anxious for him to lead an ideal life that included Sonya. Still, Sonya's offer and his rejection of it troubled Lev and the next day he wrote in his diary:

> Yesterday she spoke of going somewhere. I did not sleep all night. I have gotten very tired.

Lev had betrayed Sonya when he made the secret will and now he betrayed himself by refusing her offer. In angry frustration he turned on her and shouted that she felt differently from him in every single thing. Sonya asked in her diary:

> In what? . . . We both believe in God, in goodness, in humility before God's will. We both abhor war and the taking of life. We both love to live in the country. We both dislike luxury—. Only I do not love Chertkov but I love Lev Nikolaevich. And he does not love me but loves his idol.

Sonya received another blow when the government allowed Chertkov to return to Telyatinki for a visit from his mother without specifying the length of time he might stay. This was essentially the lifting of his banishment from the province of Tula. Sonya became so agitated at the news that Lev, to distract her, agreed to go with her on a visit to their son Sergei on Sergei's birthday. Sergei was living in Nikolskoe, half a day's journey from Yasnaya, and the two days away were a happy respite for both Tolstoys. Lev noted in his diary that "Sonya was in a wonderful mood" and she wrote rapturously in hers:

> For two days I have been close, close to my Levochka. We went to the station and he himself wanted to hold my arm.

They returned to Yasnaya on 30 June. The next day Chertkov appeared and he, Lev and Sasha met in Bulgakov's office, now known as the Remington room because of the typewriter. Sonya was alarmed to hear them mentioning her name:

> Lev Nikolaevich, Sasha and Chertkov began some secretive conversation of which I heard very little but the frequent mention of my name. Sasha came around to see whether I was listening to them and, seeing me, broke into a run saying that I had probably heard their talk or plotting

from the balcony. . . . Then I went openly into the room
where they were sitting, exchanged greetings with Chertkov and asked, "Again a plot against me?"

As Bulgakov wrote in his diary:

Yasnaya Polyana has turned into a kind of fortress with
secret meetings, parleys and so on.

Chertkov was now confident enough to attack Sonya to her face
and she recorded in her diary on 1 July how he had waylaid her
on the stairway and shouted at her:

"You are afraid that I shall expose you by means of the
[Lev's] diaries. If I had wanted to I could have smeared
you and your family with dirt as much as I pleased," a
nice expression for a supposedly respectable man. "I have
enough connections and opportunities to do so, and if I
have not done so it is only from affection for Lev Nikolaevich." . . . Chertkov shouted that if he had a wife such
as I he would have shot himself or have run away to America. Then, going down the staircase with my son Lev, Chertkov said spitefully about me, "I do not understand such
a woman who devotes all her life to the murder of her
husband."

Soon after this encounter Lev visited Chertkov at Telyatinki
and Sonya made a scene on his return. Then there happened one
of those transient flashes of their former selves. Sonya went to
Lev as he prepared for bed and asked him to promise never to
leave her secretly. "I am not planning to," he said, "and I promise
never to go away from you. I love you." His voice broke and Sonya
fell into his arms. They assured one another that their love was
as strong as it had ever been. After she had left Lev, Sonya felt
an impulse of gratitude and returned to thank him for the load
he had removed from her heart. Back in her own room she was
surprised to hear the door open. It was Lev. "Don't say anything,"
he begged her. "I simply want to tell you that our conversation
tonight has been a joy to me—a great joy." [13] Again they embraced
and kissed and Sonya wrote in her diary ecstatically:

Mine, mine, cried my heart and now I shall be calmer
and come to my senses, I shall be kinder to everyone and
shall try to be better in my relations with Chertkov.

Lev simply noted:

Late in the evening I had a very good conversation with her.

He was becoming circumspect in kind or sympathetic mentions of Sonya. Chertkov copied his diary and pointed out the error of trusting Sofya Andreevna.

Sonya did try to be calmer but Chertkov's constant presence, his arrogant domination of Lev and his subtle undermining of Lev's affection for her provoked another quarrel. Lev refused to listen to Sonya's complaints and angrily asked her to allow him to sleep. Once more Sonya ran from the house and would not return with young Lev, saying that her husband had thrown her out and so only he must fetch her back. Young Lev ran to his father with this message, but Lev was reluctant to go to his wife— a reluctance that angered his son, who told him impatiently that it was his duty to go.[14] Lev seemed bewildered by his son's reaction, but he went to Sonya in the garden and escorted her to her bedroom. Again they wept and embraced but the next morning Lev noted in his diary:

> Am barely alive. . . . The worst of all was Lev Lvovich; he scolded me as if I were a bad boy and ordered me to go into the garden after Sofya Andreevna. . . . I cannot look at Lev calmly, I am still in a bad state. Poor Sonya has calmed herself. It is a distressing illness.

In a repentant mood Sonya drove to Telyatinki with Bulgakov to pay a courtesy call on Chertkov's mother. As they drove together Sonya began to weep quietly and to beg Bulgakov to persuade Chertkov to return Lev's diaries. "Let him copy all of them," she said, "but just give back to me Lev Nikolaevich's original manuscripts. You know his former diaries were kept by me. Tell Chertkov that if he gives back the diaries to me, I shall rest content. I shall be sympathetic toward him then, he will come to our house as before and we shall work together for Lev Nikolaevich and devote ourselves to him. You will tell him this? For God's sake, tell him!" Bulgakov found Sonya's request reasonable and in Telyatinki sought out Chertkov at once. He found him closeted with Sergeenko; when Chertkov heard Bulgakov's message he became very upset. "You don't mean to say," he asked, "that you told her straight away where the diaries are?" To show how this idea disgusted him Chertkov made an ugly face and stuck out his tongue. Bulgakov said that he had told nothing because he knew nothing. "Ah, that is excellent," cried Chertkov, jumping to his feet and opening the door. "Please go now. They are drinking tea there, you are certainly getting hungry and here we are talking." Bulgakov heard the lock click as the door was shut.[15] He could not have been surprised when Chertkov told him later that it had been decided not to return the diaries.

Once more Sonya was disappointed. She was even more distressed when she looked for Lev's current diary and discovered that he had hidden it from her, thus ending abruptly the dialogue of their thoughts that had lasted for nearly all their marriage. Her wild despair prompted Lev to force a compromise on the diary impasse: He asked Chertkov to return all his diaries in order that Lev could deposit them in a Tula bank where they would be accessible only to himself. Before relinquishing the diaries Chertkov assembled his wife, her sister, Sergeenko, the Goldenweizers and Sasha and together they carefully copied all the passages that were critical of Sonya.[16] Such was Chertkov's sense of his obligation as guardian of Tolstoy's writing.

After requesting the return of his diaries, Lev wrote Sonya a letter promising to show his current diary to no one and telling her that the other diaries would be in the bank. Sonya made her own comments in the margin of the letter. Lev wrote:

> As I loved you in my youth, so, in spite of various reasons for coolness, I have loved you unceasingly and I love you. The reasons for this coolness were (I do not speak of discontinuing marital relations—such discontinuing only removed falsely expressed, not real love). . . .

Here Sonya commented:

> Of course the coolness resulted mainly from the cessation of marital relations due to Lev Nikolaevich's illness and old age. Who should know that better than a wife?

Lev went on to say that their present coolness was due to her character, which had recently become "irritable, despotic and unrestrained," and to their different objectives, his spiritual and hers material. Sonya might have reminded him of her offer to go away and live as he wished but she read on to a more palatable paragraph:

> My appreciation of your life with me is thus: I, a deeply depraved man, vicious in sexual attitudes and no longer

young, married you, a pure, good, intelligent girl of eighteen and, in spite of my filthy, vicious past, you have lived with me, loving me, a difficult, hard-working life for fifty years, giving birth, nursing, bringing up the children and looking after me, not yielding to those temptations which could have so easily taken hold of any strong, healthy, beautiful woman in your position. But you have always lived so that I have nothing for which to reproach you. . . . This is a true description of my attitude toward you.

At this point Lev's letter became confused. He agreed to give up seeing Chertkov for Sonya's sake but then he wrote:

If you do not accept these conditions for a kindly, peaceful life, I shall take back my promise not to leave you.

Sonya noted in the margin that he had not proposed any conditions. Toward the end of the letter Lev pleaded:

Think quietly, darling friend, listen to your heart, feel, and you will decide everything as it ought to be.

Sonya wrote in the margin that what she was to decide upon had not been mentioned. Lev ended his letter:

My darling, stop torturing, not others, but yourself because it is yourself who suffers a hundred times more than anyone. And that is all. Lev Tolstoy. 14 July in the morning.

Because of the kind paragraphs in Lev's letter, Sonya called it a "happy day." Her half victory over the diaries availed her little, however. On 17 July Chertkov persuaded Lev to write yet another will in his own hand, this time to Goldenweizer's dictation, the previous will having turned out to be insufficient legally. Sonya had not lost her sixth sense and the next day asked Lev if he were not hiding something from her. What was it? Had he betrayed her? If Sonya had been less distraught she might have stated her case without accusations that undermined her cause, but Sonya could not speak calmly. Her agitation became so pronounced that on the nineteenth Lev arranged for a doctor and a psychiatrist to examine his wife. The doctors found a temporary condition of hysteria. Lev told Bulgakov afterward that Sonya would definitely have a normal old age. Sasha was listening to this and interjected, "That is not likely to happen." "Why not?" her father retorted.

The medical men had no specific therapy for Sonya except the suggestion that she should live apart from her husband, a suggestion neither Lev nor Sonya was ready to accept. Sonya was quieter but suspicions still tortured her and, indeed, the matter of the will was not over. Goldenweizer had forgotten to dictate the words, "being of sound mind and in possession of all my faculties." One more time the document had to be rewritten, signed and witnessed. Lev refused to go to Telyatinki again for this purpose, but met Goldenweizer and others in the woods near Yasnaya. There Lev sat on a tree stump and wrote and signed his final will. Because it was legally improper to make a will without an heir, Lev left his works to Sasha with the understanding that she would give them to the public domain. He mentioned but did not put in writing that Sasha understood that during Sonya's lifetime she would retain her copyrights but after her death these would go to Sasha to be made free to all. Chertkov was appointed the custodian of all of Tolstoy's writings.

Lev rode home with a fresh burden of guilt. As a gesture of appeasement toward Sonya he sent Chertkov a note asking him not to visit Yasnaya for a while, but even chance was against the troubled household. Chertkov decided to ride to Yasnaya for tea and chose a different road from that taken by Lev's messenger. When Sonya heard that he was in the house she put her head in her hands and sobbed, provoking Sasha to spit on her mother and shout at her, "Phew, the devil knows how these scenes get on my nerves." [17] Sonya ignored this rudeness and went stoically to preside at the tea table. There was a white cloth, the samovar and a large bowl of red raspberries, but everyone, including Chertkov, was depressed. Later Bulgakov wrote in his diary:

> When I recall that evening, I am struck by Sofya Andreevna's intuition: she seemed to feel as though something terrible and irreparable had just happened.

Lev certainly felt that way. The next day he wrote in his diary:

> It is awful, my health is very bad but my bad health is nothing compared to my mental state. Well, what of it? *Je m'entends.* [I know what I mean.] I am sick at my stomach. I was not able to stand my ground against the demands that I take care of it.

He asked God to help him to do his will but he added that it seemed to him that his concessions to Chertkov hurt both himself and Sonya and that "I want to try some other way." Lev was not entirely lost to Sonya; however, Chertkov, Sasha, Golden-weizer, Strakhov and Sonya herself, by her nervous collapses, had worn him down and he had not been able to "stand his ground."

4.

The more Lev's conscience was tormented by his guilty secret, the more withdrawn he became from Sonya. Again and again he replied to her questions with, "I do not choose to discuss that," or he simply kept silent. Sonya pleaded, wept and made angry demands to know what was happening behind her back. Nothing hurt her so much as Lev's refusal to communicate with her. She clung to the small habits of conjugal life that survived—dinner, when she could fuss over Lev's appetite, short walks in the garden after dinner, caring for his clothes, doing his mending and giving him an oil enema when necessary. Once she took a drastic step. Exhausted by the summer heat—it had been 29°C. (84°F.) in the middle of July—and tired of her own excessive emotion, she resolved to leave home for a while. She would give herself a rest from Chertkov and Lev a rest from "my presence and my suffering soul." She announced to the family that she was leaving for an indefinite time, pushed aside by her husband and spat upon by her daughter.

Sonya considered staying in a Tula hotel for a while, or the Moscow house, but in the station in Tula she met Andrusha with his children and his new wife. Andrusha warmly supported his mother. How could Sonya resist his pleas to return with them to Yasnaya, even though she dreaded facing what she believed would be Lev's derision. At home she sneaked at once to her room and lay down. To her astonishment Lev came to her. He was badly shaken and said, "I absolutely could not live without you. It was exactly as if I had crumbled into pieces. We are too close to one another and we have grown too much together. I am so grateful to you for coming home, my darling. Thank you." As so many times before, the old couple held one another, kissed and spoke of their love.

Sonya begged Lev to trust her more and not to arouse her fears and suspicions. When she mentioned Chertkov he became confused and silent. That very day Sasha had approached Goldenweizer with the alarming news that Lev Nikolaevich was considering telling his wife about his will. Goldenweizer hastened to Lev to warn him that on no account should he speak of the matter to his wife. When Lev asked him why not, Goldenweizer gave two reasons: First, giving in to Sofya Andreevna's demands only provoked further demands and, second, her knowing about the will would give her a real basis for hating Chertkov. Lev backed down but Sasha and Goldenweizer were still uneasy, particularly when Lev escorted Sonya affectionately in to dinner. Separately they saw him alone to remind him to beware of kindness from his wife—it was simply a ruse by which to get her way. Chertkov, alerted to Lev's warm attitude toward Sonya, wrote to Lev that he had "indubitable proof" that Sonya and her sons planned to declare Lev senile so that they could invalidate any will he might make. Lev replied that this was an exaggeration but the insinuations from so many people confused him.

It was at this time that Lev began keeping a secret diary, "just for myself alone." In his first entry on 29 July he noted:

> If the suspicions of some of my friends are justified, an attempt is being made to gain her way by being affectionate. For several days now she kisses my hand which she never did before and there are no scenes and no despair.

Just as Sonya's hysteria had played into her enemies' hands now they used her affectionate manner to suggest evil motives. But in his private diary Lev set the blame squarely where it belonged:

> Chertkov has drawn me into a struggle and this struggle is painful and repellent to me.

Reinforcement for Lev's momentary reasonableness came from the disciple Biryukov who came for a visit to Yasnaya and was horrified that Lev had made a will and kept it a secret from his wife and family. He pointed out the conspiratorial way in which it had been made. Would it not have been more in the spirit of Lev's convictions to gather his family together and tell them his wishes? In the secret diary Lev noted on 2 August:

> I understand my mistake only too well. I should have summoned all the heirs and declared my intentions—not kept it a secret.

Lev now resolved to do just this but he did not dare act without Chertkov's approval. He wrote his disciple a letter that created panic at Telyatinki. Chertkov replied at length, insisting that under no circumstances should Sonya know about the will as she and her sons might succeed in some moment of Lev's weakness, perhaps even on his deathbed, in getting him to renounce his intentions. Chertkov was bold enough to describe for Lev Sonya's secret thoughts and to explain what her intentions really were with regard to her husband's work. He said that one of Lev's sons had waved the short story, *The False Coupon*, in the air and cried, "We'll get a hundred thousand rubles out of this if we get a kopek." Tanya Tolstoy, in her book *Tolstoy Remembered*, mentions that she questioned the brother accused by Chertkov and he vehemently denied ever speaking such words or having had such a thought.

Goldenweizer and Anna Konstantinova, Chertkov's wife, also wrote urging Lev to have the most serious suspicions concerning Sonya's motives. This officious interference in his private life hurt Lev and he wrote back saying that things were not so bad as they imagined. To Chertkov he wrote that he was well and happy and that everything at home was quiet—a quiet that did not last. Sonya could not rest knowing that Chertkov, her daughter and many others had more knowledge of her husband's plans than she, his wife. Lev kept his rigid silence when she questioned him and Sonya taunted him with being bound to Chertkov by homosexual love. As proof she read him a sentence from one of his youthful diaries:

> I have so often fallen in love with men; for me the main indication of love is simply fear—fear of offending or not pleasing the loved object.[18]

This use of his diary angered Lev and he locked himself in his room while Sonya, unembarrassed by the presence of Sasha and Bulgakov, wept and begged him to forgive her and open his door. This scene and the pressure from Chertkov's letter wore down Lev's resistance. The following day, 12 August, he wrote to Chertkov:

> Both last night and this morning I thought about your letter of yesterday which aroused in me, mainly, two feelings: disgust at the evidence of crude self-interest and insensitiveness which I either did not see or saw and forgot, and grief and remorse that I hurt you in my letter in which I expressed regret about what had been done. And the conclusion I then came to from your letter was that

Pavel Ivanovich [Biryukov] was wrong and I also was wrong to agree with him and that I fully approve of your actions but am still dissatisfied with my actions; I feel that there might have been a better way for me to act although I do not know how. And now I do not regret what was done, i.e., writing the will that was written, and can only be grateful to you for the interest you have taken in this matter.

Once more Lev capitulated before the father figure who was momentarily able to ease his troubled conscience.

Chertkov accepted Lev's apologies but left nothing to be taken for granted. He wrote to Lev the following brutal advice which he claimed to have obtained from psychiatrists. Three rules should be followed in treating Sonya or anyone mentally deranged: First, avoid her during hysterical scenes; second, never give in to demands, as this only provoked further demands; third, make Sonya understand that there were limits beyond which she must not interfere.[19] Lev noted in his diary:

He is right about effective methods of dealing with sick people.

Lev now tried to achieve complete emotional detachment from Sonya. He told Bulgakov that when he could feel compassion for his wife he rejoiced. "One ought to have pity for her and I rejoice when I succeed—I even made a note about it." Lev was looking at Sonya and her "insanity" as he might have looked at an object under a microscope, with cool detachment. When a ray of real compassion warmed his heart, one or the other of Sonya's enemies was quick to quench it. On 19 August he wrote in his diary:

Just now I met Sofya Andreevna, she was walking very quickly and seemed terribly upset. I became very sorry for her. I told them to watch over her secretly and see where she went. Sasha told me, however, that she does not walk without a purpose but that she is spying on me. I became less sorry for her.

To underscore her suggestion, Sasha gave her father a book on paranoia in which she underlined any comments that could apply to her mother's behavior. The book impressed Lev and he resolved not to cater to his wife but to maintain a calm silence before all her questions and accusations. He withdrew even the bridge of anger.

The embers of the old affection were stirred when Lev, Sonya and Sasha visited Kochety and Tanya's presence had a benign influence. Tanya was distressed by the constant demands her mother made on her father (would he promise never to be photographed with Chertkov, would he promise never to show his diaries to anyone since she no longer saw them and so forth), but Tanya was always kind and gentle with Sonya and she compensated for Sasha's rudeness. Sonya relaxed and when she had to return to Yasnaya on business she and Lev were loath to part. They kissed one another tenderly and Sonya had not been gone long when Lev confessed to Tanya that he missed his wife. "She was very touching when she said good-bye," he said. "The pity I feel for her makes me love her so much. I wrote her a little letter." The letter was from his heart:

> Kochety, 29 August 1910
>
> You touched me deeply, dear Sonya, by your good and sincere words on leaving. How good it would be if you could conquer in yourself that—I do not know how to say it—that which tortures you. How good it would be for you and for me. I do not stop thinking about you. I am writing what I feel and I do not want to write anything superfluous. Please write.
>
> Your loving husband,
> L. T.

Sonya was pleased when she received Lev's letter, but then wept at the words suggesting that she should overcome something in herself. She wrote in her diary:

> He has a single aim and wish and that is that I should master myself and, obviously, allow Chertkov's proximity.

Sonya's reply to Lev was plainly distraught and confused:

> 31 August 1910
>
> . . . I received your letter and Tanya's this morning which made me very happy. So many cares and anxieties fall on me here that I become a little crazy, the more so as, the same as in Kochety, I get up early and go to bed late. The weather is delightful, but Yasnaya Polyana has made a kind of strange impression on me. Everything has completely changed, that is, I have changed my view of everything. As though I have buried something in my

life and must begin life anew. And like after a funeral, such as Vanechka's, for a long, long time one is heartsick for the loss of a beloved being, so now this wound, the loss of happiness and serenity, which fate so unexpectedly sent me, hurts. Here, for the time, being in a familiar situation and without a great number of strange eyes before whom I'm ashamed, pressing on me since there is neither knowledge nor interest in the source of my grief, it would seem that I would begin to be peaceful. I have always been sincere, in spite of my numerous shortcomings. I sincerely loved you and love you and I expressed to you warmly and sincerely that I deeply regret that I cause you suffering.

Sonya had lost the habits of happiness. Her behavior was out of control and without sense. She had bought a toy gun and shot it from her window; she invited a priest to come to the house and sprinkle with holy water every room that Chertkov had entered, that his evil spirit might be exorcised.

In early September she spent another week at Kochety, but this visit was spoiled by quarrels and she returned home more upset than ever. She wept before strangers and talked freely of the third person who had destroyed her marriage. When family or friends visited and she thought they were critical of her and too sympathetic toward Lev, she read them "shameful" entries from her husband's youthful diaries. Sonya had staved off a nervous breakdown for the fifteen years since Vanechka's death; now she had no physical, emotional or mental reserves to draw upon. She went to pieces tragically and at a time when her husband desperately needed her commonsense to help him resolve his own confusions. Varvara took note of all of Sonya's indiscreet words and foolish acts and reported them to Telyatinki; from there they were sent on to Lev with slanderous inventions added by Chertkov. Lev was cold to this tattling at first and told his daughter Tanya, "Thanks be to God that it is of no importance to me, but it has a bad effect on my feelings for her. They should not do this." Gradually, the bombardment of true and false information had its intended effect and Sasha was pleased to write to Bulgakov:

There has been a change . . . in Lev Nikolaevich himself. He himself has begun to feel, partly influenced by letters from good friends, that it is no longer possible to put up with giving in as, strange to say, this neither appeases nor calls forth loving feelings as it would seem that it should but, on the contrary, increases hatred and malicious acts.[20]

Bulgakov was not taken in by this letter; his eyes were open and he knew who it was who committed malicious acts. A week earlier he had written in his diary:

14 September. . . . It is clear to me that she [Sonya], as a sick and elderly woman, should be treated with more delicacy than Chertkov or Aleksandra Lvovna sometimes show her. . . . Both Vladimir Gregorevich and Aleksandra Lvovna somehow suffer from blindness in this relation. The former's purpose is the moral destruction of Tolstoy's wife to get control of all of his manuscripts, the latter is either in conspiracy with him or, as females do, hates her mother and devotes herself to conflict with her as a kind of sport. Neither one or the other reflects credit on her. Varvara Mikhailovna pretends to be equally devoted to mother and daughter, but passes on every latest, awkward, hysterical word of Sofya Andreevna's, thereby inciting her [Sasha] to further warlike actions. Both Goldenweizer and Sergeenko are assisting Chertkov. The picture is appalling and disheartening.

How appalling even Bulgakov could not guess. Lev had finally swallowed the most outrageous of Chertkov's slanders and believed that Sonya was planning to declare him senile. On 22 September he wrote in his secret diary:

I am going to Yasnaya and horror seizes me when I think of what is waiting for me there.

Again he resolved that whatever Sonya's questions or demands he would refuse to reply to her. Lev was often referring to Sonya's "illness" and "insanity" but he himself showed signs of an emotional disorder: stony silences, a blank face without any expression of feeling, the obsession that his wife destroyed his creativity and ability to work and, finally, delusion. In August he had noted in his secret diary:

Today I thought as I recalled our marriage that there was something fatal about it. I was never even in love.

When Sergei Tolstoy read this entry after his father's death he made a note in the margin saying that it could only be attributed to the failure of his father's memory in his eighty-second year.

On the morning of the Tolstoys' forty-eighth wedding anniversary Sonya came to breakfast in an elegant white dress. Bulgakov met her in the garden and offered his congratulations. Sonya gave him her hand, but she asked, "For what? It is such a sad—" Unable to finish her sentence, she covered her face with her hands and walked away. After dinner, however, she wanted Lev to be photographed with her. No sooner were the pictures taken than Sasha made a noisy scene. In a screaming voice she asked why her father had allowed himself to be photographed with his wife and not with Chertkov. She told Lev, "It is inconsistent to sacrifice the interests of both your friend and your daughter for the sake of an unbalanced woman." When Chertkov learned of the photography session, he used it as an opportunity to send Lev a chiding letter. Lev wrote in his diary:

> A letter from Chertkov full of reproaches and accusations. They are tearing me to pieces. Sometimes I think that I should go away from all of them.

Lev was annoyed by the pettiness of Chertkov and Sasha; on the other hand, his sympathy for Sonya had become mechanical rather than heartfelt. He told Bulgakov, "She is in a dreadful, pitiful state. I am making an effort to disentangle myself from this situation." Lev had nursed his hostility against Sonya until she had become his enemy. Her affectionate overtures irritated him. He spoke with detachment to Bulgakov but fumed in his secret diary:

> These expressions of love, this loquaciousness and constant interference. It is still possible to love, I know this, but I cannot. . . . My hostile feeling for her is terribly distressing but I cannot overcome it when she begins this talking, endless talking, talking without end and without sense or purpose. . . . Today I felt very strongly the need for creative work but I see that it is impossible . . . and this is because of her, because of my persistent feeling about her and my inner struggle.

Lev's inner struggle wore out his physical health and Sonya discovered him in convulsions. In all he had five seizures, some so violent that his whole body was flung crosswise on his bed. Sonya held on to his feet and prayed aloud, "Lord! Just not this time, just not this time!" She turned to Sasha and explained pathetically, "I suffer more than you; you lose a father but I lose a husband of whose death I am guilty." Sasha did not speak; she remained calm with her lips pressed tightly together.

When Lev was resting after his seizures, Sonya tiptoed into his darkened room and accidentally made a noise. Lev asked, "Who is it?"

"It's I, Levochka."

"Why are you here?"

"I came to see you."

"Ah." [21]

Sonya was badly frightened. She faced squarely the knowledge that Lev would not live much longer and she became increasingly frantic to set things right between them, to communicate with him without irritating him, to show him her love and to reach his heart if she could not reach his head. Only a few weeks earlier he had told her that he could not live without her; now when she opened his study door he asked coldly, "Can't you leave me in peace?" Sonya slipped away and resorted to letters, hoping that he would read where he would not listen. She wrote him that she was convinced that he had made an agreement with Chertkov, an evil act which would deprive his children of his copyrights, and she begged him to reconsider what he had done under the influence of "that wretch." She wrote:

> Every day you ask me about my health, how I slept, as though you were sympathetic but I am not able to stop suffering because every day there are new blows which sear my heart, which shorten my life and which torture me unbearably.

Lev called Sonya's letters "insane." He ignored them, remained outwardly coldly civil and kept his anger for his diary:

> She knows about some will, leaving something to someone, obviously concerning my works. What torment she suffers for their money value. . . . But this is obvious and better than when she talks exaggeratedly about her love, falls on her knees and kisses my hands. It is awful for me.

Lev sat on a volcano of suppressed rage. Sonya alone could not have aroused such a white heat of anger. Her hysteria, her foolish accusations, her normal need to know her husband's plans and to share his old age, all this both irritated Lev and shamed him— but a good part of his anger was probably at Chertkov and had been accumulating ever since the disciple's return from England. Certainly a proud and courteous man like Lev must have resented the nannylike rebukes from a younger and inferior person, rebukes often given in front of family and friends. Certainly Lev must have recoiled from Chertkov's presumptuous interference in his personal life, the letter about the "horrors" of his marriage, the file kept in order that Chertkov could write his own version of the Tolstoys' home life, the sheer effrontery of informing him of his wife's secret thoughts and intentions. And the will, the will so against Lev's principles that he felt sick to his stomach after he failed to stand his ground against it, sick at being coerced. But Lev's diary shows that he did not believe that anger was permissible against Chertkov, a disciple who had suffered exile for him and whose approval, when given, had such a satisfactory stamp. Violent anger must go somewhere and once more it was Sonya who was blamed by Lev for his double bind, as he had chosen to blame her in 1884. Subconsciously he may have realized that it was more dangerous to vent his feelings on Chertkov, who brooked no disagreement, than on the wife who loved and forgave him in between their quarrels. When Sonya stopped quarreling and tried to be conciliatory she removed the pretenses for anger and it seems that Lev began to hate her for her love.

At times the old relationship took him unawares. He brought Sonya a pear, admonishing her to be sure to eat it, and she took comfort. Such moments were rare. Like Sonya, he began to talk indiscreetly to visitors. He described his marital problems and talked of his longing to leave home forever. On 20 October Mikhail Novikov, a peasant to whom he poured out his troubles, confessed that he took the whip to his own wife. The next day Lev wrote in his secret diary:

> I keep remembering Novikov's words, "When I used the whip she got much better" and Ivan's "It is our way to use the reins" and I am annoyed at myself.

Ivan was the Yasnaya coachman and Sasha had passed on to her father Ivan's sympathy for Lev Nikolaevich's troubles with the Countess and his recommendation that Lev should handle her as they did in the country. "If a woman plays the fool, her husband uses the reins on her—she becomes like silk." A few days later Lev admitted in his diary that he could not stop thinking of Novikov's words.

Sasha also told her father that Sonya was negotiating with a publisher to sell all his works for one million rubles.[22] There seems to be no foundation for Sasha's accusation and she herself does not mention it in her books. When Sasha reported Lev's coldness toward Sonya to Telyatinki Chertkov was encouraged to boldly send Lev a copy of his (Chertkov's) letter to the Rumanian disciple Dosev, in which Chertkov called Sonya a woman who hated her husband's soul and who had lost her mind from egoism, malice and cupidity. He reminded Lev that Dosev was one among many who believed that Tolstoy should leave home. Chertkov's letter came on 22 October. On the twenty-fourth Lev sent a short note to the peasant Novikov asking him:

> If it should happen that I came to you, would you be able to find me a place in your village, warm but small and detached.

Two days later Lev mentioned to his old follower, Maria Aleksandra Schmidt, that he was thinking of leaving home. Maria Aleksandrovna rebuked him for the selfishness of such a thought and Lev admitted in his diary that it was a temptation that his conscience would not permit. The following night he was lying in bed awake and heard Sonya moving in his study. There was a noise of papers being shuffled as though she were going through his desk and Lev assumed that she was looking for his will. When he sat up in bed and lit a candle Sonya saw the light and opened the door. She asked him if he felt all right and when she left Lev experienced what he later described as "disgust and rage." Precipitously, he made a "firm resolve to go." He wrote a cold letter to Sonya, wakened Sasha and Dr. Makovitsky and told them he was leaving the house secretly. While they packed for him he went to the stables and arranged for the horses. Shortly before six in the morning of 28 October the eighty-two-year-old Lev, accompanied by Dushan Makovitsky, left Yasnaya Polyana forever.

Chapter Ten

SO MANY THINGS FALLING ON SONYA, 1910–1919

1.

Sonya spent a restless night and did not fall asleep until early morning. It was eleven o'clock, just five hours after Lev's departure, when she came downstairs from her bedroom. She went directly to her husband's study and when she did not find him there she ran to the Remington room and from there to the library. She was already frightened when she met Sasha and Bulgakov in the library. In his diary for that day Bulgakov described in detail how Sonya received the news of her husband's flight.

"Where is Papa?" she asked.

"He has gone," Sasha replied calmly.

"Where to?"

"I do not know." According to Bulgakov, Sonya's knees sagged and she leaned against a doorway. Clasping her hands, she begged Sasha to tell her more. For reply Sasha handed her mother Lev's letter. "My God," Sonya whispered as she tore open the envelope. She read the first line of the letter, "My leaving will grieve you," and flung it onto the library table. "My God, what is he doing to me?" she whispered, as if to herself, and ran from the room. "Read the letter," Sasha called after her. "Perhaps there is something there." Sonya made no reply but moments later a servant came, crying that Sofya Andreevna was running toward the pond. Sasha turned to Bulgakov and said, "Follow her. You are in boots." When she had put on her boots Sasha ran past Bulgakov puffing like a steam engine with her skirts bustling. When they reached the pond

Sonya was sinking, her face upward with open mouth and water covering her. With the help of one of the servants who had followed, Sasha and Bulgakov pulled Sonya onto a small dock and took her to the bank. Sasha ran for dry clothes while Bulgakov and the cook led Sonya slowly toward the house. Once she suddenly sat down on the ground and said quietly, "I just want to sit a little bit. Let me sit." A servant then brought a chair and in this Sonya was carried to the house. At the door she instructed the cook to go to the station and find out to where Lev Nikolaevich had purchased tickets. She also gave the cook a telegram to be addressed to Lev on his train: "Return at once. Sasha." The cook showed the wire to Sasha, who telegraphed her father to ignore all communications that were not signed Aleksandra. She also wired her brothers and Tanya to come home at once.[1]

By 29 October the family had assembled. Sergei was appalled by the change in his mother. She greeted him in her dressing gown with disheveled hair. Her face was not one he knew but old, shriveled and trembling. Her eyes could not keep still. None of her children could understand the fluctuations in Sonya's behavior; at one moment she pressed Lev's little pillow to her bosom, the one that she had made for him, covering it with kisses and crying, "Darling Levochka, where are you laying your tired head now? Hear me. You know that distance means nothing." Moments later she would cry out, "He's a beast. It would be impossible to act more cruelly—he deliberately wanted to kill me." Sonya warned her children that if they did not allow her to drown herself she would find another way to die. The family decided to keep her under constant surveillance and sent for a psychiatrist and a nurse from Moscow.[2]

Tanya and all her brothers, except Sergei, desperately wanted their father to return home. When Sasha admitted that she knew his whereabouts (Lev had told her in secret that his first destination would be the Optina Monastery), the children decided to write to him. Sasha agreed to transmit their letters and one from Sonya. Andrusha wrote on behalf of himself, young Lev and Misha. He spoke of their love and sympathy for their father, but he added firmly:

> As a conscientious duty I must warn you that your final decision is killing Mother.

Ilya begged his father to remember his forty-eight years of marriage and be considerate of his wife:

Write to her, give her the opportunity for her nerves to get stronger and then—then as God grants.

Tanya was puzzled. She wanted to see Lev's flight as a final pilgrimage of the soul, but she was vividly aware of her mother's suffering. She chose not to take sides and wrote:

Dear, precious Papenka,
You have always suffered from a great amount of advice—therefore I shall not give you advice. You, like everyone, must act in the way that you think necessary. I shall never condemn you. About Mama, I tell you that she is pitiable and touching.

Sergei's short letter supported his father, telling him that Lev's position had been desperate and Sergei believed that he had chosen the right way out. At the time Sergei believed that his father was fulfilling an "ardent dream" to live a holy life and to make a final search for truth.[3] But, except for Sasha, all the children were badly shaken and confused. It was Ilya, the sensitive son who had always been closest to his father, who wrote the most plausible explanation for Lev's sudden flight from home. Ilya suggested that, because of his will, his father found himself in a position that was

. . . truly hopeless. To tell everything to his wife was impossible because this would have hurt his "friends." To destroy the will was still worse. His "friends" had suffered for his convictions, morally and some of them even materially; they had been exiled from Russia. And he felt that he had an obligation to them. And, on top of this, there were still his fainting spells, his progressive forgetfulness, the clear consciousness of his nearness to the grave, the increasing nervousness of his wife, who somehow felt in her heart the unnatural aloofness of her husband and did not understand it. And if she asked him what it was that he hid from her? Either he told her nothing or he told her the truth. But this was impossible. What was he to do?

Ilya wrote that his father had always had a dream of once living a holy life in poverty and simplicity, the dream that Sergei believed had finally lured his father from home. Ilya thought that the dream served only as an excuse, a choice between two evils:

Harassed, ill in body and mind, he started forth without any object in view, without any thought-plan, merely in order to hide himself somewhere, wherever it might be, to get some rest from the moral tortures which had become insupportable to him.

Lev's insupportable moral tortures may not have been caused by Sonya's hysterical behavior alone nor by her rummaging through his desk, probably looking for a will that she suspected existed, but also by the truth that he had, indeed, made a will—a secret, unfair will that would cause pain and hardship after his death. Until Chertkov interfered, Lev had wanted to leave the disposal of his works to his heirs as stated in his 1895 diary, but he had not been able to stand his ground against Chertkov. In choosing Chertkov's side, Lev had become divided against himself and his first flight from home was when he tried to believe that he was someone other than his true self. He wrote in his diary that he had never loved his wife and that he could not stop thinking about horsewhipping her.

In February 1910 Lev described for Bulgakov a dream which, as recounted in Bulgakov's diary, can be looked upon as a prophetic allegory to Lev's situation:

He had dreamed that someplace he had picked up an iron stake and set off to somewhere with it. And there he saw a man who crept up behind him and slandered him: "Look, there goes Tolstoy! How much harm he has brought to everyone, the heretic!" Then Lev Nikolaevich turned and with the iron stake he killed the man. But in just a moment he evidently rose from the dead because he moved his lips and said something.

With the iron stake Lev killed the true self that was dogging his heels. This was necessary in order that he might be at peace with the self who was Chertkov's. When Sonya opened his door on his last night at home, anxious because she saw his candle burning, the true Lev moved his lips. He was not dead. Lev's flight from home could be seen as more of a flight from himself than from Sonya; if he had lived, it might have been the catalyst that brought him back to her.

When Lev wrote his letter to Sonya in the early hours of 28 October, he was striking at himself with his iron stake:

My leaving will grieve you. I am sorry for this, but you must understand and believe that I cannot act differently.

My position at home is becoming, has become, insufferable. Besides everything else, I cannot live anymore in
these conditions of luxury in which I have been living
and I am doing what old men of my age usually do: leaving
the life of the world in order to live the end of their days
in solitude and quiet.

Please understand and do not come after me, even if
you find out where I am. Your coming after me would
only make your position and mine worse, and would not
change my decision. I thank you for your forty-eight honor-
able years of life with me and I beg you to forgive me
for all that I have been guilty of against you just as I
with all my soul forgive you for everything that you were
guilty of against me. If you wish to communicate with
me, communicate with Sasha. She will know where I am
and will pass on to me what is necessary; she cannot
say where I am because I have her promise not to tell
anyone. I have instructed Sasha to gather together all
my things and manuscripts and send them to me.

Lev Tolstoy

After this letter Lev made one more strike against himself. Although
his first letter to Sasha was mild (he begged her to control her
temper when talking to her mother) in the second letter to her
he wrote that he could no longer tolerate Sonya's

. . . spying, eavesdropping, these everlasting reproaches
and the unnatural hatred of the man who is closest and
most necessary to me, with this clear hatred of me and
the pretense of love.

He wrote that he wanted only one thing and that was to be free
of his wife and of her lies, pretense and malice. His true self was
alive, however, and at the end of this letter he wrote, "You see,
dear, how ill I am. I do not hide it."

When Sonya replied to the letter Lev left for her she ignored
its cold manner and poured out from her heart:

29 October 1910

Levochka, sweetheart, return home, darling, save me from
a second suicide. Levochka, friend of all my life, I will
always do everything that you want, I will cast aside entirely any luxury, I shall be friendly with your friends, I
will undergo a cure, I will be gentle, darling, darling,

come back. You know you must save me and you know what it says in the gospels, one must never on any grounds forsake one's wife. Darling, sweetheart, friend of my soul, save me, come back if only to say good-bye before our eternal separation. Where are you? Where? Are you well? Levochka, do not torture me, sweetheart. I will serve you lovingly with all my being and soul, come back to me, come back; for God's sake, for the love of God of which you always speak, and I will give you such humble, selfless love! I honestly and firmly promise, sweetheart, we shall always be friendly, we shall live simply and where you want and as you want. Well, good-bye, good-bye, perhaps forever.

Your Sonya [4]

Sonya demonstrated at once that she meant to keep her word and she took positive steps to make Chertkov her friend. She sent Bulgakov to Telyatinki to beg Chertkov to come to her and be reconciled and she gave Sasha a telegram to send to her father telling him of this step. She asked Bulgakov to reassure Chertkov that her invitation was without ulterior motive. Bulgakov was hopeful that at last there might be peace between the two. "But, alas," he wrote in his diary, "Chertkov did not change his cautious character, alien to sentiment." "But why should I go?" Chertkov asked. "In order that she humble herself before me and ask my pardon? This is a trick of hers in order to ask me to send a telegram for her to Lev Nikolaevich."

The Tolstoy sons and Tanya were astounded at Chertkov's refusal. They could not believe that he would not relent in the circumstances and they sent Dr. Berkenheim, a family friend and an older person than Bulgakov, to persuade Chertkov. But Chertkov had no desire to relieve any of Sonya's sufferings. He wrote his true feelings to Lev, saying that words could not express his joy at Lev's departure and that his whole being was convinced that it was the right course of action. Even now Chertkov seemed to be wary of the strength of Lev's attachment to Sonya; he warned Lev to feel no qualms concerning his wife, that his flight was making things better for everyone and most of all for Sofya Andreevna. Chertkov did not rely on his letter alone. From Sasha he knew that Lev was presently at Optina and he sent Sergeenko to visit him and strengthen his resolve. Sergeenko described to Lev Sonya's reaction to his letter, her attempt to drown herself, her hysteria and he added that Sofya Andreevna had instructed Andrusha to find his father at all costs. The news did not cheer Lev and he noted in his diary:

I was very depressed all day and also physically weak.

The next day Sasha arrived with the family letters. Except for Sergei's, Lev found them painful. He wrote one reply to all the children but sent his thanks only to Tanya and Sergei, the two who had not urged his return. To Sonya's letter he replied:

> 31 October 1910
> Our meeting and even more my return *now* is completely impossible. Everyone tells me that for you it would be harmful in the highest degree, and for me it would be terrible, since my situation now on account of your excited state, irritability and sick condition is even worse than before if that is possible. I advise you to reconcile yourself to what has happened, to settle yourself in your, for the time being, new position, but above all to accept treatment.

Lev's words were not affectionate but there was hope in the fact that he underlined the word "now." There was even more hope in this sentence toward the end of his letter:

> Try to turn all your energy, not toward getting what you want—my return now—but toward becoming peaceful in yourself and your soul, and you will obtain everything that you desire.

Even when writing to Chertkov Lev did not rule out his return to Yasnaya but said that he had written to his wife, not refusing to return to her, but making it a condition of his return that she should become calm.

As soon as Sasha joined Lev at Optina she began to urge him to leave the monastery for fear that Sonya would find him there. Sasha warned her father that Sonya had sworn never to be so stupid again, that she would never let him out of her sight but would sleep at his door. Sasha, Varvara (who had come with her) and Dr. Makovitsky began planning where they should go next. Lev was obviously not pleased with their plans and Sasha took him aside to talk to him alone. Afterward she remarked thoughtfully that her father seemed to be regretting his decision to leave home. But Lev, as Ilya observed, was exhausted in both body and mind and he obeyed Sasha's wishes.[5] On the last day of October they left for Novocerkassk, a town just north of Rostov, where they hoped to stay with Maria Nikolaevna's daughter, Lev's niece. They were only about one hundred miles southeast of Tula when they were forced to stop. That night Lev wrote in his diary in a tremulous hand:

> We had a good trip, but after four o'clock I began to shiver. My temperature was forty degrees [104° F.] and we stopped at Astapovo. The kind stationmaster has given us two fine rooms.[6]

Lev had pneumonia. Sasha ignored a promise to let the family know if her father fell ill but wired to Chertkov and, realizing how much responsibility she had taken upon herself, she also sent a wire to Sergei in Moscow asking him to send Dr. Nikitin, a family friend. In the meantime, the family at Yasnaya remained in ignorance. Although Chertkov confided to Bulgakov that he was leaving for Astapovo to join Lev, he first extracted Bulgakov's promise not to inform Sonya or any of the children. Lev's whereabouts were no longer a secret, however. The world press was gathering around the stationmaster's house and only the isolation of Yasnaya kept the family uninformed. It was a kind reporter, K. V. Orlov of *The Russian Word*, who telegraphed them:

> Lev Nikolaevich taken ill at house of Astapovo stationmaster. Temperature 40 degrees.

2.

Sonya took charge at once. She thought of everything that her husband might need including the little pillow from which she had not parted since his flight. She hired a special train in order not to wait for the scheduled train and on 2 November she, her psychiatrist, her nurse and her children Tanya, Ilya, Andrusha and Misha arrived at Astapovo. Sergei had already come from Moscow and seen his father. The family held a conference in the railway car which was shunted onto a siding. Sasha told them that Lev wanted her to wire his sons begging them to prevent their mother from coming because his heart was so weak that he feared a meeting would be fatal. The children decided that because of their father's request to Sasha he should not be told that Sonya was in Astapovo; Ilya, Andrusha and Misha agreed not to see him so that he could think that they were with their mother. Sonya agreed to this with sorrow, saying that she did not want to be the cause of her husband's death.

Sonya's position could not have been worse. The two people who had tried so persistently to come between her and her husband, Chertkov and Sasha, were with him while she, who had cared for him through all his other illnesses, was ostracized. Her family, Chertkov and the world at large said that Tolstoy had fled home to escape from his wife. Sonya also believed this. In her despair she accepted the cruel verdict of her enemies. She longed to beg Lev's forgiveness, to be given another chance. Her final humiliation was that her bitter vigil outside the stationmaster's house was kept in front of the entire world. Reporters and photographers swarmed around the station, around the house where Lev lay and around the Tolstoy railway carriage. When Sonya stood peeking pathetically through a window trying to catch a glimpse of her husband, she was photographed. She noted in her diary:

> I exhaust myself walking around the little house where
> L. N. lies.

She wept as she wandered around the station and reporters asked her questions. Poor Sonya was only too glad to pour out her heart to them. Who else was listening to her?

The children did not allow their mother to send a message to Lev, not even under the guise of having been sent from Yasnaya, but they did permit her to send him the little pillow which she had brought. Lev wanted to know at once how the pillow had arrived. Dr. Makovitsky, after stumbling over his reply, said that Tatyana Lvovna had brought it. Lev asked to see his daughter and the overjoyed Tanya ran to her father's bedside.

"How well you look, and stylish," Lev said, and Tanya told him that she knew his poor taste. They both laughed and then Lev asked:

"And Mama, with whom is she staying?"

"With Andrei and Misha."

"And Misha?"

"Yes. They all agree that she should not be allowed to come to you until you want her to." Surely this was the point at which to tell Lev that his wife was in Astapovo but would not disturb him until he sent for her. Tanya had the heart to do this, but not the will; her much stronger-willed sister had frightened her into silence. Lev asked again about Andrei and Tanya told him:

"Yes, and Andrei. They are very dear, the younger boys, very worried, poor things, trying in every way to calm their mother."

"Tell me, what is she doing? How does she occupy herself?" Lev's voice broke with emotion when he spoke and Tanya became alarmed. She suggested:

"Papenka, perhaps it were better for you not to talk; you are upset."

"Tell me, tell me," Lev retorted, "isn't this for me the most important thing?" Tanya told him about the doctor they had for their mother and Lev wanted to know if he was a good one. Tanya assured him that he was and that they also had a very good nurse.

"Does she like her?"

"Yes."

"Well, more. Does she eat?"

"Yes, she is eating now and trying to keep healthy because she lives in the hope of being together with you."

"Did she receive my letter?"

"Yes."

"And what did she think of it?"

"She was mainly reassured by the excerpt from your letter to Chertkov in which you wrote that you would not refuse to return to her if she should become calm." [7]

Lev fell into a deep sleep after this conversation but his intense emotion when speaking of Sonya frightened Tanya. She and her brothers decided that Sasha was right in keeping their mother away from their father. The doctors—the Tolstoys did not leave Lev to the care of Dr. Makovitsky alone but, besides Dr. Nikitin, sent for another family friend, Dr. Berkenheim—were giving Lev morphine and he drifted in and out of sleep. Shortly after his talk with Tanya he woke and wrote in his diary for the last time:

> 3 November. The night was bad. I have lain in a fever for two days. On the second Chertkov came. They say that S. A. [Sofya Andreevna]. . .

Lev did not finish the sentence about Sonya but went on to mention those who had come to see him. The last words of the entry were:

> So much for my plan. *Fais ce que doit, adv [ienne que pourra.* Do what one must, come what may. The sentence

was unfinished.] It is all for the best, both for myself and for others but chiefly for myself.

Lev failed rapidly. In moments of delirium he cried out, "To escape—escape." His family assumed that he was escaping from Sonya; it was only later that Ilya understood that his father was fleeing his own insupportable "moral tortures." Evidence for this is that at Astapovo Lev tried to change his will. On 5 November he told Tanya, "So many things are falling on Sonya. We have managed badly."

"What was that, Papa? So what? Soda?"

"Sonya, on Sonya. So many things are falling on her." With a beating heart, Tanya asked if he would like to see Sonya but Lev had already dropped into a morphine-induced sleep. When he woke he asked to dictate to Dr. Nikitin. Lev began his dictation with an order to abandon all his plans but then became confused. He was obviously tormented that Nikitin could not understand what he wanted. "Why can't you understand?" Lev asked Sergei and Tanya, who also sat with him, "Why don't you want to understand? It is so simple. Why don't you want to do it?" Sergei saw that his father was frustrated by his inability to make himself clear. Later Sergei became convinced that the plan Lev wanted to abandon was his will.[8]

Meanwhile Sonya roamed the little station platform or sat in the railway station writing in her diary. She noted sadly:

> There seems to be little hope. I am torn to pieces by my conscience, by waiting for a terrible end and by the impossibility of seeing my beloved husband.

On 6 November she wrote:

> Painful expectation. I cannot remember anything well.

In a lucid moment Lev said to Sergei, "I am afraid I am dying. It is hard." Another time he called out in a loud voice, "Seryozha!" Sergei ran to the bedside but could not understand what his father was saying. Dr. Makovitsky was certain that it was a whole sentence and he wrote down the words he managed to catch, "Truth . . . I love all . . . all of them." Tanya and Sasha decided that Lev had tried to say, "I love truth very much. I love truth." More probably Dr. Makovitsky took down the correct words and Lev was trying to say that the truth was that he loved all of them— his wife and children, his friends and disciples. During the night of the sixth Lev was restless. When the doctors proposed a morphine injection he emphatically refused. "I do not want morphia!" These were his last words. Soon afterward the doctors managed to give him an injection and he fell asleep. Around 2 o'clock on the morning of the seventh it was decided to assemble the family. At last Sonya was permitted to see her husband. She entered the room calmly, stood for a moment looking at Lev and then went to his bedside and knelt. She kissed his forehead and murmured "Forgive me" and some words of love. Later she comforted herself that Lev had heard her. Sergei was certain that his father remained asleep but Tanya noticed that after her mother spoke Lev gave a few deep sighs. Sonya might have been right that he sighed in recognition; so often he had responded with a sigh when she came to see him— "Ah, Sonya" or simply, "Ah." The sighs did cause the others to fear that he might be waking and would see his wife, so Sonya was hurried from the room. She was not allowed to return until ten minutes before the end. Once more she knelt at the bedside and murmured. Lev gave a final, long sigh and breathed no more. One of the doctors said, "A quarter to six." Soon afterward, on 7 November 1910, the telegraph at Astapovo rattled off two words that were transmitted around the world:

Tolstoy dead.

3.

Sergei and Dr. Makovitsky washed the body and dressed Lev in his gray peasant blouse. They opened the doors of the little house and over a thousand people walked past the body. Sonya sat by the bed; her face was quiet but her head shook pathetically. Leonid Pasternak, an artist and friend, the father of Boris Pasternak, came to make a drawing, the sculptor Mercurov made a cast and the photographers were busy outside the house. On 8 November Sergei, Ilya, Andrusha and Misha carried their father's coffin onto the funeral train. The next morning the peasants from Yasnaya Polyana met the train and bore the coffin to the house. Chertkov had given instructions that it should not be taken inside but left only a few minutes at the entrance. Sonya and her sons changed his orders and Lev was brought into the vaulted room and the coffin opened. Early the next morning, while it was still dark and the room was lit by candles, the people came to say good-bye. Many kissed Lev's hand or forehead and said, "Good-bye, Lev Nikolaevich" or "Thank you, Lev Nikolaevich." At half past two in the afternoon the coffin was closed and carried to the spot in the woods where the green stick of the Tolstoy brothers' childhood fantasy was supposed to lie hidden. There Lev was buried without priest or religious rite, as he had requested. Sonya was calm, quiet and did not weep. Chertkov was not present. That night Sonya opened her diary once more to write two terse paragraphs describing Lev's flight and illness. The last lines were:

> They did not admit me to see Lev Nikolaevich, they held me by force, they locked the door, they broke my heart. 7 November at six o'clock in the morning Lev Nikolaevich died. 9 November they buried him at Yasnaya Polyana.

Sonya never wrote in her diary again, but she recorded her grief in her engagement diary:

> We buried Lev Nikolaevich. . . . Terrible, sleepless nights. Unbearable anguish, conscience-stricken, weakness, pity for the sufferings of my dead husband. . . . I cannot live. . . . Gloomy and awful is the life ahead of me. . . . All the days are the same, anguished.

Although grieving, Sonya was not idle. Many visitors came to Yasnaya Polyana and she took them through the house and to her husband's grave. She was calm with strangers; with friends and family she wept and spoke of her repentance. Even Goldenweizer pitied her. After Lev's death she was no longer hysterical; hysteria had been her desperate effort to communicate with him. She worked on her editions and finished her autobiography, giving her side of the story to prove that Lev had loved her but that others had come between them. This was unnecessary. In their diaries, Sonya's and Lev's, is the record of Lev's struggle against those who wanted to come between him and his wife and the record of their love for one another. Other words also survive to testify to the Tolstoys' love and partnership—and not only the words of those like Fet who knew them in the happiest decades. Leonid Pasternak's acquaintance with the Tolstoys began in 1898. After their deaths he wrote:

> In many respects she [Sonya] was outstanding, a notable person fit for Lev Nikolaevich. Thanks to her critical abili-

ties she was able to understand artistic work and to assist her husband in his literary work. Sofya Andreevna was herself an outstanding personality.

Maxim Gorky observed the Tolstoys closely during Lev's illness in the Crimea. He wrote later that Lev Tolstoy was one of the most complicated of the great men of the nineteenth century and that his wife played a role that was "incontestably difficult and responsible." He called Sonya a "person of strength and sincerity." N. N. Strakhov, closer to the Tolstoys than either Pasternak or Gorky, wrote to Lev in 1895 that he was aware that the deepest bonds existed between Lev Nikolaevich and Sofya Andreevna:

> Bonds stronger than those between children and father and mother, the merging of two people into one.[9]

Except for Sasha, the Tolstoy children were troubled by their part in keeping their father and mother apart during Lev's last illness. Tanya wrote in her diary:

> Sergei says sadly that much irreparable harm has been done and much has been neglected and that it cannot now be repaired. The fault was partly in my indolence and partly in my scruples which made me afraid of boring him, of taking him away from people who, it seemed to me, were more interesting and necessary to him than I was.

Tanya had had too much respect for Chertkov and too little realization of the extent of Sasha's hostility toward their mother. When Tanya finally understood the role that Sasha had played in keeping Lev and Sonya apart at the end, Tanya could not speak of her younger sister without bitterness and sorrow.[10]

Ilya wrote in his memoir about his father:

> It was terrible that she [Sonya] was not permitted to go to her dying husband. This was his wish and the doctor's advice, but it seems to me now that this was a mistake.[11] It would have been better if she had gone to him when he was still conscious. Better for him and for her.

And the last sentence of Ilya's book is:

> If those people who stood nearest to my father in the last year of his life had known what they were doing, perhaps things would have turned out differently.

Sasha and Chertkov continued to work against Sonya. In 1913 they requested possession of all the manuscripts that Sonya had placed in the custody of the Historical Museum. To support their request Chertkov wrote a letter to the minister of education saying that some people believed that Sofya Andreevna's difficult relations with Lev Nikolaevich were due to illness and hysteria; Chertkov felt it his duty to insist that the disagreements were due to Sonya's financial interests in her husband's literary property. He and Sasha urged that they be given possession of all of Tolstoy's manuscripts in order that his wife would not utilize them for her own advantage. Chertkov and Sasha were not successful. On 6 December 1914 the Senate ruled that all of Tolstoy's manuscripts be handed over to his widow. Less than two months after receiving them, Sonya gave the manuscripts to the perpetual custody of what is now the Lenin Library. After Sonya's death Chertkov arranged for Aylmer Maude to translate *Hadji Murat* and then sold the copyright of the novel to an American publisher—thus earning for himself the income that he had persuaded Lev to deny his children and grandchildren. Chertkov also earned money from a book he wrote describing Tolstoy's last days, a book which Sergei described as a "one-sided diatribe against my mother."

Sonya was not alone in her old age. Tanya Kuzminsky and Tanya Sukhotin returned to Yasnaya when they were widowed and Sonya had the company of her three Tanyas; her beloved sister, daughter and granddaughter. Sasha was finally reconciled with her mother and came on frequent visits to Sonya's delight. The Tolstoy sons did not neglect their mother; in fact, Yasnaya was seldom for long without a visit from a member of the family. The last tragedy for Sonya to bear was the death of thirty-nine-year-old Andrusha from pleurisy and hepatitis. He died at Yasnaya on the night of 23 February 1916—the anniversary of Vanechka's death, as Sonya recalled in her diary. After the revolution, Nikolai Obolensky, his second wife and their three children moved into the annex; Yasnaya was nationalized and Kolya became the manager.

Sasha was at Yasnaya when in late October 1919 Sonya fell ill with pneumonia. She had first caught a chill washing windows and standing wet in the cold, autumn wind. Sergei received the word in Moscow that his mother was dangerously ill; it would have taken him several days to get a travel pass if he had not applied to a friend in the Kremlin for assistance. He had to wait only twenty minutes before he received the following permission:

In view of the extremely serious illness of Sofya Andreevna Tolstoy, wife of Lev Nikolaevich Tolstoy, her son, Sergei Lvovich Tolstoy, is permitted to leave Moscow urgently for . . . Yasnaya Polyana. All railway and military authorities are ordered to render every kind of assistance to him for the length of his journey and he is permitted to travel by freight or military convoy or passenger train.

The pass was signed by the president of the Council of the People's Commissars, V. Ulyanov (Lenin).

Sonya was a good patient, grateful to all who cared for her. When Sergei brought her wine she wanted to drink to his health. Her daughter Tanya asked her whether she ever thought of Papa and Sonya replied, "All the time. I live with him and torment myself that I was not good enough for him. But I was faithful to him in body and soul. I married at eighteen and I never loved anyone but him." Sometimes her mind wandered, but when Sergei asked her if she knew him she answered, "Of course, I know all my children." Another time she said to Sergei, "One ought to go without grieving like the peasants." On 2 November Dr. Nikitin came from Moscow and Sergei told his mother that now she would get better. "I am very weak," Sonya replied. When Sergei wished her goodnight she could not answer. After she was no longer able to speak her large, dark eyes followed her sister and children as they moved around her bedside. Sasha could not bear the suffering in those wide open eyes and left the room. On the last night it was Sonya's sister Tanya who sat with her—Tanya with whom she had run and skipped around the house at Pokrovskoe carried away with exuberance, Tanya who could always raise Sonya's spirits. In the next room Sergei and his sisters sat listening to their mother's hoarse breathing. At four-thirty in the morning they heard a rattle, then silence. Outside snow was falling. It was bitter cold when, a day later, Sonya's children carried her coffin to the churchyard on her last journey from Yasnaya Polyana.

NOTES

CHAPTER ONE

1. Lev conversation with N. N. Gusev quoted in *Young Tolstoy, Notes from Contemporaries*, Ch. V, p. 93.
2. Lev diary 17 March 1847.
3. It was usual in Russia at this time for the younger son to receive the family home, and in Lev's case Yasnaya Polyana was his choice. The four Tolstoy brothers gave their sister a share equal to theirs in the division of their father's considerable properties, even though according to law daughters could receive less.
4. Lev diary 17, 18 April 1847.
5. Lev conversation with Paul Biryukov quoted in *Tolstoi's Love Letters*, p. 122 and Lev diary May 1858, April 1861, 9 July 1908 and 14 July 1909.
6. Lyubov's mother, Sofya Kozlovsky, had created a scandal at court where she was a maid of honor. Married to the alcoholic Prince Kozlovsky, she eloped with the man she loved, Aleksandr Islenev. "I am his wife before God," she said, but their marriage was not legal and divorce impossible. The otherwise irreproachable characters of Sofya and Aleksandr won them acceptance within their circle. They were naturally sensitive to their situation, however, and anxious for their daughters to marry men who could secure their position in society.
7. *My Life at Home and at Yasnaya Polyana*, Part I, Ch. 10, p. 62.
8. *Young Tolstoy, Notes from Contemporaries*, Ch. XV, p. 455.
9. *L. N. Tolstoy, Complete Works*, Vol. 13, *War and Peace*, Book I, Ch. V.
10. *My Life at Home and at Yasnaya Polyana*, Part I, Ch. 15, p. 91.
11. Sofya had died after fifteen years living with Aleksandr Islenev.
12. Andrevna is a familiar form of Andreevna.
13. Note 99 to Sonya's diary for 1891.

CHAPTER TWO

1. *Sketches of the Past*, Part I, Family Life, 1862–1870.
2. Lev diary May 1858 and 16 February 1859.
3. Sonya diary 9 October 1862.
4. Selections from A. A. Fet's autobiography printed in *L. N. Tolstoy, Contemporaries' Recollections*, Vol. I, p. 79.
5. *Tolstoy Remembered*, p. 190.
6. *My Life At Home and at Yasnaya Polyana*, Part I, Ch. 24, p. 151.
7. Same, Part I, Ch. 24, p. 159.
8. *Sketches of the Past*, Part I, Family Life, 1862–1870.
9. *My Life at Home and at Yasnaya Polyana*, Part II, Ch. 11, p. 219.

CHAPTER THREE

1. Lev diary 11 April 1863.
2. *Tolstoy Remembered*, p. 33.
3. Although the Tolstoys had nurses and governesses for their children, and later tutors, Sonya was directly involved in all their care. She looked after their physical well-being, nursed them when they were sick and supervised their studies and social and cultural development.
4. *Tolstoi's Love Letters*, p. 104.
5. *My Life at Home and at Yasnaya Polyana*, Part II, Ch. 18, p. 264.
6. Same, Part II, Ch. 22, p. 290.
7. *Father, A Life of Lev Tolstoy*, Ch. 27, p. 268.
8. The Centenary Edition of Tolstoy's works includes "A Comedy in Three Acts" which the editors say was apparently an incomplete version of *The Nihilists*, the final version not being preserved.
9. *Father, A Life of Lev Tolstoy*, Ch. 27, p. 269.
10. *The Russian Messenger*, also translated *The Russian Herald*, was a literary journal that came out monthly from 1856 to 1906. During the lifetime of its first publisher, Mikhail Katkov, it printed most of the major Russian writers; at one time both *War and Peace* and *Crime and Punishment* were appearing in the *Messenger*. After Katkov's death in 1887, the journal became a mouthpiece for reactionary political views.
11. Sonya letter to Lev 25 November 1864.
12. A. A. Fet letter to Lev 16 June 1866, Lev letter to Fet 7 November 1866.
13. Last sentence from *The Diary of Tolstoy's Wife, 1860–1891*, 10 March 1865.
14. *Sketches of the Past*, Part 1, Family Life, 1862–1870.
15. Sonya diary 10 August 1866.
16. Y. F. Samarin was a Slavophile, an essayist, orator and reformist member of the government who drafted Alexander II's proclamation liberating the serfs.

17. *Russian Thinkers*, The Hedgehog and the Fox, p. 55.
18. *The Diary of Tolstoy's Wife, 1860–1891*, 12 September 1867.
19. I. S. Turgenev letter to P. V. Annenkov 13 April 1868.

CHAPTER FOUR

1. Samara was the name of a province in central Russia and of its capital, a city on a bend in the Volga. The steppes of Samara, vast, treeless plains, stretched eastward from the Volga toward the city of Orenburg. Today the province and capital city are called Kuybyshev.
2. Lev letters to Sonya 18 June and 16–17 July 1871.
3. Lev letter to N. N. Strakhov 23–24 September 1873.
4. In Plato's dialogue *Phaedo*, the body is a lyre and the soul is the harmony.
5. Lev letter to Aleksandra (Granny) Tolstoy 15–30 December 1874.
6. Untreated meningitis, and in 1875 there was no effective treatment, is usually fatal. Those who survive without treatment are sometimes mentally retarded.
7. It is highly unlikely that Sonya survived peritonitis without surgery or antibiotics. She probably had a severe intestinal infection.
8. Optina Monastery was in the Kaluga district, about sixty miles west of Tula. Shamardino, a convent, was a few miles from Optina.

CHAPTER FIVE

1. In spite of her problems feeding her first child, Sonya nursed most of her babies, Masha and Sasha being the exceptions.
2. Lev notebook 27 and 30 September 1878.
3. Of the thousands of words Lev wrote about his religious beliefs, I quote one from his youth and one from maturity:

    At age twenty-seven he wrote in his diary that he dreamed of founding a new religion, "a Christian religion but stripped of faith and mysteries, a practical religion which does not promise a blessed future but gives bliss on earth."

    At age seventy-three, in reply to his excommunication, he wrote to the "Czar and his Advisors" a letter beginning: "I believe in God, whom I understand as Spirit, Love and the Source of everything. I also believe that he is within me and I am within him. I believe that God's will is clearly and understandably expressed in the teachings of a man, Christ, whom to believe to be God and to pray to I consider a supreme blasphemy."
4. Sonya's notes 31 January 1881.
5. I have been careful not to "diagnose" the type of depression that afflicted Lev nor to explain its cause. For such a complex personality this would have been difficult in his lifetime, let alone a hundred

years later. The reference books that helped me recognize that during the years 1881–1884 Lev's depression was more than one of the blue moods to which he was prone all his life are: *The American Psychiatric Association's Diagnostic and Statistical Manual*, Third Edition, known as DSM-III, *The Merck Manual*, Fourteenth Edition and *Up From Depression* by Leonard Cammer, M.D., Simon and Schuster. Because symptoms are the same in many illnesses, the DSM-III's cross-referencing was important.

6. I have translated the Russian word *prazdnost*, which can mean idleness, inactivity or emptiness, as "futility"—which seemed to combine all three meanings and to express what Lev appeared to be feeling.
7. Lev letter to Sonya 1 March 1882.
8. *Father, A Life of Lev Tolstoy*, Ch. 37, p. 403.
9. Lev letter to M. A. Englehardt December 1882 or January 1883.
10. Lev letter to Sonya 29 September 1883. Her reply 30 September 1883.
11. Lev diary 9 April 1884.
12. Lev diary 3 May 1884.
13. Lev diary 22 May 1884.
14. Lev diary 18 June 1884.
15. Lev diary 14 July 1884.

CHAPTER SIX

1. See Note 5, Chapter Five.
2. Lev took the name of his novel from Beethoven's Violin Sonata in A major, Opus 47, 1803, which figures in the plot. The sonata was so called because of its dedication to the French violinist Rodolphe Kreutzer, who apparently never played it.
3. Lev diary 24 July 1889.
4. *Dostoevsky, Reminiscences*.
5. *Leo Tolstoy* (Simmons).
6. Lev letter to N. N. Gay 18 December 1890.
7. Sonya diary 19 July 1887.
8. An explorer, author and journalist, George Kennan was employed in 1885 by *Century Magazine* to write on the exile system as practiced in Russia. He was a first cousin of Thomas Lathrop Kennan, who was a grandfather of the diplomat and historian George Frost Kennan. Kennan's article in *Century Magazine* was titled "A Visit to Count Tolstoi."
9. "A Visit to Count Tolstoi."
10. Lev diary 28 August 1889.
11. Lev diary 7 August 1889.
12. *Countess Tolstoy's Later Diary, 1891–1897*, 27 May 1891.
13. Lev diary 7 September 1889.
14. Lev notebook 9 December 1889.

15. This sentence from *Countess Tolstoy's Later Diary, 1891–1897*, 23 April 1891.
16. *The Diary of Tolstoy's Wife, 1860–1891*, 5 January 1891.
17. Beginning at "He told me that his feet . . ." taken from *The Diary of Tolstoy's Wife, 1891–1897*, 7 February 1891.

CHAPTER SEVEN

1. Sonya contributed part of her earnings from her editions toward the famine relief and also raised money for Lev's work by publishing appeals in the newspaper. Sonya's first appeal brought in 13,000 rubles ($6,500) in two weeks.
2. Passports were required between provinces within Russia as well as for travel abroad.
3. Last two words taken from *Countess Tolstoy's Later Diary, 1891–1897*, 1 February 1895.
4. Sonya diary 21 February 1895.
5. The Chapter "Death of Vanechka" from *My Life*, Book 7, pp. 21–41, published with Sonya's diaries.
6. This and following six quotations from Lev diary 12 March 1895.
7. Lev diary 27 March 1895.
8. Sonya letter to Lev 12 October 1895.
9. Lev diary 13 October 1895.
10. The Dukhobors were a religious sect founded in the eighteenth century with beliefs something like those of the Quakers (pacifism, nonviolence and refusal of military service). They lived in simple, industrious communities. The letter signed by Lev's disciples protested the government reaction to an incident in the Caucasus when the Dukhobors decided to burn what weapons they owned for self-defense, knives and shotguns. Members of the sect gathered around a huge bonfire singing psalms and were dispersed by government troops, Cossacks, who flogged them brutally—some to death.
11. Sonya telephoned Lev while he was staying at the Olsufevs', wealthy aristocrats who quite naturally would have been among the first to install a telephone. There is no mention of a telephone at the Moscow house and Sonya probably went to the post office to make her call.
12. Lev letter to V. G. Chertkov 13 October 1897 and Lev diary entry 16 July 1897.
13. After glancing at *Aphrodite*, Lev asked, "What kind of art is this?"
14. Sonya diary 20 July 1897.
15. Sonya diary 22 July 1897.
16. In 1897 and 1898 Sonya mentioned Taneev 97 times, compared to 59 mentions during the remaining twenty-one years of her life.

NOTES

CHAPTER EIGHT

1. In 1898, with support from the anarchist Prince Kropotkin, English Quakers and Tolstoy, the Dukhobors were permitted to emigrate to Canada. Even in the new world they had difficulties with their host country, mainly because they lived in isolated communities, making their own provisions and refusing trade with others. Some Dukhobors carried their belief in simplicity to the extreme of becoming nudists. Another simple Christian sect that Tolstoy befriended was the Molokans, so called because they drank milk in Lent, a custom forbidden by the Orthodox church. Tolstoy got to know the Molokans in Samara; when the government separated them from their children in an effort to keep the sect from growing, they appealed to him for help. Tolstoy and his daughter Tanya were successful in having the children restored to their parents.
2. *Tolstoy Remembered*, p. 170.
3. Sonya diary 28 August 1898.
4. Konstantin Pobedonostsev owed much of his influence to his closeness to Czar Alexander III, whose tutor he had been. Tolstoy was a thorn in Pobedonostsev's side for some years; the question of excommunication was raised in 1888, but the Holy Synod did not take action until late in 1900 when the case was finally presented and voted upon.
5. See note 3 to Ch. Five.
6. Gotthold Lessing (1729–1781), German philosopher, dramatist and critic. Lev refers to his remark, "At the most only one bad woman exists in the world. It is unfortunate that each man considers his as being this unique one."
7. Sonya diary 10 October 1902.
8. Sonya diary 27 January–7 February 1902.
9. Sonya diary 13 March 1902.
10. Note 56 to Sonya 1902 diary.
11. Lev notebook 27 March 1908.
12. *Tolstoy Remembered*, p. 177.
13. Lev letter to A. M. Bodyansky 12–13 March 1908.

CHAPTER NINE

1. Sasha had bought Telyatinki, a small estate of 200 acres, in 1905. In 1908 Sasha sold half of this property to Chertkov.
2. *L. N. Tolstoy in the Last Year of His Life*, p. 335.
3. *Tolstoy Remembered*, p. 249.
4. By law the copyrights of Lev's works were his until he legally transferred them or until his death, in which case they would pass to his heirs. He permitted Sonya to publish his works written before 1881 and he permitted Chertkov, and anyone else, to publish his works

written after 1881, but the permissions were not legal and lasted only so long as Lev did not retract them. At his death his works would go to his heirs and, for all his protestations to the contrary, it seems that this was what Lev wanted until he succumbed to Chertkov's pressures.

5. Sonya diary 26 October 1909.
6. *My Recollections*, Ch. 29, p. 253.
7. *L. N. Tolstoy in the Last Year of His Life*, p. 179.
8. *Tolstoy Remembered*, p. 246.
9. Lev diary 27 May 1910.
10. *Sketches of the Past*, Part IV, Ch. 1.
11. *The Final Struggle*, p. 102.
12. Sonya diary 26 June 1910.
13. Sonya diary and Lev diary 7 July 1910.
14. Sonya diary 10 July 1910.
15. *L. N. Tolstoy in the Last Year of His Life*, p. 293.
16. Same, p. 298.
17. Sonya diary 23 July 1910.
18. Loose sheet dated 29 November 1851 and placed in 1851 diary.
19. *The Final Struggle*, Sergei Tolstoy Notes, p. 235.
20. *L. N. Tolstoy in the Last Year of His Life*, p. 338.
21. *L. N. Tolstoy in the Last Year of His Life*, p. 382.
22. Lev secret diary 19 October 1910.

CHAPTER TEN

1. From the beginning of Chapter Ten to here *L. N. Tolstoy in the Last Year of His Life*, pp. 398–400.
2. *Sketches of the Past*, Part IV, Ch. 1.
3. Children's letters, same.
4. Sonya wrote in all four letters to Lev after his departure, but this is the only one he received.
5. In Ilya's memoir he wrote that Lev's sister, Maria Nikolaevna, told him after her brother's death that she was certain that Lev had every intention of remaining in Optina but that Sasha had upset his plans. "When she came with her friend [Varvara]," Maria Nikolaevna told Ilya, "they began examining the map of Russia, considering an itinerary to the Caucasus. Levochka sat, looking pensive and sad. Sasha tried to cheer him: Never mind, Papa, all will be to the good. Her father replied bitterly: Oh, you women, women. What will be good about it?"
6. Astapovo has been renamed Lev Tolstoy.
7. Tanya's conversation with Lev is quoted in *Sketches from the Past*, Part IV, Ch. 2, from a letter Tanya wrote to her husband the same day.

8. *The Final Struggle*, Sergei Tolstoy's preface, p. 37.
9. S. Rozanova's introduction to the Moscow edition of Sonya's diaries quotes the remarks by Pasternak, Gorky and Strakhov.
10. *Tolstoy Remembered*, p. 246.
11. This was Lev's wish when he hoped to recover and feared the excitement of facing Sonya. We cannot know what his wish would have been if, when he knew he was dying, he had been told that Sonya was close by and eager to see him.

BIBLIOGRAPHY

IN RUSSIAN

Tolstoy, L. N. Complete Works, Centenary Edition (90 Vols.). Moscow-Leningrad: Government Publishing House. (Includes literary work, essays, diaries, notebooks and letters.)

Tolstaya, S. A., *Diaries*. Moscow: Belles-Lettres Publishing House, 1978. (Besides the diaries and notebooks, the edition includes a chapter from Sonya's autobiography, *My Life*, and the essay *L. N. Tolstoy's Marriage*. The editors' notes quote extensively from Sonya's letters and from *My Life*. This autobiography, a many-volumed work called by Sonya "the best writing I have ever done," is not to be confused with a brief autobiography written shortly after her husband's death at the request of a publisher and later translated and published by the Hogarth Press as *Countess Tolstoy's Autobiography*.)

Tolstaya, S. A., *Letters to L. N. Tolstoy*. Moscow-Leningrad: Academy Press, 1936.

Bulgakov, Valentin. *L. N. Tolstoy in the Last Year of His Life*. Moscow: Government Publishing House, 1960.

Eykhenbaum, B. M., ed. *Young Tolstoy: Notes from Contemporaries*. Leningrad: Writers' Publishing House, 1929.

Gusev, N. N. *Chronicles of the Life and Creative Work of Lev Nikolaevich Tolstoy*. Moscow: Government Publishing House, 1958.

Kuzminskaya, T[atyana] A. *My Life at Home and at Yasnaya Polyana*. Tula: Tula Book Publishers, 1960.

Tolstaya, Aleksandra. *Father, A Life of Lev Tolstoy*. New York: Chekhov Publishing House, 1953.

Tolstoy, I[lya] L. *My Recollections*. Moscow: Belles-Lettres Publishing House, 1969.

Tolstoy, S[ergei] L. *Sketches of the Past*. Moscow: Government Publishing House, 1949.

L. N. Tolstoy, Contemporaries' Recollections. Moscow: Belles-Lettres Publishing House, 1978.

IN FRENCH

Acouturier, Gustave, trans. *Léon Tolstoi, Journaux et Carnets*. Paris: Gallimard Press, Vol. I, 1979; Vol. II, 1980; Vol. III, 1985.

IN ENGLISH

Bulgakov, Valentin. *The Last Year of Leo Tolstoy*. New York: The Dial Press, 1971.

Kennan, George. "A Visit to Count Tolstoi." *The Century Magazine*. Vol. XII, 1887.

Kuzminskaya, Tatyana A. *Tolstoy As I Knew Him*. New York: The Macmillan Company, 1948.

Maude, Aylmer, trans. *The Final Struggle. Countess Tolstoy's Diary for 1910*, with preface and notes by S[ergei] L. Tolstoy. New York: Octagon Books, 1980. (Note: Maude's translation of Sonya's 1910 diary is not complete, but I used *The Final Struggle* for Sergei Tolstoy's preface and extensive notes.)

Sukhotin-Tolstaya, Tatyana. *The Tolstoy Home*. Diaries of Tatyana Sukhotin-Tolstaya. London: Harvill Press.

Tolstoy, Alexandra. *A Life of My Father*. New York: Harper and Brothers, 1953.

———. *Out of the Past*. New York: Columbia University Press, 1981.

Tolstoy, Count Ilya. *Reminiscences of Tolstoy*. New York: The Century Company, 1914.

Tolstoy, Sergei. *Tolstoy Remembered by His Son*. London: Weidenfeld and Nicolson, 1961. (Note: A considerably abridged translation of *Sketches of the Past*.)

Tolstoy, Tatyana. *Tolstoy Remembered*. London: Michael Joseph, 1977.

ADDITIONAL READING IN ENGLISH

Bayley, John. *Tolstoy and the Novel*. New York: The Viking Press, 1966.

Berlin, Isaiah. *Russian Thinkers*. New York: The Viking Press, 1978.

Biryukov, Paul. *Tolstoi's Love Letters*. Richmond: The Hogarth Press, 1923.

Crankshaw, Edward. *Tolstoy, The Making of a Novelist*. New York: The Viking Press, 1974.

Dostoevsky, Anna. *Dostoevsky, Reminiscences*. New York: Liveright, 1975.

Gifford, Henry. *Tolstoy*. London: Oxford University Press, 1982.

Simmons, Ernest. *Leo Tolstoy*. New York: Vintage Books, 1960.

Stillman, Leon, ed. *Leo Tolstoy, Last Diaries*. New York: Columbia University Press, 1960.

Tchertkoff, Vladimir. *The Last Days of Tolstoy*. London: William Heinemann, 1922.

Tolstoy, Alexandra. *The Tragedy of Tolstoy*. London: George Allen and Unwin, Ltd., 1933.

Tolstoy, Nikolai. *The Tolstoys, Twenty-Four Generations of Russian History*. London: Hamish Hamilton, 1983.

Troyat, Henri. *Tolstoy*. Garden City, New York: Doubleday & Co., 1967.

Werth, Alexander, trans. *The Diary of Tolstoy's Wife, 1860–1891*. London: Victor Gollancz, 1928. (See Author's Note, p. 12.)

———. *Countess Tolstoy's Later Diary, 1891–1897*. London: Victor Gollancz, 1929. Reprinted by Books for Libraries, New York: Freeport Press, 1971. (See Author's Note.)

Wiener, Leo, trans. *Tolstoy on Education*. Chicago: The University of Chicago Press, 1967.

Since this book was completed, two important translations of the Tolstoys' diaries have appeared.

Christian, R. F., ed. and trans. *Tolstoy's Diaries*. Vol. I: 1847–1894. Vol. II: 1895–1910. New York: Charles Scribner's Sons, 1985. R. F. Christian has an unusual rapport with Tolstoy and this is a discerning selection from the diaries.

Porter, Cathy. *The Diaries of Sophia Tolstoy*. New York: Random House, 1985. The first complete translation in English of Sonya's diaries, with an introduction by R. F. Christian. The translations read smoothly, but Cathy Porter's view of Sonya is very different from mine, and this difference shows in our translations.